CÚ CHUI

AN IRON AGE HERO

CÚ CHULAINN
AN IRON AGE HERO

DARAGH SMYTH

IRISH ACADEMIC PRESS
DUBLIN • PORTLAND, OR

First published in 2005 by
IRISH ACADEMIC PRESS
44 Northumberland Road, Dublin 4, Ireland

and in the United States of America by
IRISH ACADEMIC PRESS
c/o ISBS, Suite 300
920 NE 58th Avenue
Portland, Oregon 97213-3786

Website: www.iap.ie

© Daragh Smyth 2005

British Library Cataloguing in Publication Data
An entry can be found on request

ISBN 0-7165-3325 1 (cloth)
ISBN 0-7165-3326 X (paper)

Library of Congress Cataloging-in-Publication Data
An entry can be found on request

Printed in Ireland by
Betaprint Ltd

To my own clan-
Alison, Eoghan, Duncan, Caer,
and not forgetting Aurora

Contents

Translator's Note
and Acknowledgements

This translation took five years and has been a daunting task.

I took edited Irish versions from eight stories. Each of these stories represents a chapter in the book. Six of the chapters are from edited Irish editions and have been published by the Dublin Institute of Advanced Studies under the heading of Mediaeval and Modern Irish series. Two other chapters are from the book of Leinster volume 2, edited by R.I. Best and M.A. O'Brien and are also published by the Dublin Institute of Advanced Studies. In one story 'The Wasting Sickness of Cú Chulainn', I began translating direct from the edited version by R.I. Best and Osborn Bergin of Lebor na hUidre or the book of the Dun Cow, but later reverted to Myles Dillon's edition of the same story from the Mediaeval and Modern Irish series.

The translation was assisted by notes and vocabularies at the end of each relevant volume in the Mediaeval and Modern Irish series. However throughout the task the literary arm I most relied on was the Royal Irish Academy's Dictionary of the Irish Language.

The underscript of each chapter gives the original Irish heading for the story.

Cú Chulainn has been translated before and surely will be again. The previous translations into English, to my knowledge, are: The *Cuchullin in Irish Literature* by Eleanor Hull in 1898 and *Cuchulain of Muirthemne* by Augusta Lady Gregory in 1902. In the former case it is a work of compilation and edition and in the latter, a comparison between the Irish text and the 'translations that have already been made'. This is in no way to demean the work of these scholars and particularly in Augusta Gregory's case as her book still on the bookshop shelves after one hundred years testifies.

Joseph Dunn's *The Ancient Irish Epic Tale–The Tain* (1914), and Thomas Kinsella's *The Tain* (1969) both contain stories wherein Cú Chulainn is the main protagonist. He may well be seen as the main character in the Tain.

This book is an attempt to put our hero's life into context whilst admitting that more chapters could have been added. I also admit errors throughout are none other than my own.

I wish to thank Fergus Kelly, Director, School of Celtic Studies for sample checkings at various points in the translation. And to Fergus Gillespie, assistant keeper of the Genealogical Office for his advice on this endeavour as in others, also to Sean Ó Cadhla, School of Languages, Dublin Institute of Technology, for relevant suggestions. To Paddy Boyle for introducing me to Drumanagh, Co. Dublin, and to the late Dr. Diarmuid McDaid, who collated later translations from the sagas with earlier versions.

I would also like to thank my son Eoghan, who typed up all the handwritten work on the computer and who helped out when electronic problems reared their head.

Finally I would like to thank my wife Alison, who translated many chapters from Thurnneysen's *Die irishe Helden und Konigsage* in order to understand more clearly a scholarly analysis of the work, and who also translated the only full translation by Christian J. Guyonvarc'h, from the French, on the Death of Cú Chulainn.

Though deeply grateful to all the above the translation here is for better or worse my own responsibility.

Introduction

Cú Chulainn is the greatest Irish hero. Sometimes referred to as the Irish Achilles, he continues to exercise a hold on the people of Ireland. He is called the first hurler in Ireland by sportspeople and the son of the sun god Lug by romantics; either way he cuts a swathe through Irish consciousness, affecting both its history and its mythology. He straddles both warrior traditions in Ireland – the Ulster or Red Branch one and the Fenian one. His statue in bronze by Oliver Sheppard stands in the General Post Office, Dublin, as the embodiment of revolutionary independence. He is to be found on many a mural in Northern Ireland as the embodiment of Loyalist resistance to the 'Men of Ireland' (*Fir hÉrend*). He was 'the most beloved hero' of Patrick Pearse's school of St Enda's in Dublin.

For many scholars he remains an historical character. Tigernach hua Braein, the 11th century abbot of Clonmacnoise, describes him in the Annals of Tigernach as the greatest of Irish heroes: "The death of Cú Chulainn, the bravest hero of the Irish, by Lugaid, son of the three hounds, king of Munster and by Erc, king of Tara, and by the three sons of Calatin of Connacht. Seven years was his age when he followed the kine of Cualnge, but twenty-seven years was his age when he died."

Professor Declan Kiberd in his book, *Irish Classics*, mentions a category whose 'narrative generates a myth so powerful as to obscure the individual writer and to unleash an almost superhuman force'.

He mentions the Cú Chulainn story as an example, together with the lament for Art Ó Laoghaire and Dracula.

Cú Chulainn's re-emergence as part of the Irish cultural renaissance of the late 19th century is expressed both on stage, in literature and in the anti-colonial militarism, particularly of Pearse, who used the myth of Cú Chulainn to dynamize the movement towards independence. Patrick Pearse believed that he could revitalize the spirit found in Cú

Chulainn and in the Irish sagas and mould them to gain independence. Pearse equated Cú Chulainn's sacrifice with that of Christ and it was this blending of the ancient Ulster hero with Christ that he found so potent.

Pearse blended the pre-Christian Cú Chulainn and the boy corps of Emain Macha (Armagh) with the *teglach* (community) of St Enda of Aran.

This educational system developed an ethos or community spirit, which would produce a Colmcille or a Cú Chulainn. Pearse stated that: 'we must re-create and perpetuate in Ireland the knightly tradition of Cú Chulainn'. Interestingly, he blends Cú Chulainn into the Fianna cycle of legends as though he were one of the *Fir hÉrend* (men of Ireland) ignoring the fact that the *Fir hÉrend* were seen by Cú Chulainn as the enemy. Thus mythology is not an historical narrative but rather a blending of narrative, created so as to transform history or pre-history into potent myth and legend.

For the educationalist Pearse 'Cú Chulainn was our greatest inspiration at Cullenswood House' (St Enda's).

Yeats, our foremost poet, also saw in Pearse a strong identification with Cú Chulainn:

> When Pearse summoned Cú Chulainn to his side,
> What stalked through the Post Office? What intellect?
> What calculation, number, measurement, replied?

Yeats also identified with Cú Chulainn. In a letter from his wife George to a Mr. Oliver Edwards, two years after the poet's death in 1941, she writes:

'...have you ever studied the Cú Chulainn of the plays up to the Hawk's Well and the Cú Chulainn of the Hawk's Well to the last play? I decided recently that at the same moment before the writing of Hawk's Well, the poet, probably unconsciously had begun to identify himself with Cú Chulainn.'

Considering that *At the Hawk's Well* was written in 1917, this identification was to last for the rest of his life, as, shortly before his death, he wrote 'Cú Chulainn Comforted', a poem in which his own demise can be compared to Cú Chulainn.

Thus as Pearse fused the Ulster cycle with early Christianity, Yeats fused the Ulster cycles together to produce plays, amongst which were *At the Hawk's Well, The Only Jealousy of Emer* and *On Baile's Strand*.

2

In founding the Celtic Mystical Order Yeats desired to set up an order which he could control, into which members could be initiated and where through the process of 'participation mystique', those initiated could draw up visions of figures from Irish Legend.

The death of Cú Chulainn, together with the 'marriage' of Lug and Dechtine, were part of the initiation rite of the Celtic Mystical Order.

At the second meeting of this order, a vision of Cú Chulainn reputedly appeared together with other personages from Irish Mythology. The insignia of this order was designed by Sarah Purser and showed Cú Chulainn and three waves.

The name of Cú Chulainn comes up constantly either in conversation or in public talks; this year whilst attending the annual commemoration at Beal na mBláth, in Cork, for Michael Collins I was struck by the mention of Cú Chulainn's name. Dr Pat Wallace mentioned it in a quote from Alice Stoppford Green. The quote was: 'During the reign of terror his (Michael Collins's) name became a household word, to be uttered with admiration and awe, whilst he himself assumed the heroic dimensions of a Cú Chulainn.'

So what about the hero himself, aside from his impact on literary and political notables?

Some would argue that Cú Chulainn was of the Setantii, an ancient tribe settled between present day Liverpool and Preston. Ptolemy places the 'harbour of the Setantii' near the mouth of the river Ribble, which flows down from the dales into Preston and into the Irish Sea, at the firth, which the Romans called the Belisima Aestuarium.

This is derived from the fact that Cú Chulainn's first name was Sétanta. The racial origins of Cú Chulainn remain open to conjecture. Some would say that he was of the Érainn, or pre-Gaelic race. However it is possible that the Érainn were a branch of the Picts or Cruithin. The Picts are regarded as the aboriginal peoples of these islands, and various customs such as head hunting and painting their bodies seem peculiar to them. In one version of the Táin Bó Cúalnge, Cu Chulainn is called the Cú Glinne Bolg, or the Hound of Glen Bolg, a glen possibly in Co. Louth. The Fir Bolg may be seen as being racially twinned with the Érainn.

The Cruthin are also known as the Dál nAraidi, who, with the Uí Echach, occupied Antrim and Down and north Louth. Their line was matrilineal; thus Cú Chulainn's father or Uncle Conchobar mac Nessa took his surname from his mother Ness.

The connections with the Uí Echach are interesting. The Uí Echach, or the horse people, are associated with Tara Fort, which overlooks Millin Bay and South Bay on the Ards Peninsula, Co. Down. The dominant tribe was known as the Ard Echach. They gave their name to Arda, the old name for the Ards Peninsula. Another branch of this tribe is the Uí Echach Cobo whose territory, known as Mag Inis (Lecale, nowadays), is where Conchobar mac Nessa is said to have had his palace. Conchobar's foster father was Fergus mac Roich (ro-ech – great horse) and Cú Chulainn's father or foster father was Sualtam mac Roich, placing Cú Chulainn within the Uí Echach ruling dynasty.

The Uí Echach were a branch of the Dál nAraidi, and thus were Picts. The Uí Echach are sometimes referred to as the Uí Echach Ulaid. Although the Uí Echach were not of Ulaid stock, they adopted the suffix to show that they were the dominant tribe in Co. Down. The Ulaid gave their name to Ulster and it has remained thus ever since.

After his birth, Cú Chulainn was taken to Dún Imrith, a fort situated either within the Fews range of mountains, Co. Armagh or on the plain of Louth. His castle at Dún Delca (Dundalk) still stands outside the town of Dundalk to which it gives its name. His territory extended from the Fews (Sliab Fúait) to Dún Delca.

He went to court Emer Manach at Rathmooney and Drumanagh, in north Co. Dublin.

He trained in arms under Scáthach in her fortress at Dún Scáthach on the Isle of Skye. On his return from Skye he sailed to Rúad, who was king of the Western Isles (Scotland), on the night of the *Samain* (hallowe'en) in order to meet his foster brothers Conall Cernach and Lóegaire Búadach who were collecting tribute there. He married Emer at Emain Macha, the ancient capital of Ulster.

Although there are many written descriptions of Cú Chulainn, he would appear to have been small, black-haired, possibly bearded. He had grey-blue eyes. He had a cast in one eye.

He fought at many places in single combat during the Táin, the most notable of these battles being on the banks of the river Dee at Ardee, Co. Louth, against his companion Fer Diad. After his death he was taken from Knockbridge, Co. Louth, to his fort at Dún Delca and presumably he was buried there, overlooking his ancient territory of Dundalk bay, the Cooley mountains, Slieve Gullion and the Fews.

CHAPTER 1

The Conception of Cú Chulainn

Compert Con Culainn

Conchobar and the nobles of Ulster were at Emain. They were joined by a large flock of birds on the plain of Emain. They grazed the earth, leaving neither grass nor root nor anything at all. The Ulaid or Ulster warriors were weary watching them destroy the land. They gathered nine chariots together and so one day they went hunting them. Hunting birds was a custom among them. Conchobar was in his chariot with his daughter Dechtine, who was of marriageable age. She was the charioteer to her father. The rest of the Ulaid escorted them, including Conall, Loeguire and Bricriu.

The birds flew before them, over Sliab Fúad, [the Fews] across Edmon south of the Fews and across Brega or the plain of Meath. There were no enclosures at that time on the plain, no ditches nor pens nor cashels, nothing but the level plain. Lovely and fine was the flight of the birds and their song. They were close to two hundred birds, a silver chain between each two of them, each twenty following separately, nine score in all. Towards nightfall, three birds separated themselves from the rest. They went before the rest to the Brug at the Boyne. Night fell on the Ulaid. Moreover it snowed heavily upon them. Conchobar told his men to unyoke their chariots and to start looking for shelter.

Conall and Bricriu went searching. They found a new house and went in and found a couple there. They were made welcome. They went out to their people. Bricriu said that it was not worth their while to go to the house without food or clothing. Moreover, even though it was a narrow house they went in all the same. They brought their chariots with them. They did not take anything more into the house. Suddenly they saw a cellar door opposite them, and by the usual meal-time the men of Ulster were merry and drunk, and in good humour. Later one of the Ulaid said that there was a woman in the pangs of childbirth. Dechtine went to her; she assisted her and [the woman] bore a son. At the same time there was a mare at the door of the house and she gave birth to two colts. Later the Ulaid held the child and brought the foal as gifts to the boy. Dechtine nursed the child.

When morning came, they found themselves east of the Brug. There was nothing to see, no house, no birds, only the horses, the child and the foal. Later the boy came to Emain, and the child was nursed there. Soon after, they were all laid low with disease. The child died from this disease. Great was the lamenting at the grave. Great was Dechtine's sorrow at the loss of her foster son.

She had need for a drink on returning from the funeral rites. Drink came in bronze vessels. Dechtine asked for a drink and the drink was brought in a cup. As she drank, a small creature slipped into her mouth with the liquid. She swallowed the creature and it vanished. She fell asleep there for the night. In her sleep a man addressed her. He said that she [Dechtine] would have a perfect pregnancy, and that it was he who had brought her towards the Brug, and that it was he who would guard her. The son was to be nursed by her, he had brought her to Brú na Boinne and Sétanta was to be his name. He himself was the avatar of Lug mac Etnenn, and the foal would be nursed with the child.

So it was that the daughter became pregnant. A question hung over the Ulaid as to who the father was. They thought that as Conchobar had been drinking heavily he had passed the night with his daughter. Later Conchobar betrothed his daughter to Sualtam mac Roich. She was greatly ashamed to go to the man's bed whilst she was pregnant. When she went walking around she was stabbing and striking and shaking her perfectly healthy womb. Later the man [Sualtam] went with her. She was promptly pregnant again. She bore a son.

Later the Ulaid were gathering at Emain Macha when the son was brought in. After this, they were disputing as to which of them should rear the boy. They submitted their judgement to Conchobar. Conchobar said: 'Take the child to you, O Findchóem.' Later Findchóem saw the boy. 'This child is the love of my heart,' said she, 'so that he shall be the same to me as Conall Cernach is.' 'There is little between them in your eyes,' said Conchobar, 'namely between your own son and the son of your sister.' So it was that Conchobar recited the following verse:

> Becfoltach of glorious virtue,
> Dechtine's good must exist,
> [this house] has protected me
> and my seven chariots,
> and before the horses set out for a long chase
> in the cold,
> and after it has refreshed those in attendance,
> let Sétanta be taken away.

'Take you the boy,' said Conchobar to his sister. 'She will not nurse him,' said Sencha, 'for it is I who will not permit it, I who am strong, am skilful, am noble, am nimble, am a learned man, am wise. I am not forgetful. I address a king, I prepare my words; I adjudge the size of battalions coming against Conchobar, the victorious in battle. I adjust the laws of the Ulaid, and I do not rouse them against me or against one another. I do not invoke any foster-father except Conchobar.'

'Even I may take him,' said Blai Bruigu. 'He will not die from injury or neglect with me, my rightful position is supported by Conchobar. I summon the men of Ireland. I can nourish an army for a week or ten days. I support with skill and with wrath. I support those through both insult and honour contests alike.'

'This is shamelessness,' said Fergus. 'I have chosen powerful heroes, it is I who will nurse him. I am strong, am skilful, am a messenger, I shall bring him up to distinction rather than wealth. I am strong before a feat of arms and when valour is required, I am a worker against reproach. I am worthy of foster-children. I am the protection against all evil. I do damage to the strong, I look after the weak.'

'Whosoever listens to me,' said Amergin, 'cannot turn away. I am a worthy nurse to a king. I am praised before every rank for my valour, for my intelligence, for my fortune, for my age, for my eloquence, for the nobility and courage of my children. For whomsoever reigns, I am the poet, I am worthy of the respect of the king. I slay every warrior who fights from the chariot. I do not give praise to anyone but to Conchobar. I do not assemble against anyone but against an enemy of the king.'

Conchobar said: 'There is no profit in all of this. Let Findchóem take the boy and reach Emain and find Morann.' Afterwards they went out to Emain and the boy was with Findchóem. Later Morann arrived at Emain and gave a judgement: 'Conchobar has handed over the boy to Findchóem since she is a relation. Sencha can invoke eloquence. Blai Briugu can nourish him, he was carried to the knee of Fergus. Amergin was his foster-father. Conall Cernach was his foster-brother; two breasts on his mother, two on Findchóem. Let it be that all the following will instruct him – the charioteers, the king, the *ollaves*; on account of this the boy will have a multitude of friends. An honour contest will be arranged between all, he will win the fights in the fords and against all the battalions.' Later it is done; Amergin and Findchóem have responsibility for the boy. And he is reared at Dún Imbrith on the Plain of Muirthemne.

CHAPTER 2

The Boyhood Deeds
of Cú Chulainn

Incipiunt macgnimrada Con Culainn

'At this time the fosterling was,' said Fergus, 'in the house of his
father and mother at Airdig on Mag Muirthemne, and was
being told the stories of the youths at Emain. For it is thus that
Conchobar spends part of his time as king here, so that the king and
the kingdom are centred here. So that he rises at first light, and
settles questions and cases concerning the province. After this, the
day is divided into three parts. The first third begins at once, over-
seeing the youths performing feats and playing games. The second
third of the day is playing board games. The last part of the day is
spent eating and drinking, and then everyone goes to sleep. Singers
and minstrels arrive with soothing music to calm. Although I am
exiled I give my word,' said Fergus, 'that there is not in Ireland or
Scotland a young warrior the equal of Conchobar.'

And he related to the boys the stories of the youth and the company of youths at Emain: 'And the little boy addressed his mother
and beseeched her so that he might partake in the games at the playing fields of Emain. 'It is too early, little boy,' said the mother, 'to be
a warrior with the champions of Ulster, wait until you are old
enough to be placed under the safeguard of Conchobar and the protection of the warriors.' 'I cannot wait that long, O mother,' said the
little boy, 'for I wish to be instructed in the use of weaponry at
Emain.' 'It is far from here to the place of instruction,' said the
mother. 'Sliab Fúait is between you and Emain.' 'I will bring great
esteem upon Emain,' said he.

'The little boy went then and took his sporting things for
pleasure. He took his bronze hurling stick and his silver *sliotar* and
his javelin for casting, and his death-causing fiery dart, and finds

out ways to shorten the journey. One of his deeds is to strike the ball with his stick, so that it goes into the distance. Moreover, when he struck again, the second strike or puck was no shorter than the first. He cast his javelin and threw it and took his course after it. He took his hurling stick and ball and his javelin. And he always caught the ball in mid-air before it reached the ground.

'He went on to the place of assembly at Emain, to the place where the youths were. One hundred and fifty youths were there about Folloman mac Conchobar, practising feats on the plain of Emain. The little boy went among them into the centre of the playing field at Emain, and got the ball from them with his feet, and didn't allow it to go further up his leg than his knee nor further down than his ankle. And he held it close between his two legs. And neither a spear nor a blow from them nor a strike nor a thrust reached him. Then he took the ball over the goal. No sooner was he looked upon than he was gone. It was a cause of wonder and awe with them. "Well done boy," said Folloman mac Conchobar. "A mighty strike against all there, and a warning of death and fire is given by me to you, coming as you do to the games without protection, striking all in a single blow, so that the king and all the young warriors know that it is a champion of Ulster there. "Yet", says Conchobar, it is not customary to come to the games without protection and surety."

'Then they all strike together. One hundred and fifty hurling sticks are pointed towards the top of his head. One hundred and fifty balls are held and driven out. Moreover, one hundred and fifty balls are sent in the direction of the little boy. With his wrists, his arms and the palms of his hands he fields the hundred and fifty balls. He stops one hundred and fifty fiery toy spears. He defends himself with the side of his shield and drives back the boyish spears. He is rightly a master warrior, for fifty kings' sons are overthrown by him. 'Five more ran past by Conchobar and myself as we were playing board games,' said Fergus. 'the chief games of the assembly of Emain, with the little boy in hot pursuit. Conchobar placed his hand on the little boy. "Well," said he, "I see that it is not a frail contest that you conduct with the warrior youth." "Indeed, for great was the company against me," said the little boy, "and I have not received the respect due to a stranger from your young warriors." "What do you mean? Who are you?" said Conchobar. "I am little Sétanta mac Sualtam, the son of Dechtine your sister, and it is ill becoming of you that I should meet with such ill treatment." "What do you mean, little boy?" said Conchobar. "Did you not know that the warriors here are under an injunction to offer protection to strangers?" "I did not know it," said the little boy, "for had I known it, I would have been more heedful." "Good then, boys," said Conchobar, "protect this little boy," "Indeed we will," they said.

'The little boy was then under the protection of the warrior youth. He then scattered them with blows from his right hand and lays them down again. He throws to the ground fifty kings' sons and, according to their fathers, they seemed to be dead, which was not so, as they had simply turned the colour of death from the direct blows to their bodies and to their legs. "Well, indeed," said Conchobar, "What are you doing to them now?" "I swear by the gods whom I worship," said the boy, " that until they all come under my protection and defence, I will not take my hands from them, so that they will all end up under the ground." "I will place the warrior youth under your protection then," said Conchobar. "Then we are agreed about it," said the little boy.

'Then,' said Fergus 'the warrior troop went under his protection and security. He carried out these deeds when he was but five years of age. He shattered the sons of champions and battle warriors at the gates of the *liss* and the fort as well, so that understandably there is awe and amazement at how much he has completed. For he has cut down a four-pronged fork, he has killed a man or two or three or four so far on this Táin and he has just turned seventeen years of age.'

Then Cormac Con Loinges, son of Conchobar, spoke: 'The year after that, when he was six, the little boy carried out another act.' 'What did he do?' said Ailill. 'There was a smith from the borders of Ulster by name of Culann; it was customary for Conchobar to be feasted, and Culann went to Emain to invite Conchobar. He said that Conchobar should not take a large force with him, just a small number, as his territory and landholding were modest. All he had was a sledge-hammer, his anvil, his hand and his tongs. Conchobar said that he would come with a small band of his followers.

'Culann returned to his fortress in order to attend on Conchobar, and to prepare the food and drink for him. Conchobar stayed on at Emain until the proceedings were over and the day came to an end. He put on his light cloak for travelling. He then went to bid farewell to the young warriors. Thus he went to the green. What he saw was unusual: one hundred and fifty youths at one end of the green and, at the other end, a single youth. The boy took the goal shot on his own, against one hundred and fifty of the youth. It was the 'hole' game that they played. This was a game of hitting the ball into the hole, as played on the green at Emain. Now they were hurling and he was parrying the hundred and fifty balls that were coming towards the hole. They were hurling and he was defending without error, so that not a single ball was put into the hole; now there was mutual pulling of clothing, and he struck one hundred and fifty balls at their outer garments, and not one of them was able to take the pin from his cloak. They were wrestling together and they were all thrown onto the ground by him, and none of their number could either reach or seize him. When Conchobar saw the little boy he said: "Alas, O young heroes, you see before you the little boy who has come from my own land. O, were but the deeds of the young warriors of the same excellence as [those of] this young warrior!" "It is not proper to say that," said Fergus, "as the excellence of his parents has borne fruit in the deeds of this young warrior. Send for the boy so that we can take him to the fort for a drink at the feast." The little boy is summoned to Conchobar. "Well, little boy," said Conchobar, "come to the ale-drinking feast with us." "Indeed I will not," said the little boy. "Why then?" said Conchobar, "for you have your fill of feats and pleasant games in the company of youth, and you will not go as you never tire of games. And it is long for people to be waiting without food." "Leave a trail," said the boy, "and I will go after it." "You do not know the way," said Conchobar, "so I will point out the common track of the horses and the chariots."

'And Conchobar came then to the house of Cualann the smith. The king was attended upon and received with respect, with affection and gifts, as he was entitled, from the nobility, with customary kindness. Reeds and fresh rushes were laid down. They begin drinking and making merry. Culann asks Conchobar: "Well, O king, has anyone been summoned to follow you to this fort?" "Indeed no one has," says Conchobar, forgetting about the little boy who was following him. "Why do you ask?" says Conchobar. "Because I have a good war hound, and when [he is] released, nobody dares to enter within an area of a hundred hamlets. As for travellers and visitors, except for me, he knows none. He has the power and strength of a hundred." Then Conchobar said: "Open the fortress so that this cantred can be protected by the hound." The dog was released from his chain, and he makes a circuit of the smith's country. He goes as far as the mound and from there watches over the fort, with his head on his paws; fierce, barbarous, furious, uncouth and surly, that dog-like beast there.

'As regards the youths that were there at Emain, they stayed there until it was time to disperse. Each went to the house of his father and mother, or of his foster-father or foster-mother. Then the little boy took to the track of the host until he reached the house of the smith. He shortened the way by pucking with his hurley and ball. When he reached the green about the fort in which Conchobar and Culann were, he was throwing and striking nothing but the ball. The hound observed the little boy and barked at him, so that the whole country heard the yelling of the hound. And it would not please the hound to eat him in parts, but to swallow him whole, thus his chest expanded, as did the width of his neck, so that he could consume the boy. The boy struck the ball and aimed it at the dog, so that it shot into his throat, crashing through his innards and out through his anus, and then he seized him by his feet and struck him about the pillar-stone, so that bits of him were strewn about the ground. Conchobar heard the yelling of the hound: "Alas, O youth," said Conchobar, "that we came to drink at this feast." "Why?" said the Ulaid. "Because the little boy who promised to follow me, the son of my sister and Sétanta mac Sualtam by name has fallen by that hound." All the famous Ulaid rose at once and opened wide the door of the fort and went out to meet him. Quick as they reached the place, Fergus reached it faster than they. He lifted up the boy from the ground by the top of his shoulders and brought him to Conchobar. And Cualann came out and saw his dismembered hound. It was a crushing blow to him. He went back into the fort after that. "Your father and mother are always welcome here," said Culann, "but not you." "What have you against the boy?" said Conchobar. "Unfortunate that you come today to consume my ale and food, since all the life has been taken away from my good dog. That was a good member of my family that you took from me, he guarded my cattle, my flocks and my property." "Do not be wild at me, dear Culann," said the little boy, "for my word will be honoured." "What promises have been given, O son?" said Conchobar.

"If," said the boy, "a similar hound gives birth to a hound yonder in Ireland, I will rear it like a father. In the meantime, I will be your hound protecting your flocks, your cattle and your property." "Well, have you given your word, little son?" said Conchobar. "Indeed," said Cathbad, "we could not have done better. In the meantime, why not take Cú Chulainn as your name?" "No," said the little son, "for I prefer my own name: Sétanta mac Sualtam." "Don't say that, little son," said Cathbad, "since all the men of Ireland and of Scotland will call you by that name, and the mouths of the men of Ireland and of Scotland will utter your name." "Well then, that's fine with me," said the little boy, "to have that honorary title placed upon me, namely Cú Chulainn, after the hound that was killed, belonging to Culann the smith."

'Now the little son,' said Cormac Con Loinges, the son of Conchobar, 'was only six years of age when he carried out that act which killed the war hound, an act which no one in this territory would dare contemplate, nor should it be necessarily wonderful or surprising, that at the age of seventeen he cut a four-pronged shaft, besides killing two or three or four men on the Táin Bo Cuailnge.'

'The little boy did a third feat the year after killing the hound,' said Fiacha mac Fir Aba. 'What did he do?' said Ailill. 'Cathbad the druid was instructing his pupils to the north-east of Emain. The company consisted of eight pupils being instructed in druidic verse. One of them questioned the teacher as to what omens the day held and whether they were good or bad. Cathbad answered: "Any young warrior who takes up arms today will be famous and world-renowned, but will be short-lived."

'Cú Chulainn was performing feats and, though he was to the west of Emain, he heard what was said. He put down everything he had and went to the sleeping chamber of Conchobar. "Best wishes to you, O warrior king," said the little son. "What is this, a greeting followed by a request?" said Conchobar. "So what do you seek, little son?" said the king. "I want to take up arms." "So who instructed you?" "Cathbad the druid," said the boy. "He would not deceive you," said Conchobar.

'Conchobar gave him two spears, a sword and a shield. He brandishes and smashes the weapons into small fragments. Conchobar brings him two more spears, a sword and a shield. He arranges them, then bends, brandishes and wields them so that they too are reduced to small fragments. There were fourteen sets of weapons at Emain for the youth in attendance and for the company of youth who were being trained in weaponry. Conchobar took these weapons of assault to him, he showed his particular prowess after this by disintegrating the lot of them.

'"These weapons are no good, O master Conchobar," said the little son, "they will not satisfy me." Conchobar then gave him two spears, a shield and a sword from his own weapons. He struck and brandished them so that they quivered and shook, so that the pointed end of the weapons reached against the butt ends; but they did not break, they held up to him. "Good indeed are these weapons," said the little son, "I am well-suited for them. Welcome the king whose arms and armour these are, welcome the land from which he comes." Just then Cathbad the druid comes into the tent and asks "Is the little son taking up arms?" "So it would appear," says Conchobar. "It is not my wish that this mother's son takes up arms this day," said Cathbad. "Why so, was it not you who instructed him?" said Conchobar. "Indeed it was not me," said Cathbad. "Why, you imp" said Conchobar, "weaving your lies!" "Don't be enraged, O master Conchobar," said the little son, "as I was simply inquiring from the pupils what the omen for the day was, and it was said that, should a little boy take up arms that day, he would be noble, honourable and short-lived." "That is true," said Cathbad, "and you will be noble and famous, and your life will be brief." "What good is it to have illustrious fame for a day and a night unless famous tales of my exploits live after me?" "Then," said Cathbad, "proceed in this chariot on your first adventure."

'Cú Chulainn takes off in the chariot and, as is his custom, he gives it a severe testing, so that it is reduced to small fragments. He then went off in a second chariot and it ended up like the first. And again he did the same to the third chariot. There were seventeen chariots for the youth that were in attendance and for the company of youth that were with Conchobar at Emain: none of them could withstand the onslaught of the little boy. "These chariots are not good, O father Conchobar," said the little boy, "they are not a match for me." "Where is Ibar mac Riangabra?" said Conchobar. "I am here," said Riangabra. "Get my two horses yonder and yoke them to my chariot," said Conchobar. Now the charioteer gets the horses and yokes them to the chariot. Then the little boy mounted the chariot, he struck the chariot about him, and it withstood him and did not break. "Good indeed is this chariot," said the little boy, "well is it suitable for me." "Good wee lad," said Ibar, "allow the horses to graze now." "It is too early yet, Ibar," said the little boy. "Let us go about Emain today, today on the first day of my taking up arms, so that I can show my dexterity at arms." They came three times around Emain. "Allow the horses to graze, O little boy," said Ibar. "It is too early yet," said the little boy. "Let us come before the boy troop, so that they can greet me on this my first day to take up arms."

'They went before the plain on which the boy troop was. "So these are the arms you have taken up," said each. "Indeed that is so," said he. "Great your victory, your first wounding and your triumph," said they, "but it is too early for you to take up arms simply because of distinctions gained at sport." "I will not part from you, but it has been predicted that I will take up arms today." "Allow the horses to graze now," said Ibar. "It is too early," said the boy. "And where does this great road yonder go, which passes by us?" said the boy. "Why would you go there, fine fellow?" said Ibar. "Well, it is the principal road in the province and I would like to know where it goes." "It goes to Áth na Foraire in Sliab Fúait [fews mountains]", said Ibar. "Why is it called Áth na Foraire?'" said the boy. "It is known as the 'ford of the watchman or look-out," said Ibar, "for it is there that the Ulster heroes are on the look-out and keep guard for any young heroes that may come from outside the territory, in order that they may challenge them to combat. Single combat is the custom here, so that the province is defended by one warrior. Moreover, should poets come to Ulster and be dissatisfied there, then they are given jewels and precious gifts. And further, should any poets come to Ulster, it is the duty of the sentry to protect them as far as Conchobar's bedpost and this sentry is the subject of the first official composition on reaching Emain." "Do you know who is guarding today?" said the boy. "I do indeed," said Ibar. "It is Conall Cernach, the warrior champion and son of Amergin, the legendary king of Ireland." "Let us go so that we may reach the ford," said the boy.

'They went until they reached that part of the ford where Conall was. "Arms have been taken up yonder," said Conall." "Indeed they have," said Ibar. "May there be victory, triumph and first wounding then," said Conall, "but it is too early for you to assume arms, as you have as yet performed no great deeds, yet whosoever shall will protect and benefit all of Ulster and all the youth against those who encroach on her; the nobles of the province will answer his call." "So what do you do here, master Conall?" said the little boy." "Guarding and protecting the province," said Conall. "Rise up and come now, dear Conall," said the boy, "and allow me to take on the duty of guarding and protecting the province." "No, little boy," said Conall, "you are not capable of combat against a strong warrior." And the boy replied: "Nevertheless, I will go southwards to the banks of Loch Echtra today, in order to redden my hands with the blood of friends or enemies." "And I will go with you," said Conall, "as you come alone into the borderlands." "No," said the little boy. "Indeed I shall go, for the Ulaid would blame me were I to allow you to go alone towards the borders," said Conall.

'The horse was got for Conall and yoked to his chariot, and he went as a protector to the little boy. When Conall came abreast of him, it vexed him that Conall would not allow him to carry out his bloody desires. He lifted a handful of stones and threw them towards the chariot-yoke of Conall, so that it broke the chariot-yoke in two, and Conall fell to the ground, so that his shoulder blade was separated from his shoulder. "Why did you do that, boy?" said Conall. "It was I who threw it in order to test the accuracy of my cast, and also I cast it to see if I have the making of a warrior at arms." "Bad *cess* on your throw and bad *cess* on yourself, and whether or not the enemy takes your head, this far and no farther will I come as your protector." "This indeed has been my desire," said Cú Chulainn, "since there is a *geis* (taboo) on the Ulaid not to pursue the chariot of one whom they are protecting." Then Conall went back north again to Áth na Foraire.

'As regards the little boy (Cú Chulainn), he went south to the banks of Loch Echtra. He was there until the end of the day. "Dare we say it, little boy," said Ibar, "but it is timely now for us to be returning to Emain, for they started pouring out drinks, carving meat and apportioning both a while ago, and your place among the nobles will be kept for you, namely between the feet of Conchobar; and in the house of Conchobar there is no place for me, except between the messengers and the jugglers, and nothing for me to do but to be brawling with them." "Get the steeds from the enclosure," said the boy. The charioteer assembled the horses and came to the boy in the chariot. "What hill is that and what is the summit above it called?" asked the little boy. "Just there that is Sliab Moduirn [Mountains of Mourne], and the white cairn yonder on top is known as Findcharn," said Ibar. "That cairn there is truly beautiful," said the boy." "Beautiful indeed," said Ibar. "Come this way so that we may reach yonder cairn," said Cú Chulainn. "Well, you are one nice troublesome man I see," said Ibar, "for this is my first expedition with you, and I hope it is my last until the day of judgement and, if I ever reach Emain, my only one." They went to the top of the hill. "Well now, Ibar, show me Ulster from each direction, as I do not know the territory of my father Conchobar." The gilly showed him Ulster from every direction. He pointed out the mounds, the open spaces and the hills in each part of the territory. He instructed him as to the names of the plains, the forts and the landmarks in the province. "Well done, Ibar," said Cú Chulainn, "and what is that angular plain with vales and hollows at our back to the south?" "That is Mag Breg," said Ibar. "Show me the buildings and the mounds on that plain." The gilly pointed them out to him: Tara, Telltown Cleittech, Cnogba and the Brú of Mac Ind Oc, and the fort of Nechtan Scéne. "Are they the sons of Nechtan who boast that there are not more members of the Ulaid alive today than have been slain by the sons of Nechtan?" "They are indeed," said the gilly. "So let us go to the fort of mac Nechtan," said the little warrior. "Pity that you should say so," said the gilly, "for it is a foolish thing to say that, and whoever goes there it will not be me." "You shall go dead or alive," said Cú Chulainn. "I will go alive," said Ibar, "and I will leave dead from that fort known as Dún mac Nechtan."

'They went as far as the fort and the boy alighted from the chariot onto the green. Thus he was on the green by the fort, and upon the green was a pillar-stone with an iron collar around it. This was the collar of valour, with a message incised in *ogam*, which said that there was a taboo placed on any warrior coming to the green to challenge anyone to single combat. The little boy read the *ogam*, placed his two arms around the pillar-stone, on which was the collar, and threw the collar into the pool close by. "Methinks," said Ibar, "that things have not improved, and that you will find on this green the things that you have been searching for – the signs of death and destruction." "Good, Ibar," said Cú Chulainn. "Arrange the rugs and covering of the chariot so that I can get a little sleep." "Alas," said the gilly, "for this is the territory of the enemy, and not a field of delight." The gilly then spread the rugs and coverings of the chariot, and the little boy fell asleep on the green.

'Then Fóill mac Nechtan Scéne came onto the green. "Do not unyoke those horses, gilly," said Fóill. "I am not attempting to do so," said Ibar. "These are just the reins I have in my hand." "Whose horses are they?" said Fóill. "The two horses of Conchobar," said the servant, "the two piebalds." "I recognise them" said Fóill. "And who took them to this territory?" "A soft little boy who has taken up arms and who has come to the borders to display his form," said the gilly. "Never will that fellow achieve victory or triumph," said Fóill, "for, were it known that he was capable of action, it is dead rather than alive that he would return northwards to Emain." "Indeed he is not capable, for he is only in his seventh year." Then Cú Chulainn lifted his face from the ground, he placed his hand on his face and his body became purple with anger from the crown of his head to the ground. "Truly I am ready for action," said the boy. "It would seem to me that you are not," said Fóill. "Soon shall you know," said Cú Chulainn, "but let us get to the ford, let us rise with our arms, for all I see here is a coward, and I do not threaten to kill charioteers or messengers or those without arms." Fóill leaps forth for his weapons. "Be on your guard against that man, little boy," said Ibar. "Why?" said Cú Chulainn. "Because that's Fóill mac Nechtan I see," said Ibar, "and he is injured neither by the point nor by the sharp edge of a weapon." "Why say that to me, O Ibar?" said Cú Chulainn, "for I will take a sling with me, so that I can cast an iron ball, and it will pierce the shield plate and his forehead, and the ball will be so heavy as to go through his skull and out through the back of his head, and the sky will be visible through it." Fóill came out. Cú Chulainn then took out the handle of the sling and cast the missile, so that it passed through the shield and the head and the back of the head with equal force, so that blood spilled down the back of the head, and so that the head was separated from the lower neck.

'The son of the chief came out onto the green: Tuachall mac Nechtan was his name. "Well now, I see that you have been boasting," said Tuachall. "I do not boast about the killing of one warrior," said Cú Chulainn. "I would not boast yet, as you will fall by me," said Tuachall. "Away then and get your weapons, since it is nothing but a coward that approaches me," said Cú Chulainn. The man dashed for his weapons. "You should heed our warning about your opponent," said Ibar. "Who is that?" said Cú Chulainn. "That man is Tuachall mac Nechtan, and unless you fell him with the first blow from the first throw from the first encounter, you will not capture him, for he is very cunning, and possesses weaponry with both keen points and edges." "Don't say that to me, dear Ibar," said Cú Chulainn, "for I shall carry in my hand the broad-bladed spear of Conchobar, the poisonous spear, and it shall strike the shield over his breast and break through three ribs, and go into his side and pierce the heart in his chest. For it will be cast at a foreign settler and not at a freeman. And he will require neither medical treatment nor nursing when I have finished with him." Tuachall mac Nechtan came out onto the green and Cú Chulainn cast the broad-bladed spear (*manais*) of Conchobar at him, and it struck the shield over his breast and broke three ribs in his side, and pierced the heart in his chest. His head was cut off then before his body reached the ground.

'The youngest of the clan came onto the green, namely Fandle mac Nechtan. "They were foolish people that you fought with there," said he. "Why so?" said Cú Chulainn. "Come out into the water where your feet will not reach the bottom," said Fandle. Then Fandle leapt across the pool. "Be wary of him, little boy," said Ibar. "Why is that necessary?" asks Cú Chulainn. "Well, I see Fandle now and he got his name from *Fannall*, which means "swallow", after the way he flits across the sea, and no swimmers on Earth can compete with him." "There is no point in saying that to me, O Ibar," said Cú Chulainn, "for, as you know, we at Emain are close to the Callan river. And when the warrior youth leave their feats and games, and when they cannot cross the water, I carry them, one on each palm of my hand, and two of the boy troop on my shoulders; so that not even my ankles get wet." They encounter each other on the ford, and Cú Chulainn fights Fandle back and forth across the water, and overthrows him with a direct blow with Conchobar's sword, and severs his head from the lower neck, and lets the trunk of the body go with the stream and takes the head with him.

'After that they went into the fort and ravaged the dwelling and set fire to the surrounding buildings. Then they turn round back to Sliab Fúait and take the three heads of the sons of Nechtan with them.

'They saw a herd of wild deer before them. "Whose is that abundant herd of fierce cattle yonder?" said the little boy. "They are not cattle," said Ibar. "They are a herd of wild deer that wander the hidden ways of Sliab Fúait." "Let us goad the horses to see if we can capture any of them," said Cú Chulainn. The charioteer urges on the horses, but the king's horses are too fat to keep up with the herd of deer. Cú Chulainn left the chariot, and ran swiftly and vigorously after the deer, and caught two of them, then tied them to the shaft of the chariot.

'Then they went towards the assembly place at Emain, and on their way they saw a flock of white swans beyond them. "Are those tame or wild birds, O Ibar?" said Cú Chulainn. "Indeed they are wild birds," said Ibar, "a flock of swans that come from the stones and rocks of the islands out in the great sea, and graze on the open plains of Ireland." "What would be better, O Ibar, to bring them alive or dead to Emain?" "It would be more worthy to bring them back alive, for it is not everyone who can bring them back alive." Then the skill of the little boy brings eight birds to a standstill, and soon after that he brings sixteen to a standstill. He loops them, flying as a flock, by string to the shafts of the chariot. "Bring those birds with you, O Ibar," said Cú Chulainn. "You do," said Ibar. "Why is that necessary?" said Cú Chulainn. "Just bring them to me." "I cannot move from where I am," said Ibar, "for the strength and vigour of the horses would cause the chariot wheels to cut me to pieces, or else the stags' antlers would pierce and wound me." "Then you are not a true warrior, O Ibar. However, I will stare at the horses and they will keep a straight course. And I will look across at the deer, and they will bend their antlers from fear and trembling, and you will step down over the horns."

'They went on until they reached Emain. There Leborcham, the daughter of Aí and Adairce, noticed them. "A single warrior there," cried Leborcham, "and terrifyingly he comes. The chariot contains the blood-red heads of the enemy and, flying above, beautiful shining birds delay its progress, and along the shafts of the chariot fierce wild stags are bound, tied and fettered. And unless he is attended upon, all the young Ulaid will fall by him." "We know that chariot warrior," said Conchobar. "He is the little boy who is the son of my sister, who went to the border county to redden his hands, and who never has enough of combat, and unless he is attended upon all the

21

youth of Emain will perish by him."

'A meeting advised that women should be allowed to meet the boy, these women to number one hundred and fifty, comprising ten women and one hundred and forty stark naked at the same time. The chief woman leading them as they exposed themselves to him was Scandlach. Then all the women came out and appeared naked before him. The boy lowered his face against them and turned his face towards the chariot so that he would not see their unashamed nakedness. He then raised himself into the chariot and soon after is put into three vats of cold water in order to drown his anger. The first vat he was put into, he demolished two of its staves and two of its hoops, which sounded like the breaking of a nutshell. The second wet his hand, and the third he endures. Then the anger abated and a cloak was put around him. And he returned to his natural shape, making a whirling motion from his head to his feet. Seven toes in each of his two feet, seven fingers in each of his two hands, seven pupils in each of his two royal eyes, and seven rays flashing from each of his pupils. Four dimples on each of his two cheeks, a blue dimple, a purple, a green and a yellow one. Fifty bright yellow locks from one ear to the other, like the wax of bees or like a pale gold brooch against the sun. A bright cropped head of hair on him. A green cloak about him, silver clasped to the tip of his shoulder. A gold threaded shirt about him. The boy was seated between the two knees of Conchobar, and the king stroked his head.

'Now by seven years of age the little lad had done the following deeds: he had overcome the champions and warriors by whom two thirds of the Ulaid had fallen, and they had not been avenged until this person had arisen amongst them. And one need not feel wonder and astonishment when he comes to the borderlands at the age of seventeen, having killed two or three or four men during the cattle raid of Cooley.'

This then is the tale of the boyhood deeds of Cú Chulainn.

CHAPTER 3

The Wooing of Emer

Tochmarc Emire

Now there was a wonderful, princely king at Emain Macha, namely Conchobar mac Fachtna Fatháig. He had dominion throughout Ulster. There was peace, justice and merriment under him. There was an abundance of nuts and acorns, game and seafood. There was authority, law and good rule throughout Ulster. There was great dignity, sovereignty and abundance in the royal house at Emain.

It is thus that the house was described. The banqueting hall of Conchobar had a great likeness to the house of the circulation of mead (Tech Mid-chúarta) at Tara. Nine beds from the fire to the wall there, thirty feet up was each bronze frontage to the house. There were carvings of red yew there. A frieze along the lower part added to it; above, a tiled roof. A frieze of silver surrounded Conchobar's bed at the front of the house; the support posts were of bronze, with lustrous gold upon the head, with inlaid carbuncles of precious stones; there was equal light both day and night there. There was a silver gong above the king's parapet in the royal household. When Conchobar beat the royal rod against the gong, all the Ulaid turned towards him. Twelve beds there, twelve beds for the charioteers and those visiting in their company.

However, there was room for all the Ulster heroes drinking in that royal house, and consent was not required from anyone. The Ulster heroes were noble, lord-like and pleasant in that house. There was much socializing in the royal house and wonderful entertainment. There were performances, music and recitations there; feats by the champions, recitations by the poets and music by the harpers and lute players.

One day the Ulaid were at Emain Macha with Conchobar, drinking from the beer barrel: a hundred measures of this were sufficient for the evening. This was the coal-hued drink. It satisfies all the Ulaid for a while. The charioteers of the Ulaid performed their feats across a rope from one door to the other in the house at Emain. One hundred and ninety-five feet long was the size of that house. Three feats the charioteers were performing: the javelin feat and the apple trick and the edge-feat.

The warriors that performed the feats were: Conall mac Amergin, Fergus mac Roich Ródanai, Lóegaire Búadach mac Conaid, Celtchar mac Uthidir, Dubtach mac Lugdach, Cú Chulainn mac Súaltam and Scél mac Bairini, from which Belach mBairdini [the Pass of Barnene] is named. The last-named was the doorkeeper at Emain Macha; the 'tale of Scél' came from Scél the great story-teller.

Cú Chulainn surpassed them all at sport and dexterity. The women loved Cú Chulainn greatly for his skill at sport, for his dexterity with his hands, for his wisdom, for the beauty of his countenance, for the loveliness of his face, for the sweetness of his voice. There were seven pupils in his royal eyes – four in the one and three in the other – seven fingers on each of his hands and seven toes on each of his two feet. His gifts were numerous. In the first place his wisdom came from the magic beam of light springing from his head ('the champion's light'), then his victory in performance, his performance at board games, his skill in judgement, his power of prophecy, his intelligence, his manner. Yet he had three failings: he was very young, he was not sufficiently grown up to rein a team of oxen, and it was easy to mock the hero for being very bold and very beautiful.

The Ulstermen held a council on account of the great love the women and daughters had for Cú Chulainn, for at that time Cú Chulainn had no wife. Advice was offered: Cú Chulainn was to choose and woo a wife. It was obvious to them that, if he sought a wife, less destruction would be done to the maidens who adored him, for a man should accept the love of a woman, especially one who would suit him. And, moreover, they were upset and afraid that Cú Chulainn might die prematurely. For that reason they desired that a woman be taken to him, in order that he would leave an heir, for they knew that only from him himself would his like be born again.

Later, nine men from each province in Ireland were summoned by Conchobar to seek a woman for Cú Chulainn. They were to search first in each fort and in each large community in Ireland for the daughter of a king or a chief or a landowner, someone who was pleasant and whom Cú Chulainn might choose and court.

The messengers came together on the day after a year, yet they found no maiden for Cú Chulainn to choose and court.

Afterwards Cú Chulainn himself went in search of a woman he knew at Luglochta Logo [the Gardens of Lug], namely Emer, the daughter of Fergal Manach. Then Cú Chulainn and his charioteer, Laeg mac Ríangabra, went in their chariot. It is the one chariot that neither the troop nor horses can follow of all the Ulster chariots, on account of its speed and its splendour, the chariot; and in it the seated champion.

Later Cú Chulainn found the maiden in a playing field with her foster sisters about her. These girls were playing around the fort of the landowner, Fergal. They were learning embroidery and needlework with Emer. Moreover, she was the one woman who of all the daughters of Ireland was worthy to be addressed and courted by him. For it is she who held the six supreme gifts, namely, an excellent shape, an excellent voice, pleasant speech, skill at embroidery, wisdom and chastity. Cú Chulainn said that of all the daughters of Ireland she was most fit for him by age, manner and race, 'for I would go with no one and would be security for no one unless she were my wife. For she is the one woman possessing all the attributes.'

It is thus that Cú Chulainn went wooing with determination.

It was dressed in his cloak for special assemblies that Cú Chulainn went to address Emer that day, so that she might contemplate his shape. At that moment the daughters were on the benches on the grass beside the fort [of Fergal] when they heard something coming towards them. It was the hooves of a horse, the clattering of a chariot, the whistling of the straps, the squeaking of the wheels, the rage of the hero, the clashing of weapons.

'Let one of you look out,' said Emer, 'to see who is coming towards us.'

'Indeed, I see there,' said Fíal, daughter of Fergal, 'two horses equally large, of similar shape, equally swift, equally bounding, prick-eared, high-headed, swift, having large reins, wide-standing, thin-mouthed, with hair plaited, having broad foreheads, very speckled, very slender, very broad, impetuous, curly-maned and curly-tailed. The grey horse, having broad hips, wild, swift, leaping, furious, skipping, long-maned, spotted, stamping, low-maned, high-headed, having a broad chest, throwing up large clods of earth all over the place with its hooves and its fourfold vigour, triumphant in vigour he overtakes a flock of birds, he strikes a course, the breath of the horses leaps from them, thirty red sparks of fire flare out of the jaws at the end of the muzzle, and down along the shaft at the right end of the chariot.

'Another horse, jet-black, hard-headed, round, slender-footed, having broad flanks, swift, well-running, with plaits, broad-backed, strong-necked, spotted, sprightly, angry, striding proudly, bounding, long-maned, curly-maned, long-tailed, having long plaits, having a broad forehead, elegant. The horse plays at fighting along a meadow. Presently it strides through the valley and sends its breath over the plain of the mid-glen. It does not leave any obstacle unturned, along a course of long distance in the land of oak.

'The chariot is comprised of wickerwork, namely a bundle of sticks. Two wheels of white copper, a chariot pole of white silver connected to a bronze white hoop. A high body to the chariot, very beautiful, it consists of hard turned tin. An arched yoke made of solid gold. With an entirely yellow plaited bridle. The chariot shafts are hard and straight as a sword.

'A dark sorrowful man there in that chariot, the most beautiful man in Ireland. A fine five-fold purple tunic about him, fastened by an inlaid gold brooch above his white breast, which when open heaves in broad blows against him. A white hooded smock is on him, interwoven with shining gold. Seven red dragon stones over the centre of each of his two eyes. Two cheeks veined with blue, and blood-red, emitting jets of fire and vapours. A ray of love flashes from his face. It seems to me that a shower of pearls is placed on his head. Black, each of his two eyebrows. A sword with a gold hilt in a sheath is against his thighs. A fiery-red spear fitted to his hand, an aggressive, keen javelin there on a shaft of forest wood, dark red and tied to the hoop of the chariot frame. A purple shield with a circular rim of silver and many interlaced figures of gold are above. He performs the hero's salmon leap, and many feats equally swift above the hero's chariot.

'There is another, slender, tall and freckled charioteer in front of that chariot. Very curly red hair is on the crown of his head. A white embroidered headband is upon his forehead, not allowing his hair down his face. There is a lock of gold hair in a bun at the back of his head. A winged cape is about him, with an opening at the elbows. A spike of red gold is in his hand.'

Cú Chulainn reached the place where the maidens were and greeted them. Emer raised up her beautifully shaped face and recognised Cú Chulainn, and said: 'You are riding about in the south,' said she, in other words make plain your intentions.

'Best wishes to you in your uncertainty, and may you be safe from every harm,' said he.

'From where have you come?' said she.

'From the said Emain,' said he, namely the plain of Emain.

'Where did you spend the night?' said she.

'We spent the night,' said he, 'looked after by a man on the cattle plain of Tethra'.

'What was the entertainment there?' said she.

'Chariot outrages were cooked there,' said he, that is, a meal was cooked [of horseflesh?].

'Which way did you come?' said she.

'Between two established woods.'

'Which way did you go?" said she.

'Easy to answer,' said he. 'Across the darkness of the sea, across the wonderful man of god, across the foam of the two horses of Emain, across the field of the Mórrígan, against the mountain ridge of the Great Pig, across the glen of plenty, between the god and the prophet, across the marrow fields of the women of the prophetess Fedelm, between the king and his wife, across the stream of the horse deity, between the king of Ireland and his champion, through the underground storehouse for cattle at Muin-Chille, across the Ailbine river, across the midden heap at the estuary, between the large tub and the small tub, towards the maidens of the nephew of Tethra, king of the Fomorians, towards Luglochta Loga' [that is, Lug's gardens].

'What about yourself, O maiden?' said Cú Chulainn.

'Easy to answer,' said the woman. 'Tara is pure, a maiden is pure, chastity is in the mind,' or as Tara is over each hill, so is Emer superior to each woman in her purity. 'A sprig that is not bent. A watchman who does not see far,' meaning each looks at her beauty but does not see it. 'The bashful woman is like the worm in the water, for when they look for the worm all they see is a string of water. For I am related to Tethra the sea god, and therefore will not depart from the rushes' [on account of her beauty]. "The daughter of a king, the flame of glory, I will not be bound to a slender youth, until that sleepy one has acquired the skills and renown of a charioteer. I desire a strong man to follow,' that is, a strong man who will be capable of pursuing her. "Whatever it will be, and without being an essential part of my adventure, his desire will carry me off from Fergal.'

'Who are the strong men pursuing you here, O maiden?' said Cú Chulainn.

'Easy to tell,' said Emer: 'Two Luis, two Lúaths, Lúath and Láth Gaible mac Tethrach, Triath and Trescath, Broin and Bolar, Bass mac Omnaig, the eight Connlas, Conn mac Forgaill. Each of these men has the strength of a troop of one hundred and the feats of nine men. Moreover the strength of Fergal himself is impossible to calculate: stronger than each warrior, more learned than each druid, keener than each poet. Manly deeds will be greater when performed by Fergal himself, everyone will be more powerful, both at games and at combat.'

'Why do you not include me among those strong men?' said Cú Chulainn.

'If you can obtain their skills,' said the daughter, 'then there is no reason why I ought not to reckon you among them.'

'I choose, O maiden,' said Cú Chulainn, 'that my swift deeds and famous feats of strength be known among them.'

'Indeed, what is your strength then?' said Emer.

'Easy to tell,' said he. 'My weakest fighting is a match for twenty, a third part of my strength is a match for thirty, on my own I can take on forty, my protection is a match for a hundred. I protect the fords, and in battle I am a monster before warriors. I leap into the multitude of the host, and the large band of armed warriors dread my face and countenance.'

'O triumphant, noble, tender and beautiful one,' said the daughter, 'You are not a powerful charioteer yet.'

'Noble indeed,' said he. "I have been reared by the hand of my master, Conchobar. Not as a little churl, striving to bring up his children. Not between a stone and a kneading trough, nor between a fire and a wall, nor upon the ground of a front yard with

Conchobar, but between charioteers and champions, between jesters and druids, between poets and wise men, between hospitallers and victuallers of Ulster, all the customs and arts have been completed by me.'

'Then who are they who have been teaching you these feats, O great one?' said Emer.

'Easy to say,' said he. 'I was trained by Sencha of fluent speech until I was strong, intelligent, noble, dexterous and a full warrior. I am wise in judgements. I am not forgetful. I address people intelligently; I prepare speeches. I decide on all the judgements of the Ulaid and I do not rouse them. All this I have learnt from the rearing by Sencha. I was taken into the family of Blai Briugu and my lawful position was fixed by them. I summon the men in the company of Conchobar, king of the province of Ulster. I entertain them for a week. I support them by gifts and by pillaging. I support their honour in contests of honour. I was a fosterling of Fergus until I killed three young warriors by strong deeds and feats of arms. Thus I am able to defend the border territories against strangers. I am cunning in deeds and feats of arms. I am a protection against every evil. I make damage at each turn through the fosterage of Fergus. I came to the knee of the poet Amergin, so that I could praise every quality the king possessed. I repelled [the enemy] by duels and by feats of arms, by wisdom, by excellence, by severity, by hacking, by courage. I repelled each charioteer and I did not strive to please anyone save Conchobar.

'Findchóem brought me up so that I was the foster-brother and equal in vigour of the triumphant Conall Cernach. For the sake of Dechtine, Cathbad of the kind face has instructed me. So that now I am a wise man well-studied in the craft of the gods of magic, so that I am a learned man with a distinct knowledge. The Ulaid reared me the same as all the rest, among the charioteer and the warrior, between the king and the ollamh. So that I am a friend of the host and the multitude, so that I avenge in honour contests all equally. Indeed, as a free man I was conceived by Lug mac Conn mac Eithliu while on an expedition to the shelter of Dechtine at the house of the Proud One at Brú na Bóinne. Moreover, yourself, O daughter,' said Cú Chulainn, 'how were you reared at Luglochta Loga [The Gardens of Lug]?'

'I was reared,' said she, 'by the distinguished Féni, in the ways of graciousness, under the injunction of chastity, with the appearance of a queen, with a fine countenance. In the company of boastful women every noble figure is judged in comparison with mine.'

'Indeed, you are one of the noble stock then,' said Cú Chulainn.

'Moreover, how,' said Cú Chulainn, 'can it not be customary for us both to meet? For until now, I have not found a woman who could hold her own in conversation with me in this way.'

'Question: do you have a wife?' said the daughter. 'Are you looking after your family?'

'No, why?" said Cú Chulainn.

'It is not lawful for me to go with a man,' said the maiden, 'in the presence of a sister that is older than I am, for I see Fíal, daughter of Fergal, close by. She is excellent at needlework.'

'Indeed, it is not she whom I have fallen in love with,' said Cú Chulainn, 'and I am not obliged to a woman who might have known a man before. And it has been related to me that yonder woman has been with Cairpre Nia Fer on a former occasion.'

Later on, as they were considering that, Cú Chulainn sees the breasts of the maiden over the borders of her smock. So that he said: 'Beautiful is the meadow, the meadow beyond the ridge.'

Then in answer to Cú Chulainn's words the maiden said: 'No one will approach this meadow, unless he kills a hundred men on each ford from Áth Scenmenn on the Delvin stream towards Banchuing and another hundred at the confines of Brega by swift-passing Fedelm.'

'Beautiful is the meadow, the meadow beyond the ridge,' said Cú Chulainn.

'No one will approach this ridge,' said she, 'unless he can perform the salmon leap and take two men with their weight in gold while slaying thrice nine men, saving one man, the one in the middle of each nine men, with each blow.'

'Beautiful is the meadow, the meadow beyond the ridge,' said Cú Chulainn.

'No one will approach this meadow,' said she, 'who does not go without sleep from Samain to Brigit"s day, from Brigit's day to Beltane or May day, and to autumn from Beltane.'

'Tell me, and it is done,' said Cú Chulainn.

'The offer is dependent on an offer being made, I will take it upon myself, I will accept it,' said Emer.

'Question: describe yourself,' said she.

'I am the other nephew of a man who goes to the wood [*ros*] of Badb,' said he.

'What is your name?' said she.

'I am the champion of the plague that visits dogs,' said he.

Afterwards Cú Chulainn went from them after some pretence at words, and he did not make any more conversation on that day. When Cú Chulainn was crossing Brega, he was questioned by his charioteer, Laeg: 'Well,' said he, 'and the words you spoke to each other, and the girl Emer, what had she to say?'

'You do not know,' said Cú Chulainn, 'what it is like to be wooing Emer, and you are heeding and concealing the conversation, so that the maidens do not understand what is being said during the courting, which occurs when Fergal is asleep, as we cannot meet with his consent.'

Cú Chulainn repeated the conversation, and was explaining it and abridging it for his charioteer.

'Emain,' he said, 'when she asked, 'Where do you come from?' It is as I have said: Emain Macha, Macha the daughter of Sainrith mac Imbath, wife of Cruind mac Agnoman, she ran against two horses of the king, after she was requested to do so; she outstrips them on the course, and gives birth to a son and a daughter at one delivery. So that Emain is called Emain [a pair of twins] after them, and the course that Macha ran is called the Plain of Macha.

'The man who was mentioned,' said he 'the man in whose house we passed the night, he is Conchobar's fisherman, namely Roncu. It is he who chases the fish that thread under the sea. It is a shoal of fish that he draws in from the sea, and it is the sea of the Plain of Tethra, the king of kings of the Fomorians, that is the plain of the king of the Fomorians.

'A cooking hearth with a young colt in it was mentioned, that is, a young animal. It is a chariot crime during nine days unless it is under the king. And it is an injunction on them to seek protection, in other words, there is a chariot taboo for nine days on a person eating horse meat.

'Going between two support lengths is mentioned: that is two mountains there, between which we have come, that is, the Fews at our west and Slieve Gullion at the east side. At Oircel [Mill-Wheel]

31

we were between them, that is, we were in the wood between them, between the two of them I judged the way.

'The way was mentioned, from the dark sea: this means from the plain of the dark sea [*muir* = sea, *themne* = dark] i.e. Muirthemne. On this sea thirty years before the Flood, and under the protection or shelter of the sea, a boat arrived on the plain of Muirthemne, which is the magical sea that drew in an armed man into the centre of the treasure cave. This man was the Dagda, who came there with his awesome club, and on the beach he uttered the following words: "Turn your hollow head, turn your envious body, turn your shield and gaze."

'Upon Amrún Fer Diad, that is, a wondrous mystery and a famous secret; it is known today as Grellach Dollaid. It is there that Dollud mac Cairbre Nia Fer is with his wounding stick. However, it was named Amrún Fer Diad before that, at a time when a hundred char- ioteers were mustering for the battle of Mag Tuired with the Túatha Dé Danann, in order to defeat and then collect tax from the Fomorians, this tax to consist of two thirds of their linen, of their milk and of their children.

' "Across the foam of the two horses from Emain": There was a wonderful young warrior with the king of Ireland. The two horses were reared by him at the fairy mound at Ercmon of the Túatha Dé. Nemed mac Nama was the name of the king there. Afterwards they let themselves down from the two horses on that fairy mound and a unique stream burst forth after them from that mound, and there was a great foam upon that stream there. And across half the country there was a great foam for a great period of time; thus it was until the end of the year. So that it was safely said that the water was brown from the foam, that is, from the foam upon the water, and it is the Uanub [foam river] that is there today.

'The field of the Mórrígan is said to be upper Edmann. The ground there is where the Dagda brought the Mórrígan and later turned his attention to her thighs. The year Ibor Boichlid slayed the sons of Garb in that field, there was misfortune in that weedy field during that year for the two sons of Garb.

'Druim na Mármuice' or the ridge of the great pig is said to be Drom Beg. The description of the pig was explained to the sons of Míl upon each hill and upon each mound in Ireland, at the time when they were planning and desiring to seize the country by force, after they had put out lies against the Túatha Dé Danann.

' "Glend na Márdaim" was said to be Glen Breoga from Breoga mac Breogan, ancestor of the sons of Míl, so it is named Glen Breogan and Mag Breg or the plain of Brega. Glen Márdaim was called the beloved ox of the son of Smirgull of the son of Tethra, who was king of Ireland and who dwelt there. Moreover, the ox died there; the women took charge of its effigy that rose up on the plain of Brega towards the back of the fort.

'It was said that the path between the god and the druid is in Mac Ind Óc, that is, the burial places of the god Óengus at Brú na Bóinne and the druid, namely Bresal Bofaith, at the east of the Brú. In between them was one woman, the wife of the smith. Thus it is between the fairy hill of the Brú where Óengus is buried and the fairy mound of Bresal the druid.

'Upon Smiur Mná Fedelm, which was another name for the Boyne, which is called after Bóand, the wife of Nechtan mac Labrad; who went in search of the secret well, which was in the front yard of the fort, with the three cupbearers of Nechtan, namely, Flesc and Lesc and Lúam. And no one came to that well without disgrace unless they came with the cupbearers. The queen went with pride and overbearing towards the well, and said that she would neither destroy the place nor bring disgrace upon it. She came to the well in a direction contrary to the sun's, feeling the supernatural power. Later, three waves burst forth and broke against her two thighs, her right hand and one of her eyes. Then she ran, avoiding disgrace, out of the mound and towards the sea. Everywhere she ran the well or spring ran after her. Segais is the name of that mound. The spring of Segais runs from that mound towards the pool of Mocha, to the elbow of the women of Nuada, being the poetic name of part of the lower course of the river Boyne, to the estuary of the Boyne after that; Bóand of Meath, she had a hundred attendants, from Find to Trim to the marrow women of Fedelm, from Trim to the sea.

'Between Triath the king and his wife was said to be Cleitech, and Fésse was there as well. For Triath is the name of the hero, the lord of the host. Moreover, it is the name of the king, the chief of a great people. And Cleithech is the hero of the battle troop. Fésse is the name of a great woman, a great housewife and spouse. And between the boar and the sow we came.

'The king of Ireland and his champion, that is Cerna, it is across from there we have come, that is, Cerna, after whom this place is called. "The fairy mound of the Círini" was its name far back in time. The name "Cerna", meaning a swelling of the body, from a wound he received; he was proclaimed Enna Aignech Cerna, king of Ireland, in that mound there. And his steward was wounded to the east of that mound there. That champion's name is forever associated with Rath Gníad at Cerna. Enna made Geise, his champion, a boy king of Emain on account of the great friendship that there was between Geise and Cerna.

'The washing place of the Horse God, as it was called, is now known as the Ainge or Nanny stream. They washed the horses of the man god [Fer Déa] there, after they came back from the battle of Mag Tuired. The Ainge, where they washed the horses of the Túatha Dé Danann, after that same battle.

'The storehouse for cattle at Manncille is now called Muincille. It is there that Mannach the hospitaller was. Moreover, there was a great cattle plague in Ireland during the reign of Bresal Bric, son of Fiachra Fobric of Leinster. Thus Mannach made a great underground storehouse there; that place is known as the upper part of Muincille today. And his cattle were confined in the storehouse and guarded against the plague. At the end of seven years he prepared a coshering feast for the king and twenty-four couples. Manncille, therefore, is the storehouse of Mannach in the upper part of Manncille.

The Ollbine was called the Ailbine then. There was a wonderful king here in Ireland. Rúad mac RígDúnd was his name and he was from Munster. He held a meeting with foreigners; he sailed out with three boats for this meeting in the direction of the south of Scotland. Now there were thirty in each boat. The fleet stopped in the middle of the sea. Neither winds nor a search for treasures had stopped them. A meeting was held to cast lots in order to determine why they had stopped, and to ascertain where at sea the boat had been becalmed. The lot fell on the king himself. Later, the king Rúad mac RígDúnd jumped into the sea. He disappeared at once, having thrown himself into the great plain. He found at once nine beautiful women. They confessed that they had stopped the boat when it had come towards them. They brought nine ships of gold to him. He spent nine nights with them, a night with each of them.

In this manner he spent his time. Meanwhile the people in the boats had no power to overcome the magic of the women. Then one woman said that it was time for her to be conceiving and that she would bear a son and visit a high place, and she would return to them before the birth of the son. The king returned to his men and took them to the women. They were carousing with the women for seven years; they left and did not revisit any place until they reached their destination at Inber nAilbine. Then they overtook the women. The men heard the sound of nine bronze instruments when they were landing their boats. Then the women went on land and left the boy behind. The landing place was stony and rocky. The men threw a stone at the boy, so that he died. The women retreated and all shouted: "Great crime, great crime," or *bine oll*. That is how Inbern Ailbine got its name.

'The midden heap at Máirimdill, as it is called, is at the back of Telltown. It is there that Lug Scimaig had a great feast for Lug mac Ethlenn to comfort him after the battle of Mag Tuired. That feast was the wedding feast for a king. For Lug was enthroned king of the Túatha Dé Danann after Nuada was killed. The place where refuse was put was on the great hill of the queen. The hill of the Máirimdill, or the midden heap at Máirimdill, that is Telltown today.

'The daughters of the nephew of Tethra, that is, Fergal Manach, the nephew of Tethra, the king of the Fomorians, they are the daughters of Fergal, who is also called the nephew of the champion.

'There are two waters in Crích Ross, they have been described before, one of them is named Conchobar, and the other is called Dofolt, or the bare-banked river. Moreover, a rope-bridge goes there from the Conchobar to the Dofolt, connecting them as one stream. I am the nephew,' said he, 'of that man there, namely Conchobar, I am the son of Dechtine, Conchobar's sister. Not only his nephew, I am his champion.

'It is the headland of Bodb or the headland of the Mórrígan. It is that Ross or headland, namely the territory of Ross. Moreover, that Bodb is the war god Bodb. It is also called Be Néid, wife of the one and the same Néid, the god of war. [Cú Chulainn continues his descriptions and explanations of the riddles].

'It has been said that "I am the hero of the plague that visits hounds." That is true, when rabies destroys, that is the plague that visits dogs. I am that hero, I am the strong memory of that plague. I am the wildness, and am the fierceness and courage in battle.

'When it was said: "Fair is the plain of Mag Alchuing," it is not Mag Breg there that is being praised, but rather the figure of the daughter. Beyond her yoke or carrying garment I have seen her two breasts against her red smock, and it is thus it was called Mag Alchuing, or the plain of the yoke, as the yoke was against the breasts of the maiden.

'It was said: "Nothing disappears nor is killed on the plain known as the hundred," which means the hundred languages of the poet. It is that which is being interpreted at this moment: that I will not reach nor abduct the maiden till I slay one hundred men on each ford of the Delvin river towards the Boyne, about Scennmenn Monach. For she is the sister of Fergal Manach, changing herself into any shape in order to destroy my chariot and bring about my death,' said Cú Chulainn.

'The sprite-like creature [Emer] will not come with me until I perform a salmon leap across three ramparts to seek her, and come to the three brothers who are guarding her, namely Ibur, Scibur and Catt, and attack thrice nine men whilst only slaying eight and not striking any of the brothers among them. I took the weight of the foster brothers in gold and silver to the fortress of Fergal.

Benn Súan [the hill of sleep] was said to be the place where the son of Roiscmilc is from. There I must slaughter without sleep from the samain, that is, *sam fuin* or summer's end. For there had been a division of the year long ago; summer from Beltane [May] to Samain [Hallowe'en] and winter from Samain to Beltane. The samain was the time when the summer fell asleep and the end of the samain was the end of summer sleep.

'*Oí-melc* [sheep's milk], is the beginning of spring, around the time when it is wet, wet in spring and wet in winter. *Oí* is the poetic name for sheep. The word *ba* after a word was said to mean a plague. Thus a plague of sheep [*oíba*], a plague of dogs, a plague of horses, a plague on people, as the word *ba* was used. Moreover *oí-melc* is the time when sheep's milk comes, so that is the time when they are milked. The word *oísc* or ewe originates from *oí sesc* or dry sheep and *oí sesc* finds its name in Roiscmilc.

'As for Beltine [Beltane], that is the fire of Bel, meaning the prosperous fire. Two fires were made each year by the druids with great incantations. Cattle were passed between the fires as a guard against pestilence. These were known as the cattle of Bel. Bel is the name of a pagan god; they exhibit all the young cattle as the herd of Bel. The cattle of Bel, afterwards known as the fire of Bel. Towards autumn, that is Lugnasa or the beginning of autumn, the earth wails and fruit comes from the ground.'

Before setting out on a course, Cú Chulainn went to a feast at Emain Macha that night. The daughters related to the landowner the conversation between the warrior youth in the splendid chariot and Emer, and they knew that it was not a solemn conversation between them, and he himself [Cú Chulainn] turned back across the plain of Brega and northwards from them. Moreover, they related to the hospitaller, Fergal Manach then, everything the maiden said. 'It is true then,' said Fergal Manach, 'the madman from Emain Macha has come, and was talking with Emer, and he has fallen in love with the girl. Be heedful then of what one has said to the other. Help will not be given to them,' said he. 'I shall prevent them, so that their desire will not come to pass.'

Afterwards Fergal Manach went to Emain Macha dressed as a foreigner, and, as a foreign messenger to the king, addressed Conchobar, and presented him with golden treasures and wine from Gall and other riches besides. Later he was made welcome. Now he stayed in their company for three days. Cú Chulainn and Conall, and the charioteers of the Ulaid as well, were praised in his presence. Then he said that the performance of the charioteers was both precise and splendid: 'but only when he [Cú Chulainn] has visited Domnall Míldemail in Scotland will his feats be more wonderful, and when he has visited Scáthach and learned the warrior arts, he will surpass all the other warriors in Europe'. But the reason he came to them was in order that Cú Chulainn would not come back again. For it seemed to Fergal that Cú Chulainn, while in love, would die through the hostility and fierceness of yonder warrior [Scáthach], and thus would not return.

Cú Chulainn agreed to go then and Fergal took him at his word. Later Fergal went off, after he had impressed upon Cú Chulainn that he desired all arrangements to be kept. Fergal went home, and the young warriors arose on the morrow and they were determined to go, and Lóegaire Búadach and Conchobar went, and some authorities say that Conall Cernach went with them.

Now Cú Chulainn went across Brega to visit the young woman. Later he addressed Emer, before he entered the boat. The maiden said that it was Fergal who had given the request in Emain Macha for Cú Chulainn to study the warrior art abroad, in order that he and Emer could not come together. And she said that Cú Chulainn should be on his guard, for Fergal would kill Cú Chulainn any time he saw them together. Each promised that they would keep their purity until they were united, unless one of them died. They bade farewell to each other and then he turned towards Alba [Scotland].

Later they reached Domnall. He instructed them at the rampart, upon a stone with a small hole under which blew bellows. They performed on them until the soles of their feet were black or grey. A course of climbing on spears, performing on their points and not inflicting suffering on their soles, also known as the binding feat of warriors on a spear point. Now the daughter of Domnall, named Dornoll of the large fists, fell in love with Cú Chulainn. She had an ugly figure. Her knees were big, her heels before her, her feet after her, large grey-black eyes in her head, locks of jet-black hair between her knees. And she had a very strong forehead on her and very rough, very red hair in a headband down from her head. Cú Chulainn refused to share her bed. She promised to avenge herself for this. Domnall said that Cú Chulainn would not be fully skilled in arms until he reached Scáthach, in Scotland, from the east. The four of them went across [to] Scotland.

When Cú Chulainn was with Conchobar, king of Ulster, and Conall Cernach and Lóegaire Búadach, Emain Macha appeared to them in a vision. Now it was impossible for Conchobar and Conall and Lóegaire to pass from that place. The daughter of Domnall conjured up an apparition in order to separate Cú Chulainn from his people; the purpose of this was to destroy him.

Other authorities say that it was Fergal Manach who placed the apparition, in order that he would not return, so that Cú Chulainn could not fulfil his pledge to return to Emain, because returning would cause him shame; moreover, if it should happen that he would go east to learn the warrior craft, that is, the usual and the unusual feats of arms, it was more likely that he would die, being alone.

Afterwards Cú Chulainn went from them, voluntarily, and he was uncertain about the strangeness and the power of the spells the daughter was causing, and it was upsetting him that he was separated from his people. Then Cú Chulainn went across [to] Scotland, he was sad and very weary from the loss of his friends, and he did not know where he would go to reach Scáthach. He promised his friends that he would return to them after he reached Scáthach, unless he were to die. He remained there, aware that he was straying about in ignorance.

Now when he was on his way, he saw a great dreadful beast like a lion coming towards him. It was observing him, but it did not do damage to him. Now each way he went, the beast observed and turned its side towards him. Then he leapt onto its neck. He did not restrain it, but went whichever way the beast did. They went for four days in that manner, and then they came to a territory in which there were inhabitants, and an island where there were youths playing by a pool. They laughed at the extraordinary harmful beast among them that was being of service to that man yonder. Now Cú Chulainn dismounted from the beast at that moment and saluted it.

Afterwards he came to a great house that was in a deep glen. There he found a beautifully shaped maiden inside. The young woman addressed him and made him welcome. 'Welcome thy coming, O Cú Chulainn,' said she. He asked how she happened to know him. She said that they were both loving foster children with Ulbecán the Saxon, 'when we were there learning melodic speech from him,' said she. The young woman brought him drink and food, and afterwards he goes away from her.

Moreover, he met a young warrior, wonderful and pleasant. He bade him welcome first. Greetings were exchanged between them. Cú Chulainn was seeking directions to the fort of Scáthach. The young warrior pointed out the direction beyond the plain of ill fortune, which was close by. On this half of the plain men would freeze fast, so it was necessary to move fast; on the other half they are lifted up against the grass and are held fast by the grass tips. The young warrior brought him a wheel and told him to run with the wheel across that part of the plain that was freezing. Moreover, he gave him an apple and told him that, as the apple follows the ground, so should he. With these he might be successful in crossing the plain. In this way he goes off across the plain that he finds before him. Further, the young warrior said to him that there was a deep glen with one slender rope across it, and that it was full of spectres having been

39

sent by Fergal to destroy him, and that this was the way to the house of Scáthach across a high terrifying stony place.

Then Cú Chulainn and the young warrior pay respects to each other. Eochu Bairche is that warrior, and it is he who instructs him on how to act in the house of Scáthach. Moreover, the young warrior forewarns him of the struggles and troubles he will suffer in the Táin Bó Cúailgne. Also he tells him of the sufferings and of the deeds and the triumphs he will have over the men of Ireland.

Cú Chulainn went then on the road across the plain of ill fortune and across the perilous glen about which the young warrior spoke to him. This is the way Cú Chulainn took to the camp where the pupils of Scáthach were. He asked them where she [Scáthach] was.

'On the island yonder,' said they.

'Which way may I get to it?' said he.

'Across the Bridge of the Pupils,' said they, 'and nobody reaches there except by a feat of arms.'

Thus it was, and two ends of the bridge were low and the middle was high, and when one stept on one end it lifted up, and on the other end it went down. Another authority says that there were a number of Irish warriors in the fort there learning feats under Scáthach, namely Fer Diad mac Damáin, Naoise mac Uisliu, Loch Mór mac Egomas, Fíamain mac Forai and countless other young warriors. However, this was not reckoned to be the version of the story at that time.

Three times Cú Chulainn tried to cross over the top of the bridge and failed. The men jeered at him. He became distorted and crossed at one end of the bridge, and then he did the hero's salmon leap and landed in the middle of the bridge, so that he came to the bridge at the other end that lifted up, and he reached the island. So that he landed there on the ground at the end of the island. He went to the fort and pushed the point of his spear against the door, so that it went through it. He was addressed by Scáthach then. 'True,' said she, 'yonder is another who has learned the skill of weapons.' And she sends her daughter off to find out who this youth is. Then Úathach the daughter of Scáthach went to him. She sees him but does not address him, owing to the amount of passion his glorious shape awakened in her, and until she had looked at him for as long as she desired. She goes to the same place where her mother was. She praised the man she saw to her mother.

'Thus the man I see with you was pleasing,' said the mother.

'That is true,' said the daughter.

'If your passion is such,' said Scáthach, 'then you should request that he spends the night with you.'

'Indeed it is not difficult for me to do that,' said Úathach, 'if that is what he wishes.'

Later the daughter serves him water and food, and attends and entertains him. She welcomes him and serves him in the guise of a servant. He [Cú Chulainn] violates her by breaking her finger. The daughter shrieked. Her cries reached the encamped army so that the people in the fortress rose up. Then a warrior arose against him, namely Cochair Cruibne, a warrior of Scáthach. He and Cú Chulainn engaged in combat for a long time. The warrior performed a battle feat and Cú Chulainn tackled him with effortless skill. The warrior fell by him and Cú Chulainn cut off his head. Scáthach was sad then, until Cú Chulainn extolled the service and manners of the man he had defeated, who was the leader of the host and her strongest warrior after him. And Úathach came then and had a conversation with Cú Chulainn.

Now on the third day the daughter gave advice to Cú Chulainn, for it was to perform heroic deeds that he was here, to go to the spot where Scáthach was training her two sons, Cúar and Cett, and that he should perform a salmon leap at her by the great yew tree where she was reclining, and that he should place a sword between her two breasts and hold it there until she grants him three wishes: that she should train him without neglect, that he should marry her [Úathach] with payment of the dowry by herself, that she should warn him of anything which might befall him, as she was a seer.

Later Cú Chulainn went to the place where Scáthach was. He places his two feet against her slender body and unsheathed his sword then, and its point is placed against her heart, and he said: 'Death is above you,'

'Your three wishes will be granted,' said she 'that is the three chosen wishes, as demanded with your breath.'

'They must be granted,' said Cú Chulainn. Then he bound her to her word. Other sources say that Cú Chulainn brought Scáthach to the shore, and they were united there and lived together, and each thing that would befall him was prophesied. This prophecy begins,

'Welcome, weary but victorious,' but then some authorities have a different version.

Afterwards Úathach passed the night with Cú Chulainn, and Scáthach trained him in warfare, that is, in the craft of arms. At that time he was with Scáthach and in the company of her daughter Úathach, and it was then that another wonderful man that was in Munster, Lugaid mac Nois mac Alamaic, a wonderful king, both comrade and foster brother of Cú Chulainn, came from the west with twelve charioteers of the high kings of Munster, wooing the twelve daughters of [Cairbre] Niad Fer mac Rois. They were betrothed before two other men. When Fergal Manach heard this, he went to Tara and asked Lugaid who was the best maiden in Ireland as concerns form, chastity and needlework. Lugaid said that he [Fergal] possessed such a maiden. Then Fergal betrothed his daughter to the king and the twelve daughters of the twelve hospitallers in Mag Breg, as well as the twelve daughters of the high kings that were with Lugaid, were also betrothed.

The king comes with Fergal to the wedding feast at the fortress. Later, when Emer was taken to the spot where Lugaid was sitting, she seizes her two cheeks and, baring her soul, confesses that it is Cú Chulainn with whom she has fallen in love, and that it is under his protection she was, and it would destroy her honour if she should be given to another. Now Lugaid did not attempt to go to the feast with Emer, for fear of Cú Chulainn, and turned back from the house.

Moreover, at that time Scáthach was fighting in other districts and it was Queen Aífe whom she was against. Both battalions assembled for battle. Cú Chulainn was bound and tied by Scáthach. She gave him a sleeping draught before that, so that he would not go into battle, so that he could not reach the battleground. This complied with her protection of him. However, Cú Chulainn awakened suddenly from his sleep. He but slept for a portion of it; anyone else would still be asleep after twenty-four hours from the draught that he alone had drunk.

Later he went with the two sons of Scáthach against the three sons of Ilsúanaig – Cúar, Ceth and Cruife, the three warriors of Aífe. He alone slaughtered the three of them, and they fell by him. There was a battle meeting on the morrow and the host came in two battle formations until they were face to face. Then the three sons of Eis Enchind, Ciri and Biri and Blaicne, three other warriors of Aífe, went into battle and were challenged to fight by the two sons of Scáthach. They used the rope feat against them. Scáthach makes an utterance at that moment and nobody knows what it is. Some thought that it was as a result of having only two sons against the three of them, and moreover she was afraid of Aífe, on account of the fact that she was the most dangerous warrior on Earth. Then Cú Chulainn went towards the two sons, and leapt on the rope and met them, and turned against the three sons, and the three met their death by him.

Aífe challenged Scáthach to single combat. Cú Chulainn went against Aífe and, having been asked what she loved most, Scáthach said that 'she loves her chariot and her two horses and her charioteer most'. Cú Chulainn and Aífe came against each other upon the rope of feats, and waged combat on it. Later Aífe breaks the weapons of Cú Chulainn, so that the longer hilt of the sword is broken. Then Cú Chulainn said: 'Alas, Aífe's charioteer and the two horses and her chariot have fallen down the glen, so that they all died.' At that Aífe looked down. Then Cú Chulainn approaches her and seizes her under her breasts, and lifts her like a burden, and took her to his own host. He intended to strike her against the earth, and lifted his unsheathed sword over her, and Aífe said: 'A life for a life, O Cú Chulainn,' said she.

'Grant me my three wishes,' said he.

'They will be granted with thy breath,' said she.

'These are my three wishes,' said he: 'hostages to Scáthach, so that there is no trespassing later on; to spend tonight with you in your fortress; and for you to bear my son.'

'I accept all,' said she. 'All will be complied with just as you say.' Then Cú Chulainn went with Aífe and spent the night with her. Later Aífe said that she was pregnant and would bear a son. 'Seven years to this day, I will send him to Ireland,' said she, 'and he will be left a name.' Cú Chulainn left a gold finger ring for him, so that he might come and seek him in Ireland as soon as his finger would fit the ring. And he said that a name would be given to him and Conlaí would be that name, and that that name would not be given to anyone else, and that he would not refuse combat with anyone.

Then Cú Chulainn returned again to his own people, and it was upon the same rope that he came. He found an old woman blind in the left eye upon that rope. She forbade him from crossing by the rope. He said that he would not have come to that half of the rope but for the huge cliffs that were below him. She demanded that he leave the way free for her. Then he let himself down the rope, adhering to it only with his toes. She went over and kicked his big toe from the rope, in order to fling him down the cliff. He notices something then and performs a salmon leap upwards again, and strikes the head off the *caillech* [old woman]. She was the mother of the last three heroes that fell by him, one of whom was Éis Énchend, and she had come in order to destroy him. Later the host went with Scáthach to the borderlands, taking hostages from Aífe with it, and Cú Chulainn remained for a while recovering there.

Later Cú Chulainn departs, having fully learned the military arts from Scáthach – between the apple feat and the thunder feat and the edge feat and the horizontal feat, the javelin feat and the rope feat, the body feat and the cat's feat and the salmon leap, the throwing of rods and the bound across hurdles, the turning of a valiant champ-ion and the *gaé bulga*, the profit of quickness and the wheel feat and the support feat and the trick performed on the breath, the great shout and the hero's scream, the stroke under restraint and the stunning blow, the cry stroke and the climbing along a lance to stretching the body against the point of a weapon, and the 'sickle chariot', and the binding of champions to the point of a spear. Later he came to the same land that he had been requested to come to, and bade farewell. Now Scáthach said then the things that would befall him. This was done through the rites of *imbas forosnai* or divination. So that the following words were said to him:

> Welcome, weary but victorious,
> all-conquering, warlike, cold-hearted,
> come so that help may be given you!
> There will not be a foretelling without a chant,
> there will not be a chant without a beholding.
> About this warrior of single combat
> awaits great danger.
> Being alone for a long time during the cattle raid of Cooley
> you will be dissipated, from fighting the warriors of Cruachain.
> Heroes will be saved by you; necks will be broken by you.
> Against the backstroke of Sétanta's blade,
> blood will flow.
> Bloody battle will sound over long distances,

spear points will shatter bones.
Wooden palisades will enclose the mighty horns of cows.
An aspen club with goodly edge will testify
to warrior feats and token flesh.
Cows from Brega will be stolen.
Hostages will swear by their people.
For a fortnight a third of the country will be full of tears,
cattle will go unherded about the roads.
A sorrowful single warrior will be against the host.
It will be difficult, to be sure, there will be a long sigh of lament.
The blood will drive a red pestilence onto many shields
of alderwood, and onto much weaponry;
The women will be red-eyed.
The battle-field will be red with the clash of weapons.
Ravens will eat well on flesh,
scald crows will traverse the ploughland.
Very strong kites will be encountered.
Portions of herds will be stolen through fierceness.
A large number will be lead away for the great host,
a large amount of blood, without flesh, will be spilt
on account of Cú Chulainn.
You will suffer injurious wounds.
You will slay a large number of unfortunate heroes.
The mill house of the lord will be plundered.
A destructive rout will bring great ruin to everyone
in Mag Muirthemne, during the wounding game.
The fiery hero will perform great deeds against the Plunderers.

Performing cold deeds with dreadful shouting –
thus the feat-performing hero goes.
There will be weeping, a company of women will be wounded.
Medb boasts of destruction to Ailill.
A sick bed awaits you;
Thy face against cruelty and fierceness.
See the white-horned bull roar against the
Brown bull of Cooley.
It will drive the wood of your ever-keen valour.
The learned son of red spear points will strike
a blow, curved and long.

Your journey will be lonely and without support.
Weakness is the cause that lays you low.
Arise, fully armoured one,
shapely in the art of many combats,
striding, raiding, oppressive,
arise in full force to the land of Ulster,
go to your Ulster maidens!
Weary, wounding warrior,
with your strong-shafted, effective, curved spear,
your brave blade will paint
in dark masses of black blood.
The Scot will know your name.
Screams and cries of a winter night,
Aífe and Úathach will lament you.
Your beautiful body laid low
by ingenious sleep-making spells.
Three years on full thirty
will be the length of your power over your enemies.
Thirty years I boast
the power of your ever-keen deeds.
Beyond that I do not add,
beyond that your life is not related.
Among a troop of triumphant women
your life will be short, this you will recognize.
I bid you farewell.

Welcome, weary but victorious.

Then Cú Chulainn went in a ship towards Ireland. This was the crew aboard the ship: Lugaid and Lúan, the two sons of Lóch, together with Fer Báeth and Láirin and Fer Diad and Drust mac Serb. They went to the house of Rúad, king of the islands, on the night of the samain. This is where Conall Cernach and Lóegaire Búadach were collecting tribute. For at that time tribute was paid from the isles [of Scotland] to the Ulaid.

Later Cú Chulainn hears wailing before the fort of the king.

'From whom is that cry?' said Cú Chulainn.

'The daughter of Rúad is being taken away as tribute to the Fomorians,' they said, 'and it is thus that there is lamenting inside the fortress.'

'Where is the daughter?' said he.

'She is below at the beach,' they said.

Cú Chulainn comes to where the daughter is, over on the beach. He demands her account of what is happening. The daughter tells him everything.

'From where do the men come?' said he.

'From that remote island yonder,' said she. 'Be not here when the outlaws come towards you.'

Now he remained as he stood, killing three Fomorians in single combat. However, the last man wounded him on the wrist. The maiden brought him a strip of cloth for his wound. Then he goes away without giving his name to the daughter.

The daughter comes to the fort and tells her father all the news. Then Cú Chulainn comes to the fort like any guest. Afterwards Conall and Lóegaire made him welcome. A great many in the camp boast of killing the Fomorians, but the daughter did not believe them. Afterwards he is made to wash by the king, and everyone in turn is presented to the daughter. Moreover, Cú Chulainn came like everybody else and the daughter recognised him.

'You will take the maiden to you,' said Rúad, 'and you will be paid a dowry.'

'No,' said Cú Chulainn, 'but, in a year and a day from now, the maiden can come after me if she wishes, and she will find me.'

Afterwards Cú Chulainn came to Emain and told his story. When he had rested himself, he came towards the ramparts of Fergal, seeking Emer. A year passed, and he got no opportunity to see her, due to the large numbers on watch. At the end of the year Cú Chulainn said: 'Indeed it is today, O Lóeg, that we have a tryst with the daughter of Rúad, but we do not know the exact spot, and we were not informed about it. Let us go to where the land borders the sea.'

Now by the shores of Loch Cúan, they see two birds on the water. Cú Chulainn takes a stone from the ground and flings it at the birds. The men run to where one of the birds is struck. When they reach there, they see two of the most beautiful women ever, Derbforgall the daughter of Rúad, and her handmaiden.

'It is bad the deed that was done, O Cú Chulainn,' said she, 'for it was to see you we came, not to be wounded by you.'

Cú Chulainn sucked the stone out from her so that blood gushed all about.

'I will not be united with you now,' said Cú Chulainn, 'for I have drunk your blood. I will give you my foster-child who is here with me, namely Lugaid Reo Derg.'

This was done.

Cú Chulainn was seeking the fort of Fergal, yet he could not reach his daughter, for she was too well guarded. So he went again to Luglochta Loga, to the fort of Fergal. And that day his sickle chariot was prepared for him and it was brought upon a difficult course. So that for the thunder feat three hundred and nine men prepared the chariot, and on the third day it was ready for Cú Chulainn. And it was called sickle [*serrdae*] either from the iron sickles that were projecting from it or from the Syrians who were the original builders of the sickle chariot.

He reached the fort of Fergal within a day, and performed the salmon leap across the three ramparts, so that he landed in the centre of the fortress, and he struck three blows inside the fort, so that eight men fell with each blow, for one man was spared from each nine, namely Scibur and Ibur and Cat, the three brothers of Emer. Fergal made a leap out of the mound towards the ramparts without escaping from Cú Chulainn, so that he was left lifeless. Cú Chulainn took Emer with him, and her foster-brother, and gold and silver, and he leapt again across the three ramparts and left with the young women. They shrieked out loud. Scenmenn steps forward. Cú Chulainn kills her at the ford, hence the name Áth Scenmenn. They go to Glond Áth. There he slays a hundred men.

'That is a great deed [*glond*] you have done,' says Emer, 'to kill a hundred armed and warlike men.'

'It will be called Glond Áth forever,' said Cú Chulainn.

Cú Chulainn reached Crúfóit, which, until then, had been called Ráe Bán. He strikes a great destructive blow against the host at that place, so that streams of blood burst forth, flowing in all directions. 'The hill is a scene of carnage today, O Cú Chulainn,' said the maiden. So that it is called Crúfóit, namely *fót cró* [the sod of gore].

At the ford over the Boyne [Áth Imfóit] he comes face to face with his pursuers. Emer goes in the chariot. Cú Chulainn urges on the chase, so that the hooves of the horses throw up sods of earth northward from the ford. He urges on the others so that the hooves of the horses throw up the sods southwards from the ford. So that this place is called Áth Imfóit [the ford with the sods from all sides].

In short, he slays at every ford one hundred men, from Áth Scenmenn on the Delvin river to the Boyne at Brega, and he fulfilled all the deeds that he promised to the young woman, and he remains uninjured all the way to Emain Macha, which he reaches at the fall of night. Emer is accompanied to the banqueting hall of Conchobar and the Ulster nobles, and is made welcome. There was a grim evil-tongued member of the Ulaid in that banqueting hall. Bricriu mac Carbad was his name. This is what he said: 'It would be displeasing indeed for Cú Chulainn,' said he, 'to have to comply with anything tonight, such as the woman he has taken with him having to spend the night with Conchobar, for it is customary for Conchobar to deflower maidens before the Ulaid, on their first night of marriage.'

Cú Chulainn becomes so furious when he hears this that the feather bed under him bursts and the downy feathers fly all about the house, and he dashes out.

'It is very difficult,' said Cathbad, 'for there is a *geis* on the king if he does not do what Bricriu has said. However, Cú Chulainn will kill anyone who sleeps with his woman,' said he.

'Call Cú Chulainn to us,' said Conchobar, 'so that we can see what we can do about his anger.'

Later Cú Chulainn arrives.

'Go' said Conchobar, 'and gather the herds that are on Sliab Fúait.'

Later Cú Chulainn went. He found the pigs and drove them together, and the wild deer, and every sort of wild animal besides, that was moving about on Sliab Fúait, and brought them as one herd onto the green at Emain. Then the fury of Cú Chulainn receded.

Then a conversation takes place among the Ulaid about this affair. The Ulstermen decide that Emer must spend the night with Conchobar, but that Fergus and Cathbad should share the same bed so that the honour of Cú Chulainn be kept, and the blessings of the Ulaid on the couple are accepted. In this way everything is complied with. The next day Conchobar pays Emer her dowry, and Cú Chulainn accepts his *eneclann* or compensation for his injured honour, and passes the night with his wife, and both remain together until death.

The leadership of the sons of Ulster is gained by Cú Chulainn then. These were the sons of Emain at that time, a poet says their names aloud:

CÚ CHULAINN

The sons of Emain were at that time
A beautiful host, at the hall of the warriors of Ulster,
About Furbaide, white the hero,
In the company of Cuscrad and Cormac.

In the company of Conaing and pure Glaisne,
About Fíachaig and Findchad,
About Cú Chulainn, hard and clear,
In the company of the son of gifted Dechtine.

In the company of Fíachna and Follomain there,
About Chacht, with Maine and Chrimtann,
With the seven Maines from the mountain of the hound,
With Bres and Nár and Lóthar.

In the company of the six sons of Fergus there,
With Ilarchless and Illand,
With Fíaman and Buinde, with Brí,
With sworded Mál and Conrí.

With quick Lóegaire and cross-eyed Conall
In the company of the two beautiful Etars,
With Mes Diad and beloved Mes Dedad,
The children of shorn Amergin.

Conchraid mac Cas from the mountain of the thrushes,
Conchraid, son of Bád Bernad Brón,
Conchraid, son of the Red son of Find,
Conchraid Súan, son of Sálchind.

Áed mac Findeirg of speckled colouring,
Áed mac Fidaig of the strong shoulders,
Áed son of Conall, the battle maimer,
Áed mac Duind and Áed mac Duach.

Fergus mac Lete of great clarity,
Fergus mac Deirg, son of Dáire,

THE WOOING OF EMER

Fergus mac Roich whom quatrains praise,
Fergus mac Duib, son of Crimthann.
The three sons of Tráiglethan of great fame,
Siduad, Currech and Carman,
Three sons of Uisliu of the battles,
Noíse, Anli and Ardán.

The three Flands, the three Finds, the three melodious Conns,
The names of the nine sons of Scíuil,
The three Faelans, the three Collas fair,
The three sons of Néill, the three sons of Síthgal.

Lón and Iliach, beautiful men,
The foster-brothers of perfect Cormac,
The three Dondgases, sons of the sons of mac Roich,
The three Dundgases and the three Doelgases.

The poets of melodious Cormac,
The nine sons of Lir mac Eterscíuil,
The three fine vigorous pipers,
Find, Eochaid and Illand.

The three musical horn-blowers,
In the company of the two Aeds and Fingin,
The three druids making sharp satire,
Atharne and Drec and Drobél.

The three cupbearers of renown,
Find, Erúath and Fatemain,
The three O'Chletigs perfect and clear,
Úath, Urad and Aislinge.

Áed and Eochaid, famous of Emain,
Two sons of fair Ilgabla,
The son of Bricriu, who generated fame
Conspicuous with the sons of Emain.

The sons of Emain.

CHAPTER 4

The Death of Aífe's One Son

Aided Óenfir Aífe

What was the cause of Cú Chulainn killing his son? Easy to tell. Cú Chulainn went for instruction in the use of arms to 'foam white' Scáthach, daughter of Ardgeme from Brittany, in order to learn the mastery of feats from her, and Aífe daughter of Ardgeme went to him, and he left her pregnant, saying that she would bear a son. 'A gold thumb-ring you will have,' said Cú Chulainn 'suitable for a son. When he is ready, he will come seeking me in Ireland, and he is not to seek directions from anyone, and he is not to tell his name to anyone, nor is he to refuse combat from anyone.'

After seven years the boy went searching for his father. The Ulaid were assembled at Trácht Éise in front of him. They saw him coming towards them across the sea in a little bronze boat, with two golden oars in his hands. There was a heap of stones by him in the little boat. He carried the stones in a staff-sling and cast a stunning blow against the birds. He performed his feats on them, and while they are alive he let them into the air again. He performs the 'jaw-feat' then, too quick for the eye to follow. He tuned his voice to theirs, so that he brought them down a second time. After that he revived them again.

'Well, then,' said Conchobar, 'woe to the land from where yonder gilly comes,' said he. 'For if great men came from the island from which he comes, they would grind us to dust, when a small boy can perform like that. Let someone go towards him, to see if he can be admitted here at all.' 'Who will go towards him? Who should it be,' said Conchobar, 'except Condere mac Echach?' 'Why should Condere go?' said everyone. 'Easy to say,' said Conchobar. 'With his sense and eloquence it is proper that Condere goes.' 'I will go to him,' said Condere.

Now Condere went just as the boy reached the strand. 'You have come far enough boy,' said Condere, 'we want to know where you are going and where your people are from'. 'I am not giving my name to anyone,' said the youth, 'and I am not avoiding anyone.' 'You will not land here, until you name yourself,' said Condere. 'I will continue in the direction that I have come,' said the youth.

The youth turned away. Then Condere said: 'Turn to me my boy, you who are of great feats, you whose blood has the makings of a man. The armoured pride of the Ulaid comes towards you. Conchobar wishes to converse with you. Put your little chariot and your javelin to the left side, for it is that [javelin] which raises the ire of the charioteers of the Ulaid. You should come and converse with Conchobar. Listen carefully to me. Turn to Conchobar, impetuous son of Ness, to Sencha, son of victorious Ailill; to Cetherir son of Fintan of the red sword-edge, to the fire of the battle wounder; to Amergin the poet; to Cumsaraid of great hosts. Welcome to a meeting with great Conall Cernach to discuss stories, with music and laughter in the company of battle heroes. Blaí the landowner would be sad and troubled should you be able to pass him, as he is a warrior. Do this, as a rebuke ill befits the great host. For so it is said: I Condere rose then and came to the warlike youth in order to detain him. But he threatened me; come then, beardless and unripe youth, unless you wish to disobey the Ulaid.'

'It is good for you to come,' said the youth. 'I will be here so that I can address you. I have cleared my throat. Allow me to make an unerring cast from the chariot. I collected a beautiful flight of birds by attacking them with little spears, without recourse to the feat of the salmon leap. I boast of my warrior deeds, although I do not choose to be under siege. Inquire of the Ulaid for permission to duel with one or with a number. Turn away again,' said the youth, 'for unless you have the power of a hundred with you, I am not capable of being restrained.' 'Good,' said Condere, 'come on later, so that someone else may address you.'

Afterwards Condere went to the Ulaid and related the conversation. 'That is not true,' said Conall, 'The honour of the Ulaid will be upheld, as long as I am active.' He went then seeking the youth. 'It is delightful, your sport, O youth,' said Conall. 'It will be less delightful against you,' said the gillie. The youth put a stone in his sling and cast it into the air, so that it made a din and a noise, and it threw Conall over. Before he could rise the youth put the shield strap upon his arms. 'Someone else against him!' said Conall. The host smiled at that.

However, Cú Chulainn was about, and in festive mood, with the arm of Emer, the daughter of Fergal, about his neck. 'Don't go down!' said she. 'A son of yours is below. Do not slay your only son, avoid slaying that impetuous well-bred boy. It is not a fair fight, nor does good counsel advise a hosting against a boy of great deeds and feats. A mighty tree like you should avoid punishing its offshoot, turn away from the hard lesson of Scáthach. If Conlaí were to sustain a challenge, it should be manfully avoided. Turn to me! Hear me! Good is my advice! Could it be that Cú Chulainn might listen? For it is obvious that it is Conlaí there, the only son of Aífe,' said the woman.

Then Cú Chulainn said: 'Steady, woman! I do not request the advice of a woman on splendid feats. The assistance of a woman is not required. We are of splendid deeds. Great is the eye of the chief. A vapour of blood upon my skin: the blood from the body of Conlaí. Beautifully the spears will suck the fair javelin [Conlaí]. What is it to be, O woman?' said he. 'For I would kill for the honour of Ulster.'

Then he himself went down. 'It is beautiful, boy, the sport you make,' said he. 'However,' said the young boy, 'it is ugly for the game, when I cannot go from you until I give my name to them.' 'What is necessary, young child, in this company,' said Cú Chulainn, 'is that you will die unless you give us your name.' 'That is true,' said the youth. The boy makes for him. They exchange blows. He gives the head of Cú Chulainn to his sword, that is, he cuts his hair with his sword. 'An end to mockery!' said Cú Chulainn. 'Thus we go to wrestle.'

'I cannot reach your belt,' said the boy. The son traversed upon two stones, and thrust Cú Chulainn between two standing stones thrice, and the son did not move either of his feet among the standing stones, and his feet remained on the stones up to his two ankles. This place is known as the track of the two feet to this day, it is called Trácht Éise by the Ulaid. Then they went fighting in the sea until the son immersed him twice. Later Cú Chulainn came out of the water, before the boy, and got the *gaé bulga*, for no one had been taught by Scáthach how to use it except Cú Chulainn. He shoots it at the boy through the water until his bowels were about his feet.

'It is true now that Scáthach did not teach me that, alas! For now I am wounded!' said the son. 'It is true,' said Cú Chulainn. Later he grabbed the boy between his arms and placed him before the Ulaid. 'Look here, my son,' said he. 'Woe, woe,' said the Ulaid. 'And it is true,' said the son. 'If I were among you for as long as five years, I would slay men that were against you in every direction and extend the kingdom as far as Rome. Since it has been pointed out to me that wonderful men are in this place, let us celebrate them.'

He placed his arms about the neck of each man then, and bade farewell to his father, and died forthwith. Now they uttered laments by his grave and his stone, and for three days, in memory of him, no calf was let to its cow.

CHAPTER 5

The Wasting Sickness of Cú Chulainn and the One Jealousy of Emer

Seirlige Con Culainn inso sís óenét Emire

A fair was held in Ulster each year, three days before the samain, [Hallowe'en] three days afterwards and three days during the samain itself. At this time the Ulaid or Ulster heroes were on the plain of Muirthemne. The fair of the samain was held every year, and nothing else in the world happens with them but games, assemblies, amusements and enjoyments, together with eating and feasting, and this constitutes the festival rites of the samain throughout Ireland. On occasion, the fair of the Ulaid was held on the plain of Muirthemne and it was held for the sake of allowing each warrior to boast of his deeds, as was usual during the samain. Moreover, it was a custom with them when holding contests at the fair to cut off the tip of the tongue of each man that he had killed and to put it in their pouch. And as the contests continued, they took the tongues from the cattle, so that their number of conquests can be increased, then one is brought for each contest and each death is shouted out in turn. It is thus that they beat their swords on their thighs when they made a contest. And their swords would turn against themselves should they make a false contest; it was natural for the demons to speak to their weapons, so that they gave guarantees swearing on their swords.

All the Ulaid came to the fair with the exception of only two, Conall Cernach and Fergus mac Roich. 'Let them hold the fair,' said the Ulaid. 'It will not be held until Conall and Fergus come,' said Cú Chulainn. For he was the foster-son of Fergus and the foster-brother of Conall. Afterwards Sencha said, 'Meanwhile we might play board games in the fort, and chant poems, and let the jugglers perform.' Afterwards that was done.

Meanwhile a flock of birds was lying low across a neighbouring loch. There was not in Ireland a flock so melodious. The women were desirous of possessing the many birds, that were on the lake. Arguments broke out among the women as to who would have the birds placed round their shoulders. Ethne Aitencháithrech, wife of Conchobar, said, 'I desire two birds around my shoulders from the flock on yonder hill.' 'We desire them all,' said the women. 'If they are given to anyone, they will first be given to me,' said Ethne Inguba, wife of Cú Chulainn. 'What will we do?' said the women. 'Not difficult,' said Leborcham, daughter of Óa and Adarc, 'for I will seek the proud and kingly Cú Chulainn.'

Afterwards she went to Cú Chulainn and said to him: 'It is a bad desire of the women that they should want these birds from you above all else.' He takes his sword and threatens her, and says: 'Have these whores nothing better to do than have us hunt these birds?' 'It is not fitting,' said Leborcham, 'to be raging against the women of Ulster, for you are the cause of the third blemish of the three, that is, being blind in one eye.' For the women of Ulster had three blemishes: crookedness, stammering and blindness in one eye. Each woman who loved Conall became crooked. For every woman who loved Cúsraid Mend Macha mac Conchobar stammered when she spoke. Likewise each woman who loved Cú Chulainn was blind in one eye, such is love. It was his custom when angry to contract one of his two eyes to the size of a heron's in his head. The other of his two eyes would protrude out to the size of a cauldron for a yearling calf.

'Get the chariot ready, Láeg,' said Cú Chulainn. Meanwhile Láeg has yoked the chariot, and Cú Chulainn goes then in the chariot and casts a stunning shot at the birds with his sword, so that their feathers follow their claws into the water. Afterwards all the birds are seized, and are given and distributed among the women. They all received the birds with one exception – Ethne Inguba. Then he turned himself to the women. 'Your desire is bad,' he said to Ethne Inguba. 'It is not bad,' said Ethne, 'to distribute the birds among the women. It is right for you,' said she. 'For among the women who would not love thee or have a soft spot for thee? For while others give you a share of their love I alone love you.' 'Indeed, your desire is not bad,' said Cú Chulainn. 'I promise you that if birds come on the plain of Muirthemne or along the Boyne river you shall have the most beautiful pair.'

It is not long before they see two birds upon the lake and a chain of red-gold between them. The birds sing a little song. They all fall asleep except Cú Chulainn, who sets out towards them. 'Listen to me,' said Ethne, 'you will not go anywhere, for these birds possess a power, in the meantime other birds will be caught.' 'Is it that I am to be denied?' said Cú Chulainn. 'Put a stone into a sling, O Láeg.' Thereupon Láeg takes the stone and brings the sling. Cú Chulainn cast his stone towards them. He missed his mark. 'Alas!" said he. He takes another stone. He cast it at the birds and went towards them. 'Truly, I am a doomed man,' he said. 'From the day I first cast weapons, I have not missed my aim – until today.' He cast his javelin at them so that it went through the wing of one of the two birds. Then they flew along the pool.

Cú Chulainn came to that place and leaned his back against the pillar. His mind was disturbed and he fell asleep beside the pillar. One of the two women, wearing a green cloak, turns to him. The other was wearing a five fold purple cloak. The woman in the green cloak went to him smiling and laughing and gave him a lash from a horsewhip. The other woman comes to him, laughs over him and strikes him in the same manner. And they were at this for a long time, each of them in turn striking him until he is almost dead. After this they went from him.

All the Ulaid find him and say that he should be awakened. 'No,' said Fergus, 'do not disturb the vision that he sees.' After that he arose from his sleep. 'What have they done?' said the Ulaid remaining with him. Meanwhile he is not able to speak. 'Carry,' said Fergus, 'this hero with the wasting sickness to Brecc, the many-coloured palace of comfort at Emain Macha, not to Dún Imrith on the plain of Louth nor to Dún Delca.' 'Take seeking Emer to Dún Delca," said Láeg. 'No,' said Fergus, 'take her to my dwelling at Téite Brecc. Meanwhile he was taken to that place so that he remained there till the end of the year without speaking to anyone at all.'

At the end of another year from the day of the vision at the samain, the Ulaid were gathering around Téite Brecc at Emain Macha. They were all there as equals, between Fergus at the wall, between Conall Cernach at his head, between Lugaid Réoderg at his pillow, and Ethne Inguba at his feet, when a man came into the house and sat in front of the large assembly, in front of the bed of Cú Chulainn. 'What has brought you here?' said Conall Cernach. 'Easy to answer,' said he, 'for if this man here were in his health, that would be surety for all the Ulaid. Moreover, when there is weakness and sickness from wounds, greater is the surety required from then on. Fearing no one, I have come to address you.' 'Let us bind together in welcoming you. We fear no one either,' said the Ulaid.

Afterwards he rises and stands up, and tells them his wondrous story accordingly:

O Cú Chulainn of long sickness
luck will not be long delayed:
You would be healed if they were here,
the daughters of Áed Abrat.

Said the wife of Labraid, Lí Ban,
standing by the side of Labraid in Mag Crúach:
'It will be the heart's desire of Fand
to be lying with Cú Chulainn'.

On the day Cú Chulainn reaches my
country,
a true love will await him:
With silver and gold in plenty,
and large quantities of wine for drinking.

Cú Chulainn mac Sualtam, were he
a friend to me until now,
perhaps he would tell what he saw
in his sleep, apart from his companions.

In Mag Muirthemne here in the south,
the nights of samain are without misfortune.

I will send Lí Ban to you,
O Cú Chulainn, with the sickness. O Cú Chulainn.

'Who are you?' said they. 'It is I Óengus son of Áed Abrat,' said he. Thereupon the man went from them, and they did not know from where he was or whence he came. Meanwhile Cú Chulainn sat up and began to speak. 'That was indeed timely,' said the Ulaid. 'Tell us what you were doing.' 'Indeed, I have seen,' said he, 'visions concerning last year's samain.' He tells everything as he has seen it. 'What will be done here, O father Conchobar?' said Cú Chulainn. 'What will be done,' said Conchobar, 'is that you will depart to that same pillar stone.'

Then Cú Chulainn went from them till he reached the place and there he saw the woman in the green cloak. 'Good then, O Cú Chulainn,' said she. 'A journey like last year's is not good,' said Cú Chulainn. 'Indeed there will be no injury to you,' said she, "nothing but returning and the seeking of friendship. Indeed for you coming and conversing,' said the woman, "with Fand, the daughter of Áed Abrat, who has been abandoned by Mananánn mac Lir, and meanwhile has given her love to you. Moreover, Lí Ban is my name. Indeed, my spouse Labraid Lúathlám of the sword has sent a message to you. He will give you the woman [Fand] in exchange for a one-day skirmish against Senach Síaborthe and against Eochaid Íuil, as well as Éogan Inbir.' 'Indeed it is not good,' said he, 'to do battle against these men today.' 'It will be a short contest then,' said Lí Ban. 'You will be healthy and you will lack nothing. For Labraid has it all ready for you, for he is the best warrior in the world.' 'Where is this place?' said Cú Chulainn. 'It is in Mag Mell,' said she. 'It is better to be going there than anywhere else,'said the woman. 'Let Láeg come with you,' said Cú Chulainn, 'for he has come in order to find out about this country.' 'Let him come along now,' said Lí Ban.

Meanwhile they went until they reached the place where Fand was. Then Lí Ban comes seeking Láeg and takes him by the shoulder. 'You will not come out of here alive unless protected by women,' said Lí Ban. "Protection by a woman is something that we are not accustomed to,' said Láeg. 'Alas and ever alas that it is not Cú Chulainn who is here now instead of thee,' said Lí Ban. 'Moreover, it is not good for me that he is not here,' said Láeg.

Thereupon they went from there until they reached the side of the island. They saw a little bronze ship on the lake before them. Afterwards they go to the ship, and they go into it, and went to the island and to the door of a house, where they saw a man before them, and Lí Ban said to him:

> 'Where is Labraid Lúathlám of the sword,
> the leader of a victorious band,
> victorious over a strong chariot body
> making redness with sharp red points?'

The man answered and said this to her:

> 'Labraid is active and eager,
> he will not be slow, he will be numerous.
> He has mustered an army, which is
> going to cause slaughter throughout Mag Fidga.'

Meanwhile they go into the house, where they saw three times fifty beds inside and three times fifty women upon them. Láeg is made welcome by all. Then all said to him:

'Welcome to you, O Láeg, both in coming here and in returning from here, and for thine own sake.' 'What will you do now?' said Lí Ban. 'Are you going to speak to Fand now?" "I will go, but only when I know where she is.' 'Easy to tell. She is in her own chamber,' said Lí Ban. Afterwards they went to converse with her and were made welcome in the same place. Then Fand the daughter of Áed Abrat arrived: Áed Abrat, that is, fire of eyelash, meaning the fire in the iris of the eye; Fand, named from a tear that comes over the eye, named thus on account of her purity and because of her beauty, and besides there was no one in the world her equal.

When they heard the sound of Labraid's chariot coming towards them, Lí Ban said 'Labraid is in bad spirits today, let us go and speak to him.' They go out and Lí Ban welcomed him and said:

> 'Welcome, Labraid Lúathlám of the sword!
> Inheritor of a fighting troop,
> swift spearman
> who smites the shields,

61

who scatters the spears,
who wounds bodies,
who slays free-men,
who seeks and slays,
hence all desire him
in destroying the hosts.
He scatters treasures,
attacking bands of warriors, welcome! Welcome, Labraid.

Yet Labraid is not quick to answer, and the daughter spoke again:

'Welcome, Labraid Lúathlám of the battle sword!
Ready to grant favours,
generous to each one,
eager for battle,
whose side is battle-scarred,
true to your word,
forceful for right,
friendly your rule,
daring with your right hand,
avenging with valiant deeds,
cuts down warriors.
Labraid, welcome! Welcome, Labraid.

Still Labraid does not answer. She chants the lay again:

'Welcome, Labraid Lúathlám of the sword!
A warrior to young men,
proud to chieftains,
who destroys with vigorous deeds,
who does battle,
who pierces young warriors,
who raises the weak,
who lays low the strong,
Labraid, welcome! Welcome, Labraid.

'It is not good of you to say this,' replied Labraid himself, and he said:

'I am neither proud nor arrogant, woman,
nor is my reason confused by intoxification of pride.
We will go to battle with numerous spear-points
on all sides,
wielding red swords against right-handed fists,
to the many tribes, to the single heart of Eochaid Íuil.
There is not any pride with us.
I am neither proud nor arrogant, woman.'

'Indeed, it is in good spirits you might be,' said Lí Ban to him. 'For Láeg, charioteer of Cú Chulainn, is here, and he brings a message from him to you that you will come with an army from here.' Thereupon Labraid made Láeg welcome and said: 'Welcome Láeg, on account of the woman you have come, and thanks to him from whom you have arrived here. Return home, Láeg," said Labraid, 'and Lí Ban will go after you.'

Meanwhile Láeg comes from there towards Emain, and tells his story to Cú Chulainn and everyone else besides. After that Cú Chulainn arises from his sitting position and puts his hand on his face, and addressed Láeg clearly, and his spirit was strengthened by the stories told to him by his servant.

Moreover, an assembly of the four great provinces of Ireland was held at that time, so that they could find someone whom they would choose as king of Ireland. At that time it was bad for them, around the hill of chiefs and princes, to be at Tara without the rule of a king over them; and it was bad for them to be without a king's rule making decisions for the community. For the men of Ireland were without the rule of a king for seven years from the death of Conaire at Bruiden Dá Derga until the great assembly of the four fifths of Ireland, in the court of Erc mac Cairpre Nía Fer, at Tara of the kings.

However, the kings held a meeting [at Tara] and at it were Medb and Ailill, Cú Roí and Tigernach Tétbannach mac Luchtai, and Find mac Rossa. The men of Ulster did not take counsel with the king on account of the fact that the alliance formed did not include the Ulaid.

Afterwards the ritual of the bull feast is initiated in order to find out who will be king. It is thus that the bull feast was carried out then: first a white bull is killed and one man takes his fill of the meat and of the broth, and, satisfied with that, sleeps, and four druids chant an incantation for finding truth over him, and it was seen from the dreams the kind of man who would be king, and from the spectre in the dream a description was made; thus the work was done. The man awoke from the dream and told the vision to the king: a strong, noble, youthful warrior with two red circles over him, standing above the pillow of a man in decline in Emain Macha.

Then they go with the news to Emain. After that the Ulaid went and assembled about Conchobar who was in Emain at that time, and about Cú Chulainn, who was in decline there. They tell their story to Conchobar and to the leading men besides. 'That resembles,' said Conchobar, 'the noble son of a good family, namely Lugaid Réoderg, son of the three Finds of Emain [the Three Fair Ones of Emain], foster-son of Cú Chulainn, who is standing at the pillow of the bed of his foster-father, consoling him, namely Cú Chulainn, who is in decline.' Then Cú Chulainn arises, gives instructions to his foster-son and said:

'Precepts of Cú Chulainn to the king of Tara

Be not seeking combat nor doing base things.
Be neither fierce, churlish nor arrogant.
Be neither fearful, violent nor suddenly rash.
Do not descend to wealth, which ruins and confuses.
Be not a spoiler of the ale feast in the house of a nobleman.
Do not delay about the borders of the enemy.
Everyone is of good repute until he is satirized.
There is no prescription for a crime.
Let memories be consulted to learn to which heir the land belongs.
Old antiquaries shall be questioned as to the worth of their conscience.
Let them find judges for kinsman and lands.
Let the genealogical trees be added to as children are born.
Let the dead be made to live by means of oaths sworn in the place where they dwelt.
Let heirs be maintained according to their proper inheritance.
Let strangers go forth under the protection of rulers.
Do not answer back nor boast.
Do not relate stories noisily.
Jest not.
Do not mock.
Do not refute old men.

Be not suspicious of anyone.
Do not make difficult requests.
Do not refuse a request from anyone.
Be gracious in giving, be gracious in lending and refusing.
Be humbly instructed by the wise.
Be mindful when correcting old men.
Follow the paternal rule.
Be not cold-hearted about friends.
Be vigorous around enemies.
Do not allow gossip to bring opprobrium.
Do not intimidate.
Do not hoard anything that is not useful.
Restrain and reprove irregular deeds.
Do not condemn the uprightness of people.
Do not dissolve a contract unless there is repentance.
Be not contentious, be not malevolent.
Be not lazy, be not weak.
Be not too eager, so that you are not vulgar.
Adhere to and follow these precepts, son.'

Then Lugaid said to Cú Chulainn:

'Let everyone know
Of these instructions;
They will not be neglected.
They will be executed.'

Then Lugaid went to Tara and was proclaimed king, and spent the
night at Tara. After that the assembly returned to their own homes.
    Meanwhile, as regards Cú Chulainn, it will be told here now. 'Go
from me, O Láeg,' said Cú Chulainn, 'to the place where Emer is,
and tell her that the *mná Sidhe* have visited me, that I have been laid
low, that I am getting better, and that she is to come and visit me.'
Then in encouraging Cú Chulainn the servant said the following:

'A warrior of great idleness
lying with the sleep of decline,
it shows that the demon
people from Tenmag Trogaigi

have injured you,
have tortured you,
with the strengths of a woman's wantonness.
Awake from the fairy sickness
return as the vigorous warrior
among the champions and the chariot-fighters,
so that you might sit up in ruddy health,
so that you might be with your companions,
so that you can set forth on great deeds.
Rise to the call of strong Labraid,
O mighty man,
Rise so that you may be great.'

After that the servant goes to the place where Emer was, and tells her about Cú Chulainn. 'It was bad of you, servant,' said she, 'to visit the *síd* without finding any means of healing your chief. Alas for the Ulaid,' said she, 'in failing to find a cure. If Conchobar would shrink from involvement, if Fergus were overcome by sleep, if Conall Cernach were wounded, Cú Chulainn would help.' Afterwards she sang a lay in the following manner:

'O son of Riangabra, alas!
although you go often to the *síd*,
no one comes hither early,
healing the son of shapely Dechtine.

Alas for the Ulaid, full of generosity,
between foster-father and foster-brother,
no one to search the brown earth
for our suffering friend Cú Chulainn.

If Fergus were deep asleep,
if the skill of any druid were of avail,
the son of Dechtine would not rest
until he got a druidic examination.
If the same Conall
were wounded and scarred,
Cú Chulainn would search the wide world,
until he got a doctor to cure him.

66

THE WASTING SICKNESS OF CÚ CHULAINN

If Láegaire Búadach were faced
with overbearing danger,
the men of Ireland would be searching the meadows
for a cure for the son of Connad mac Ilíach.

If deceitful Celtchar
Were asleep and in decline,
Sétanta would be journeying night and day
between the mounds.

If Furbaide of the warrior bands
were in deep rest,
he would search the whole world
until he found and saved him

The armies that died at Shee Truim,
no longer do they perform great deeds:
no one surpasses the Hound yonder,
until he has drunk of the sleep of the *síde*.

Alas for the wound that has seized
the Hound of Conchobar's smith:
Grief will break my heart and my bosom,
unless he comes to be healed.

Alas for the blood of my heart,
wasting for a horseman on the plain
until he comes here to the
fair at Mag Muirthemne.

Accordingly he does not come to Emain
on account of the visions that confuse him:
my voice grows weak and dies
on account of all this misery.
Months and seasons and years
without sleep under wedlock
without a sweet-voiced person
whom I have not heard, O son of Riangabra.'
                              O son of Riangabra.

Emer came then to Emain Macha to visit Cú Chulainn, and sat down by the bed where Cú Chulainn was and said: 'It is a shame for you, to be lying down for a woman's love, because constant lying down will bring illness to you.' After she spoke she sang a lay:

'Arise, Ulster warrior!
arise from your sleep in health and happiness,
behold the king of Macha of lovely form:
he will not allow a prolonged sleep.

Look at your shoulder, full of sparkle,
look at a hero ready for contest,
look at the chariots moving through the valley,
look at the warrior pieces spread out on the *fidchell* board.

Look at the heroes full of strength,
look at the girls tall and gentle,
look at the kings on a course of danger,
look at the great queens.

Look at the beginning of clear winter,
look at every familiar thing turning,
look at yourself ready to serve,
look at the cold winter without colour.

Heavy sleep is wasteful, it is no good,
it makes one weary and distressed.
A deep intoxication of sleep
leaves one weak and next to death.

Awake from the sleep of the mounds,
in a sudden rage cast off your tiredness,
with many gentle words of love,
arise, Ulster warrior!'
arise, Ulster warrior.

Then Cú Chulainn arose and placed his hand over his face, and put the weariness and the heaviness from him, and he went from where he was until he arrived at Airbe Rofir in Conaille Muirthemne.

There he saw Lí Ban coming towards him, and the daughter spoke to him and invited him to the fairy-mound. 'Where is Labraid?' said Cú Chulainn. 'Easy to tell,' said she:

'Labraid is on a clear pool
that bands of women frequent:
you will be glad to visit these people,
if there is an invitation from Labraid the Quick.

Daring, his right hand cuts down a hundred,
with knowing ability.
There, there is purple and beautiful colours
like the cheeks of Labraid.

Labraid destroys Doghead of keen battle,
Labraid the owner of the slender red sword:
He bruises the foolish bands with sharp weapons,
he cracks shields against the warriors' armour.

Brightness of the eye and skin in combat,
he does not betray friends in great need,
more honourable than the men of the mounds [síde],
this is the man who has cut down many thousands.

There are wonderful stories from young warriors
who have reached the land of Eochaid Íuil:
his hair like threads of gold,
the scent of wine on his breath.

An extraordinary man,
he carries the combat
along the length of the fierce borders:
boats and a drove of horses race
past the island where Labraid is.

Labraid Swifthand of the sword,
a man of many deeds from across the sea:
a dogfight does not bother him,
enduring as he does the sleep of the multitude.

A bridle and collar of gold upon the droves of horses,
and not only this:
silver and crystal pillars
are what his house is made of.'

'I did not choose,' said Cú Chulainn, 'the invitation of a woman.'
'Let Láeg come and see everything,' said the daughter. 'Then let him
go,' said Cú Chulainn. Láeg set out with Liban, and they went to
Mag Lúada and Bile Búada, and to the fair at Emain and to the fair
at Fidga, and there in the *síd* was Áed Abrat with his daughters.
Fand made Láeg welcome. "Why was Cú Chulainn not here?' said
she. 'It has not been his desire to come at a woman's invitation, and
moreover, only when he had received the invitation did he know it
was from you.' 'It is from me,' said she, 'and let him come quickly
to me, for today he is being put to battle.'

Again Láeg went to the place where Cú Chulainn was. 'How are
things, Láeg?,' said Cú Chulainn. Láeg answered and spoke thus: 'It
is time to come,' said he, 'the time for the battle is set forth for
today.' And having spoken to him thus he sang this lay:

'I reached a place of splendid diversion,
wonderful, though not unknown,
into a mound of twenty armies,
there I found long-haired Labraid.

I found him in that mound,
sitting down with thousands of weapons,
a beautiful mane of yellow hair on him,
bound in a golden-coloured bun.

Then, after I had recognised him
by his five fold purple cloak,
he said: "Will you go with me
to the house where Fáilbe Find is?'
The two kings are in the house,
Fáilbe Find and Labraid,
each of them with a retinue of about three
times fifty;
that was the full number in the house.

THE WASTING SICKNESS OF CÚ CHULAINN

Fifty beds on the right hand
and fifty couches,
fifty beds on the left side
and fifty platforms.

Blood-red pillars close to the beds,
bedposts of gilded white,
there before them a shining candle
with lustrous bright jewels.

Thus they are at the west door,
at the place where the sun sets,
there a brightly coloured drove of horses
with grey manes, every second one purple-brown.

At the door to the east
there are three trees of purple crystal,
from whence a flock of birds call gently
to the children of the royal fort.

At the entrance to the *liss* is a tree,
it is not unseemly against it,
the brilliant sun shines against this silver post
as though it were gold.

There are sixty trees,
their branches almost meeting.
Three hundred are fed by the fruit on each tree,
their crop almost depleted.

Moreover, there is a well there by the fairy mound
As well as one hundred and fifty bright mantles
And there is a gold-coloured pin
in the corner of each brightly coloured mantle.

There is a vat of mead for making merry
for the tryst at the household,
moreover, there is an ongoing custom, which persists,
that it should be forever full.

Now there is a daughter in that house,
the most distinguished of the women of Ireland:
she comes out with her yellow hair,
and she is beautiful and much-gifted.

She makes conversation with everyone,
it is beautiful and wonderful:
she breaks everyone's heart
from love and from charm.

And the daughter has said:
"Who is the lad whom we do not recognise?
If it is you, come hither quickly,
servant of the man of Muirthemne".

I have gone slowly,
seized with fear for my honour:
and she said, "Does he come hither,
the one son of fine Dechtine?'

Woe to him who came not, just now,
and everyone seeking him:
he might see for himself
the great house I have seen.

If all Ireland were mine
and the kingdom of yellow Brega,
I would give it all up, no weak resolve,
To frequent the place I have reached.

     I reached a place.

'That is good,' said Cú Chulainn. 'It is good,' said Láeg, 'and it is
right to go and to arrive, for everything in that land is good.' Láeg
said this, still telling of the pleasures of the Otherworld:

'I have seen a bright, free land,
where neither lies nor untruths are spoken:
There is Labraid of the strong sword arm
the king who sheds the blood of many.

THE WASTING SICKNESS OF CÚ CHULAINN

Since coming across to Mag Lúada
I have been shown the Tree of Victory:
In Mag Denna I have seized the
two serpents with the two heads.

This was the utterance of Lí Ban
At the place in which we were:
"The miracle would be
If I were with Cú Chulainn rather than thee."

Beautiful women, victorious without restraint,
the daughters of Áed Abrat:
beautiful Fand, sound with brilliance,
no king or queen her equal.

I will say, for I have heard,
that since the race of Adam, without transgression,
nowhere is there the equal
of Fand's beauty and fairness of form.

I who have seen such brilliant warriors
with weapons for fighting:
I have seen their coloured clothing,
not the dress of the commoner.

I have seen gentle women at feast,
I have seen the girls,
I have seen the clean servants
going across the wooded ridge.

I who have seen the musicians at their homes
playing music for the daughter:
had I not come out so quickly
they would have made me helpless.
I have seen the hill on which she was,
the beautiful woman Ethne Inguba,
but the woman whom I see here,
it is this woman who fascinates men.'
                                   I who have seen.

Afterwards Cú Chulainn went with her [Lí Ban] into the country with his chariot and reached the island. Labraid welcomed them and all the women welcomed them, and Fand, moreover, gave a special welcome to Cú Chulainn. 'What is to be done in the here and now?" said Cú Chulainn. 'Easy to answer,' said Labraid. "This is what we will do, we will go waving our arms about the host.' Afterwards they go from there until they reach the gathering hosts of the army, and cast an eye at them beyond. And it was innumerable – the gathering of the host. 'Rise up now,' said Cú Chulainn with Labraid. Labraid, meanwhile, left the host and Cú Chulainn waited by them. Two ravens of druidry announced him; the hosts recognized it. "It is likely,' said the host, 'the ravens' prophecy: the distortion from Ireland [Cú Chulainn] is here.'

Then the hosts pursued them until there was no place for them throughout the land. Meanwhile Eochaid Íuil comes to the well to wash his hands in the early morning. Cú Chulainn, meanwhile, has seen his shoulder through his cloak. He hurled his spear at him so that it went through him. He has killed thirty-three of them at one time. He attacked Senach Síabortha then, and a great fight ensued and Cú Chulainn killed many of them. Labraid arrived then and routed the hosts. Labraid requested him to pause from the slaughter. 'Indeed, let us go,' said Láeg, 'in case by not fighting enough he should turn his anger on us.' 'Let us go,' said Láeg, 'to where three vats are being prepared with cold water to cool his rage.' He goes and the water boils in the first vat beyond. He does not stay in the second vat, as it is too hot. The third vat is suitably hot.

When the women saw Cú Chulainn, it was then that Fand sang the following:

> 'The stately charioteer travels the road,
> although beardless and young:
> the beautiful charioteer moves along the plain
> at evening towards the fair at Fidga.
>
> The canopy [of the chariot] the colour of blood,
> does not sing fairy music
> unless harmonizing with the whirring sound
> of the chariot's wheels.

74

THE WASTING SICKNESS OF CÚ CHULAINN

The horses are steady along the chariot
all the while they are being gazed upon:
There has not been found the like of this drove of
horses:
as swift as the wind in spring.

He performs feats with fifteen golden
apples, well above his breath:
there has not been found the like of this king,
between the smooth and the rough.

Each of the two cheeks are
a shade of red as red as blood,
a shade of green, a shade of blue,
a shade of purple of light colour.

There are seven lights for each eye,
it is not a fact to be left unspoken:
the ornament of the noble eye,
the eyelashes are a dark blue-black.

A man who has been
heard of throughout Ireland,
there are not three hairs of the same colour on him,
this young beardless lad.

Blood makes his sword red
up as far as his silver sword hilt:
the shield to its boss is yellow gold
and at the rim white bronze.

He marches over men in each battle,
he goes into danger and into unguarded places:
there is not, it is said, a fierce warrior
the like of Cú Chulainn.

Cú Chulainn comes hither,
the young warrior from Muirthemne.
It is the daughters of Áed Abrat

who have brought him back from such a distance.

A drop of red blood
flows from the side of his spear-shaft.
The warrior cry from this proud one
causes the phantoms and spectres to shudder.'

Then Lí Ban welcomed him and said the following:

'Welcome, Cú Chulainn,
advancing hero,
great chief of Mag Muirthemne,
great the spirit,
honourable champion victorious in battle,
warrior at heart,
strong stone of wisdom,
red when angered,
ready for fair play in combat,
Ulster warrior of valour,
beautiful the brightness,
bright eyes for women,
Welcome.' Welcome Cú Chulainn.

'Question! So what have you done, Cú Chulainn?' said Lí Ban. Cú Chulainn answered her thus:

'I have thrown a spear
into the camp of Éogan Inbir:
I do not know
whether for victory or as the result of an unlucky deed.

For better or worse with my strength,
until now I have not cast my spear except
in fair play or in ignorance at
a man in a fog:
Or perhaps I did not strike a living being.

The white brilliant army with splendid horses
I pursue on all sides,

the people of Manannán mac Lir
are summoned by Éogan Inbir.

So whatever be my form,
when I turned, I let go my full vigour,
one man against a fighting force,
hound-like I sent them towards death.

When I heard the groan of Eochaid Íuil
it is from the heart the mouths speak:
if it truly was a man and not the
clamour of battle,
then my shot had found its mark.'
I have thrown a spear.

After that Cú Chulainn spent the night with the daughter [Fand], and stayed a month with her. And at the end of the month he says farewell to her, and she said: 'You will ask me to make a tryst and I will.' And the place they arranged for their meeting was by the yew wood at the head of the shore [Ibor Cind Tráchta – Newry, Co. Down]. This is told to Emer. Knives were made at the fairy mound in order to kill the daughter. Fifty daughters came with her to the tryst.

At this time Cú Chulainn and Láeg were playing *fidchell* and they did not notice the women there. Fand noticed the women and said to Láeg: 'Look, Láeg, and see the women.' 'What is it?' said Láeg. Láeg looked and the daughter spoke then, namely, Fand: 'Look behind thee, Láeg. Listen to the right sensible women with sharp grey knives in their right hands and gold against their breasts. See the fine form of the warriors of valour as they come across from their battle chariots. See how the clear appearance of Emer, the daughter of Fergal, changes.'

'Do not fear,' said Cú Chulainn, 'for in no way will anything come between us. Over there the strong frame of the chariot rests before me in a sunny position, I will protect you from the many and numerous warriors from the four quarters of Ulster. If the daughter of Fergal in the midst of her foster sisters boasts deeds of power, perhaps she may not dare to with me.'

Moreover, Cú Chulainn said to Emer: 'I avoid striking thee. I do not strike the hard spear in your trembling hand, nor does the slim feeble knife compress cowardly anger, for very grievous is my strength if released against the strength of women."

'A question then,' said Emer. 'What, in your opinion, Cú Chulainn, is responsible for my humiliation before the many women of Ireland and before the people of rank in general? For it is under secrecy that I have come and under great protection, for, though you boast arrogantly of mighty conflict, your attempt to abandon me may not succeed.'

'A question then, Emer,' said Cú Chulainn. 'Why is it that you will not allow me my time in the company of this woman? First among women is she, pure, chaste, bright and clever, and fit for a king. The most handsome daughter from the waves and great tides across the sea, and fair of form and of noble family, skilled at embroidery, hand-icraft and its produce, full of sense, prudence and fortitude, and with abundant horses and herds of cattle. There is nothing under Heaven she would not do to form a mutual agreement for a joint spouse. O Emer,' said he, 'you will not find a hero as fair, nor as battle-scarred or as victorious in battle, as worthy as this one.'

'Perhaps,' said Emer, 'the woman whom you follow is not a better woman. But moreover, everything red is beautiful, everything new is bright, everything high is lovely, everything bitter is familiar. Everything honourable is absent, everything known is neglected, till all knowledge may be known. O lad,' said, she 'at one time you held me in esteem. We will be happy again for I desire you.' And melancholy came over her. 'Upon my word indeed,' said he, 'thou art dear to me and you will be dear to me as long as you may live.'

'My release from you then,' said Fand. 'Better my release,' said Emer. 'Not so,' said Fand. 'It is I who will go, and it is I who have been taken advantage of, just now.' And she began a lamentation of great sorrow, and was ashamed by her abandonment, and, going through the house forthwith, she was troubled by the great love she had given to Cú Chulainn. And it is thus while she was lamenting that she composed this lay:

> 'I will go on a journey,
> whether it be best for me to be on a great adventure:
> whatever will come about, great his fame
> under whose protection do I desire to be.

It would be better for me to be here.
However, I will yield without grudge,
rather than going with you
to the wonderful sun house of Áed Abrat.

O Emer, you may enjoy the man,
for he is by you, good woman:
yet the hand reaches out,
for I must desire.

Many men sought me
between the roof and a hidden place:
our tryst was not carried through.
Thus it is I who feel righteous.

Woe to the person bringing love,
if it is not heeded:
it is better to put it away,
if one is not loved as one loves.

Fifty women came hither,
O noble Emer of the fair hair,
to fall upon Fand. It is not good,
killing her in her misery.

This day there are three times fifty women,
Beautiful maidens,
my court,
they will not abandon me.'

Then all was revealed to Manannán about what was happening: that
Fand, daughter of Áed Abrat was being oppressed by the women of
Ulster, and was being abandoned by Cú Chulainn. Afterwards
Manannán came from the east seeking the girl. He was present
there and was noticed by no one there but Fand alone. And then
Fand was seized by regret and unhappiness, she looked at
Manannán and made this lay:

'Observe the son of the warrior Lir

79

from the plains of Eógan Inber:
Manannán, high above the world,
at one time he was dear to me.

If today I would greatly lament
that my proud spirit does not love,
then love is useless,
its knowledge goes fast.

One day I was with mac Lir
in the sun house of Dún Inber:
there at that time he unceasingly said
that we would never separate.

When handsome Manannán brought me here
I was a fitting spouse:
I could not be taken
at a single game of fidchell.

When handsome Manannán brought me here
I was a fitting spouse:
a bracelet of gold he brought to me
as the price of my blushes.

It was out beyond on the heath,
fifty beautifully complexioned girls:
I have brought fifty men to him
in addition to fifty women.

There is a household that holds
two hundred people, without doubt, in the one abode,
two fifties of men, prosperous and healthy,
two fifties of women, fair and healthy.

See hither over the sea –
invisible to dull-witted mortals –
the horseman on the foaming sea:
he does not follow the long ships.

Heretofore travelling, nothing was seen
but a very singular fairy [Fand]:
your wisdom [Manannán] perceives each
slender company,
although they may be far away from you.

I wonder if it were right for me
[for there are women of foolish sensibility]
to have loved greatly;
for here I have received oppression.

Farewell to you, O fair hound!
Behold, we go from you in a dignified way.
I wish that I were not going away:
A rule is good until it is broken.

Behold, a timely rising for me:
there is one with whom it is not difficult.
Great is the loss indeed,
O Láeg, son of Riangabra.

I will go to my own spouse,
because he will not be in opposition to me:
nor let it be said that I am leaving in secrecy:
if you wish, observe.'   observe.

The daughter arose then, following Manannán, and the man
Manannán bade her welcome and said: 'Good girl,' said he. 'You
will be where Cú Chulainn is waiting now, or you will return with
me?' 'Upon my word,' said she, 'there is one of you whom I should
prefer to the other. But,' said she, 'it is with you I shall go, and not
wait for Cú Chulainn, for I have been abandoned by him. And
moreover, something else, kind person, in truth, you do not have a
dignified queen, Cú Chulainn has.' Moreover, when Cú Chulainn
saw the girl going from him to Manannán, he said to Láeg: 'What
is that?' said he. 'Easy to answer,' said Láeg. 'Fand is going with
Manannán mac Lir because she was not pleasing to you.' Then Cú
Chulainn leapt three high leaps, the three southward leaps of
Lúachair, so that he was a long period of time throughout the

mountains without drink and without food, and was sleeping each night on the Slige Midlúachra.

Then Emer went seeking Conchobar at Emain, and told him how Cú Chulainn was. Conchobar sent for the seers and the poets, and the druids of Ulster, so that they might seek, secure and bring Cú Chulainn with them to Emain. To avoid this Cú Chulainn tried killing the poets. They chanted spells of druidry in his face; then he was taken by his feet and hands, so that he recovered his senses for a while. Moreover, he was asking them for a drink then. The druids brought a drink of forgetfulness to him. As he drank the drink he did not remember being with Fand. Moreover, the drinks made Emer forget her jealousy, yet she was no better for that. Then Manannán shook his cloak between Cú Chulainn and Fand, and she never possesses him nor meets him again.

And Cú Chulainn appeared to destroy the people of the mounds then, believing that great was his devilish power, and it was so great that he was fighting with the actual demons against the people, to the extent that he was enjoying himself and showing the hidden places to them, so that they might appear to be existing. He did not believe this to be so. They say that this story shows itself to be a struggle between the demons and the people of the mounds.

CHAPTER 6

The Intoxication of the Ulstermen

Mesca Ulad

Since the sons of Míl from Spain reached Ireland, their intelligence circumvented the Túatha Dé Danann, so that Amergin Glúnmár, son of Míl, allowed Ireland to be divided. A royal poet and a royal lawgiver is thus what he was. He divided Ireland in two, and gave the part underground to the Túatha Dé Danann and the other part to the sons of Míl from Spain, who were themselves a blood sept.

The Túatha Dé Danann went into the hills and fairy regions, and, following this, to the supernatural places underground, and submitted to them. They left five men opposite each province in Ireland at increasing battle, strife, conflict and combat among the sons of Míl. In particular they left five men opposite the province of Ulster. The five warriors were: Brea mac Belgain from Drommanna Breg, [southeast Ulster], Redg Rotbél from Slemna Maige Itha [near Raphoe, Co. Donegal], Tinnell mac Boclachtnai, from Sliab Edlicon, Grice from Cruachán Aigli and Gulban Glass mac Gráci from Ben Gulban, Gurt meic Ungarb.

As befitting warriors, these men forced a division within the province of Ulster concerning its three fold division at a time when this was the best province, that is, during the reign of Conchobar mac Fachtna Fáthaig. Conchobar shared the province with his own foster-sons, Cú Chulainn mac Sualtam and Fintan mac Néill Níamglonnaig from Dún Dá Bend. This is the division that was brought into the province: from Cnoc Úachtair Fhorcha, which is called Uisnech Mide or the hill of Uisneach, to the centre of Baile Strand, Dundalk Bay, is where Cú Chulainn's share of the province was. Moreover, Conchobar's third extended from Baile Strand to Trá Tola in Ulster. Fintan's third extended from Trá Tola to Island Magee and Larne.

This was the year when the province was divided into three parts, until Conchobar held the Samain festival at Emain Macha. Such was the extent of the banquet that one hundred of the largest tubs were filled with every type of ale. The officers of Conchobar said that all the Ulstermen would not be too many to attend the banquet, such was its excellence.

A plan was made with Conchobar. Lebarcham, his messenger, was sent to meet Cú Chulainn at Dún Delga, and Findchad Fer Bend Úma mac Fraeglethain was sent to meet Fintan mac Néill Níamglonnaig at Dún Dá Bend.

Leborcham came to Dún Delga and said to Cú Chulainn that he was to address his guardian at Emain Macha. At this time Cú Chulainn was at the great feast for the people of the region at Dún Delga, and said that he would not go, but would be attending to the people of the region himself. Emer Foltchain, daughter of Fergal Manach, spoke, one of the six best women who ever traversed Ireland. 'Do nothing,' she said, 'but go and address your foster-father Conchobar.'

Cú Chulainn asked for his horses to be harnessed and for his chariot to be yoked. 'The horses are harnessed and the chariot is yoked,' said Laeg. 'Do not delay or an evil hour may hinder you from your valour. Set off when you are ready.'

Cú Chulainn took his armoury of valour and leapt into the chariot. Cú Chulainn set out, taking the most direct routes and the shortest paths, towards Emain Macha, and Sencha mac Ailella bade Cú Chulainn welcome on the green of Emain. It is thus that the welcome was expressed: 'Welcome, even welcome for coming, you who always bring good fortune to the hosts of Ulster, noble warrior and one who brings valour to the Gael, O purple-fisted, many-hosted, dear son of Dechtine.'

'The welcome of a man seeking a request,' said Cú Chulainn.

'True indeed,' said Sencha mac Ailella.

'Say what this request is about,' said Cú Chulainn.

'I will ask for sureties to satisfy me,' said Sencha mac Ailella.

'Tell me what sureties you request in return for my services.'

'The two Conalls and Lóegaire: Conall Anglonnach mac Iriel Glúnmáir and Conall Cernach mac Amergin, and Lóegaire Londbúadach.'

Pledges and sureties were offered to Cú Chulainn.

'What form should these sureties take?' said Sencha.

'The three young illustrious noble lads, Cormac Cond Longas mac Conchobar, Mess Dead mac Amergin and Eochu Cendgarb mac Celtchair.'

'I am asking,' said Sencha mac Ailella, ' that you give the third of Ulster that is in your possession to Conchobar, and with permission from you that this shall be so for a year.'

'If the province were the better for his having it for a year, that would not be difficult, for he is a source of authority that could neither be refuted nor contradicted, as he is the descendant of the kings of Ireland and of Scotland. But if the province were not the better, then there will be a skirmish and he will be returned to his third at the end of the year.'

Fintan mac Néill Níamglonnaig arrived. Cathbad the most excellent druid took care of things. He made him welcome thus: 'Your arrival is welcomed, O beautiful, wonderful warrior, O prime hero of the great province of Ulster, who does not accept pirates, foreigners and raiders from overseas, welcome O man, from the borderlands of Ulster.'

'Welcome, men seeking gifts,' said Fintan.

'That is so indeed,' said Cathbad.

'You were speaking, continue,' said Fintan.

'I will say that I may be asking for sureties to satisfy me.'

'What are the guarantees you are seeking in return for pledges to me?'

'Celtchair mac Uithidir, Uma mac Remanfisig from Fedan Chuailnge, Errgi Echbél from Brí Errgi.'

A binding agreement was then reached.

'Now what will you take in return for my pledges?' said Fintan.

'The three sons of Uisliu of great deeds, the three shining torches of valour throughout Europe, Nóisi and Ánli and Ardan.'

The sureties were bound side for side.

They came into the house in which Conchobar was, namely in Téite Brecc.

'Conchobar is king of Ulster now,' said Cathbad, 'if Fintan has given his third to him.'

'That is so,' said Sencha. 'Cú Chulainn has given his third.'

'If that is so,' said Cú Chulainn, 'he [Conchobar] is coming drinking and making merry with me, for that is my request in return.'

'What are my guarantees and requests,' said Fintan, 'when one has dared to say them?'

Each of their guarantors burst forth then, and such was the savagery that, when they arose, nine men were wounded, nine bloodied and nine were stone dead side by side. Sencha mac Ailella arose and shook the peaceful wand of Sencha, so that the Ulaid fell silent and mute.

'You quarrel too much,' said Sencha mac Ailella, 'especially since Conchobar is not king until the end of the year.'

'Stop fighting,' said Cú Chulainn, 'so that nothing may come between us at the end of the year.'

'Nothing will come for sure,' said Sencha.

Cú Chulainn bound him to it. They allowed themselves to remain for three days and nights drinking at the feast of Conchobar until it was all over. After that they went to their houses and forts and goodly dwellings.

Anyone who came at the end of the year would find that the province was a fountain of justice and abundance.

Under Conchobar there was not an abandoned fort empty and desolate, from Island Magee and Larne to the Hill of Uisnech, to the Blackwater river and to the river Drowes, without a son in the place of his father and grandfather serving the proper lord.

Then there occurred a pleasant conversation between Cú Chulainn and Emer:

'Methinks,' said Emer, 'Conchobar is now the high king of Ulster.'

'It is no harm that it should be so,' said Cú Chulainn.

'It is time to be making the banquet of kingship for him now,' said Emer, "for he will be the king forever.'

'Let it be done then,' said Cú Chulainn.

The feast was prepared so that there were a hundred vats with every kind of ale in each.

At the same time Fintan mac Néill Níamglonnach gave permission for preparing his banquet. There were a hundred vats, each with ale, which were well-prepared and ready in time. In one day the work was taken in hand, and in one day everything was ready. In one day the horses were harnessed and the chariots were yoked.

Cú Chulainn was the first to arrive at Emain. He was unyoking his horses when Fintan arrived and came before Emain. It was while

Cú Chulainn was inviting Conchobar to his feast that Fintan arrived.

'Where are my guarantors and my security, or dare one ask that?' asked Fintan.

'Here we are,' said the sons of Uisliu, arising.

'Though I am here,' said Cú Chulainn, 'I am not without guarantors.'

The Ulaid arose and savagely went for their arms. Since Sencha dared not intervene among them, they were quarrelsome. Conchobar could do nothing with them save leave them the royal palace; and his son, who was named Furbaide mac Conchobar, followed him. And it was he that Cú Chulainn had reared. And Conchobar took him aside and said, 'Good my son,' said Conchobar, 'you might be responsible for the pacification of Ulster.'

'How?' said the son.

'By wailing and grieving in the presence of your fair guardian Cú Chulainn, for when there was any stress of battle or combat on his mind he was thinking of you.' The son turned back, and made wailing and grief in the presence of his foster-father Cú Chulainn. Cú Chulainn inquired as to what ailed him. The youth said to Cú Chulainn: 'When the province is in good spirit you destroy and spoil for the sake of changing one night.'

'I gave my word,' said Cú Chulainn, 'and it will not be broken.'

'I swear,' said Fintan, 'that I will not allow the Ulaid to avoid coming with me tonight.'

'I will find excellent advice for you, if I might speak,' said Sencha mac Ailella. 'The first half of the dark night to Fintan and the second half to Cú Chulainn. That will check the little son's grief.'

'I will permit that,' said Cú Chulainn.

'I shall also abide by it,' said Fintan.

The Ulaid arose about Conchobar, and he sent a messenger about the province, summoning the people of the province to the great feast of Fintan. Conchobar himself went at the head of the innermost circle of the Craeb Ruad towards Dún Da Bend to the house of Fintan mac Néill Níamglonnach. The Ulaid came to the mustering at the feast and men from half the hamlets in Ulster arrived. Thus they came, each hospitaller with his spouse, each king with his queen, each musician with his instruments, each gallant with his lady. For if only a small company had reached the place, it was thus they were attended upon. The sleeping chambers were beautiful, ornamented and finely shaped, and well-provided. There were beautiful tall *grianáns* strewn with rushes and fresh rushes, and very long houses for the hosts; the cooking houses were wide and spacious, and the banqueting hall was speckled, with a wide door, and it was wide, ample and great, having corners and nooks and four doors. There the good people of Ulster between them find room for drinking and merrymaking. There choice portions of food and drink are served to them, so that a hundred portions of food and ale are served to each nine of them.

After that the drinking house was set out in order by Conchobar, according to the divisions of kindred, to the ranks and skills, and in a pleasant manner with a view to the arrangement of the feast. The caretakers set out the room, and the cupbearers dispensed the drinks, and the doorkeepers did the door keeping. Musical compositions are sung together with rousing songs. Their praises were sung in poems and tales. Treasures and jewels and wealth were distributed to them.

Then Cú Chulainn said to Laeg mac Riangabra, 'Arise and go forward, dear Laeg, observe the stars in the sky, find when the very middle of the night will come, for you have watched frequently for me at the borders of the foreigners' territory.'

Laeg arose and went forward. He began observing and gazing afar until midnight came. At the middle of the night Laeg came to the house of Cú Chulainn.

'It is the middle of the night now, O hound of feats,' said he.

When Cú Chulainn heard this he related it to Conchobar, for he was sitting next to him on the champion's seat.

Conchobar arose, and made for the speckled and gold drinking horn. The Ulaid went silent and mute when they saw the king standing. Such was the silence that they could hear a needle drop from the ridgepole to the floor. One of the taboos of the Ulaid was to speak before the king and one of the taboos of the king was to speak before the druids.

Then Cathbad, the most excellent druid spoke: 'what is happening, O Conchobar, illustrious high king of the Ulaid? It is that Cú Chulainn is here. It is time for him to go drinking at the feast.' 'Does he wish to impress the Ulaid by leaving the weak, the women and the young behind?' replied Conchobar.

'It will be done,' said Cú Chulainn, 'provided that the heroes, champions and battle warriors, together with the musicians and poets and their minstrels, come with us.'

The Ulaid arose, rising as one man out onto the hard-soiled green. 'Good my dear Laeg,' said Cú Chulainn,' 'take a leisurely course on the chariot.' The charioteer had the three excellent feats of charioteering at that time: turning the chariot with the charioteer's wand or stick, backing up straight and leaping across the gap.

'Good O friend Laeg,' said Cú Chulainn,' 'goad the horses on to battle.' With a warlike leap the horses of Cú Chulainn burst out. The horses of the Ulaid came in imitation, and this is the way they went, to the green of Dún Da Bend, to Cathir Osrin, to Li Thúaga, to Dún Rígain, to Olarba, by the shores of Olarba into Mag Macha, then towards Sliab Fúait, Ath na Foraire, to Port Nóth of Cú Chulainn, towards Mag Muirthemne, into Crích Saithni, across Dubid, across the current of the Boyne into Mag Breg, then towards west Meath and Seanmag Léna, into Claithar Cell, across the Brosna and little Brosna rivers of the Slieve Bloom mountains to the left side across Berna Mera, of the daughters of Treaga, which is called Berna Éle today, to the right across the Slieve Felim mountains of the daughters of Guaire, across the white stream that is called the river of the grandson of Cathbad, into Machaire Mór na mMuman, across the territory of the Martine tribe and into that of the Smertaini people, then right across the white rocks of Loch Gur, across the flowing waters of the Maigue river, to the territory of Máil mac Úgaine, into the region of the Dési Bec, into the land of Curoi mac Daire. Each forest they came across they razed and left as a flat glen. The iron wheels of the chariots cut down each wood so that the roots of the great oaks were on the territory of the plain after them. Each river and each ford and each estuary they came across was reduced to dry, bare flagstones after them, for great was the length and long the extent of the region that the horse teams with the fronts of their knees carried out of existence.

Then Conchobar, king of Ulster, said, 'We did not take this path between Dún Da Bend and Dún Delca before.'

'Upon that we give our word,' said Bricriu. 'Clearer to us a whisper than to anybody else a shout: methinks we are not anywhere at all in the land of Ulster.'

'Upon my word then,' said Sencha mac Ailella, 'it is not any-where in Ulster we are.'

'Upon my word,' said Conall, 'that is true.'

Then the charioteers of the Ulaid tightened the bridles of the horse teams from the first charioteer to the last.

Then Conchobar asked, 'Who will find the fort attached to the region in which we are?' 'Who will find it for you,' said Bricriu, 'but Cú Chulainn, for it is he who said there was not a cantred in which he did not slaughter a hundred men for every thirty hundred.'

'It is I who am responsible, O Bricriu,' said Cú Chulainn, 'and I will go.'

Cú Chulainn went to Druimm Collchailli, which is called Áine Clíach.

'Tell me, dear Laeg, do you know what territory we are in?'

'Indeed, I do not know that.'

'Truly, I know,' said Cú Chulainn. 'This is Cend Abrat, south of Sliab Cáin; here is Sliab Éblinn in the north east; Lind Lumnig, the large bright pool that you see yonder. Here we are at Druimm Collchailli, also called Áine Clíach, in the territory of the Deis Bec. To the south of us is the host at Cliu Mail mac Ugaine in the land of Curoi mac Daire mac Dedad.'

While they were thus engaged huge amounts of heavy snow fell on the Ulaid, until it reached the shoulders of the men and the shafts of the chariots. Heavy work was done by the charioteers of the Ulaid, columns of stones were raised as shelters between the horses and the snow, and they are surviving still, 'a shelter for the horses of Ulster' ever since. There is evidence for that story.

Cú Chulainn and his charioteer went about until he and Laeg reached the place where the Ulaid were.

'A question then,' said Sencha mac Ailella. 'In what territory are we?'

'We are,' said Cú Chulainn, 'in the territory of the Déis Bec, in the land of Curoi mac Daire, at Cliu Máil mac Úgaine.'

'Therefore woe to us and woe to the Ulstermen,' said Bricriu.

'Don't say that, Bricriu,' said Cú Chulainn, 'for the Ulaid will be informed by me of a way to retrace our steps, so that we may reach the enemy before the day is out.'

'Woe to the Ulaid, when a son born of a sister gives counsel,' said Celtchair mac Uithidir.

'We did not find,' said Fergna mac Findchonna, kingly hospitaller to the Ulaid, 'weakness, feebleness or cowardice in the Ulaid,
O Cú Chulainn, until tonight.'

'Alas that he goes giving counsel,' said Lugaid Lámderg mac Léti,
king of the Dal nAraide, 'without making a mark on a spot or an
edge on a weapon.'

'Apart from that,' said Conchobar, 'what do you wish?'

'We wish,' said Celtchair mac Uithidir, 'to be for a day and a
night in this territory in which we are, then to go out of this place
with its appearance of defeat, since in our case the track is not one
for the foxes of the grassland, neither is it a wilderness or a forest.'

'Then say, O Cú Chulainn,' said Conchobar, 'what is a fitting
camping place for us this day?'

'Here we are at Óenach Senchlochair,' said Cú Chulainn, 'and it
is not the season for this fair field, during this rough wintry season.
And Tara Lúachra on the slopes of Irlúachra, and the chambers and
buildings are there.'

'Then it is fitting that we go to Tara Lúachra,' said Sencha mac
Ailella.

They went then by the most direct route to Tara Lúachra and Cú
Chulainn was their guide.

Big and empty though Tara Lúachra was, no one has spent the
night before or since at that desolate place.

It was natural that when a son was born to Medb and Ailella he
was given a name. Mane Mo Épirt was the name he was given and
he was taken in fosterage to Curoi mac Daire. They came that night
to Ailella and Medb, and the nobles of the province, to drink with
them at the end of that son's first month. For they were all there,
Eochu mac Luchta and his province, also Curoi mac Daire with all
the Clanna Dedad. And it was there they all were in the company of
the wary woman Medb, the warrior woman and daughter of the
high king of Ireland Eochaid Fedlech: there were two watchmen
and two druids looking after her. These were their names: Crom
Deroil and Crom Darail, two pupils of Cathbad, the great druid.

At that time it befell the above pupils to be engaged in watching
and observing from the rampart of Tara Lúachra, on the look-out
and gazing afar from each side of the rampart. Then Crom Deroil
said, 'Has it appeared to you, as it has appeared to me?'

'What?' said Crom Darail.

'Methinks I see a great host of red armour driving hither and thither across the slopes of Irlúachra from the east.'

'It was not raw guts and blood that you were invoking,' said Crom Darail, 'especially when there is no host nor great troop there, but the great oak woods beyond, which we came to yesterday.'

'If it were they, then what causes the great kingly chariots to shake under them?'

'We did not come to these chariots here,' said Crom Darail, 'but to the kingly fortresses yonder.'

'What caused the beautiful white shields to be above the fortress?'

'They are not shields at all,' said Crom Darail, 'but are columns consisting of stones in front of the doors of the ring fort.'

'If they were columns,' said Crom Deróil, 'then what caused the quantity of pointed weapons above the great and dark belly of the host?'

'They are not points of weapons at all,' said Crom Darail, 'but deer and wild beasts of the region, with their horns and antlers above them.'

'They were not deer nor wild animals at all,' said Crom Deróil, 'for is it not the horses casting up the black sods with their hooves over our heads and into the vastness that you are seeing?'

'It is not the horses,' said Crom Darail, 'but cattle and herds from the region let go from the pens and cattle enclosures, for it is there that the birds and fowl stand still on the snow after grazing.'

'Upon my word they are not a single flock:

'If it is a flock with the appearance of a flock,
it is not birds of a single flock;
it is a cloak of speckled pale gold
that you would think is about each bird.

If it is bird points that the flocks are
across the rough glen,
then they are not the bitter
staked spears of Bodb.

Methinks it is not a shower of snow,
but it may be truly small men

92

that are in a noble gathering
with sharp points:
each man under a hard purple shield,
a vast gathering of pointed spears.'

If it is.

'And don't refute it at all with me,' said Crom Deróil, 'since it is I who am right. When they come from the edge of the woods of Irlúachair from the east, what else should make the men stoop?'
And it is thus that they were refuting and singing this lay:

'O Crom Darail, what do I see
through the mist?
Who is foredoomed to slaughter?

It is not fitting for you [said Crom Darail]
to be contentious on every point;
The bent men you say
are slow-moving bushes.

If the bushes are
silent here [and not men], [said Crom Darail]
they could not
arise and go.

If they were groves of alder
above the wood of a cairn,
they would not have traversed it
in a deceiving way, if they were dead.

Since they are not dead,
but roughly coloured, from fierce fighting,
then the living traverse the plains
and the boundary of the wood.

If they were trees on the tops of the hills,
They would not be involved in struggle,
they would not traverse the breadth of the plain
as if it were a speckled cloak.

Since they are not trees,
it is no lie;
the red arms
are those of the men of triumphs and the men of shields.

Since they are on the backs of brown horses,
the bands extend in a row;
like rocks in a swift line,
as though they were red stones.

What causes the poison on each spear point?
Truly an ale boast.
Who are they that go stooping
to yonder point?
O Crom Darail.'

Cú Roi, the son of fair- formed Dáire, heard the two druids on the outside rampart, opposite Tara Lúachra, in contention.

'The druids are not in agreement outside,' said the king of the world, Cú Roi, son of the fair-formed Dáire. Then the sun arose beyond the sphere of the Earth.

'The host is clear to us now,' said Crom Deróil. The sun rose over the hillside of Irlúachra, and thus it was that the lay was said and sung:

'I see Lúachair with many hills,
the sun shines purple-fronted on its sides;
From afar the warriors drive their chariots
between the brown moor and the trees.

If it is a flock of ravens over east yonder,
if it is a flock of heavy corncrakes,
if it is a flock of loud starlings,
if it is a flock of barnacle geese and cranes,

If it is a flock of shrill barnacle geese
if it is a flock of sharp-voiced swans,
it is far from heaven they are,
it is close to the grass they are.

O dear Cú Roi mac Daire,
O man who traverses the briny stream,
Tell us, since you know best,
what is coming around the ancient mountain?'

Cú Roi replies:

'The two watchmen, the two druids,
and in great confusion;
Their terrified eyes see
a lively fight.

 If they are the horned curly-headed cattle,
if they are the rocks with their hard surfaces,
if it is the sparse dark green wood,
if it is the roar of the sea at Muir Miss,

If they are cattle they have the appearance of cattle
and are not a single herd;
There is a fierce man with a spear dripping blood
on the back of each cow.

There is a sword on each cow
and a shield on the left side;
I see the rough and crude standards
above the cows.
I see Lúachair.'

The two druids and the two watchmen were not far away when the
white leap of Bodb burst forth from the first troop across yonder
glen. The savageness descended on Tara Lúachra so that they rose
up and no spears were left on the weapon rack, no shields on the
pegs and no swords on the rack. They all fell down. On each
thatched house in Tara Lúachra it descended in huge flakes, white
as linen cloths. It was as though the sea came towards them over the
ramparts from every corner of the world. The aspects of their coun-
tenances were changed and there was a chattering of teeth within
Tara Lúachra. The two druids fell into a swoon and into a faint, and
into a bed of sickness: one of them, Crom Darail, fell out over the

rampart and the other, Crom Deróil, fell on the other side of the wall. Notwithstanding all this, Crom Deróil cast his eye on the first group that came into the green.

The host leapt down onto the green and sat in one assembly on the open space. The snow melted and ran as liquid down thirty feet on either side of them, glowing with the heat of valorous foot-soldiers.

Crom Deróil came to the house in which Medb and Ailella were, and Cú Ruí and Eochaid mac Luchta, and Medb inquired, 'Whence comes the alarm that has come to us, from the sky above or across the sea from the west or to Ireland from the east?'

'It is to Ireland from the east, across the hillsides of IrLúachair to be sure,' said Crom Deróil. It has the appearance of a savage troop, neither Irish nor foreign. Or if it is Irishmen and not foreigners, then it is the Ulaid.'

'Is the description of the Ulaid not known to Cú Ruí yonder?' said Medb. 'For it is often that he has been on hostile expeditions and hostings and journeys in their company.'

'It will be known,' said Cú Ruí, 'provided that I get a description.'

Indeed, a description of the first troop came to them at their place of encampment. 'It is with me,' said Crom Deróil. 'Give it to us then,' said Medb.

'To the east of the fort on the outside I saw a very great kingly troop: like a king, each man in that troop. Three men are in front of the troop. In the centre among them a broad-eyed kingly warrior; his countenance, appearance and face like a full moon. A fair and narrow two-forked beard on him; ruddy yellow close-cropped hair on him held by a band at the back of his head. A cloak of bordered purple around him, a brooch of inlaid gold on his cloak above his white shoulder, a mantle of kingly satin close to his white skin, a shield of dark purple with bosses of bay-coloured gold on it, a sword with an inlaid golden hilt by him, a spear with a bright pur-ple blade in his right hand, alongside it a smaller pronged spear. On his right side – a proper warrior, brighter than snow his count-enance. On his left side a small black-browed man; greatly res-plendent that man, a fair, bright man performing a feat of jugg-ling swords above them, a very sharp, bare sword with a hilt of tusk in one hand, a warrior-like great sword in the other hand. He casts them in turn high aloft and downwards, so that they strike like a shadow against the hair and the cheek of the great central warrior. Before they reach the ground they catch the same man by the tip of their points and by the edge of their swords.

'It is a kingly description,' said Medb.

'It is a kingly people that is described,' said Cú Ruí.

'Who is that, who is that yonder?' said Ailella.

'Easy to explain,' said Cú Ruí. 'Conchobar mac Fachtna Fáthaig, a proper and worthy king of Ulster, a descendant of the kings of Ireland and Scotland, that great warrior in a central position there yonder. On his right side Fintan, son of Niall Niamglonnach, ruler of one third of Ulster: bright as snow his countenance and his face. Cú Chulainn mac Sualtaim the small black-browed man on his left side. Ferchertni mac Corpri, son of Iliach, the fair, very bright man there, plying feats of valour above them, the kingly chief poet of all the poets of Ulster there and rear guard to Conchobar when he goes to the region of the enemy. Whoever he be who might wish to hold conversation with the king, he dare not until that man has first been spoken to.'

'Lo!' said Crom Deróil. 'I saw over yonder coming from the east, three light-footed warriors attired in military dress. Two of them were youthful, the other had a two-forked dark crimson beard. They did not carry the dew from the grass, so swiftly and light did they travel, as if the great host did not see them.'

'It is a mild, light and peaceful description,' said Medb.

'It is a mild and pleasant description of the people,' said Cú Ruí.

'Who are they?' said Ailella.

'Indeed,' said Cú Ruí, 'not difficult to answer. Three noble youths of the Túatha Dé Danann there: Delbáeth mac Eithlend and Óengus Óc mac in Dagda and Cermait Milbél. They came at the end of the night to the ever-growing conflict and battle, they mingled themselves among the host, so that it is true that the troops did not see them, the troops there, and that they are observed by them.'

'Here from the east and beyond,' said Crom Deróil, 'I see the warrior- like band of full valorous deeds, with three distinguished warriors taking precedence before them. A very brown furious warrior there, and a fair comely warrior, and a mighty strong and stout-of-arm warrior with close cropped ruddy-yellow hair on him, like the top branches of a silver birch at the end of autumn or his hair compared to the bright sheen of pale gold brooches, a swarthy brown two-forked beard on him, similar to the length of a warrior's arm. Like the purple of the foxglove or the glowing embers of a fresh fire his countenance and face. Three warrior-like russet shields on them; three great broad-headed spears with spear shafts with them; three heavy swords for dealing vigorous blows with them; three beautiful crimson garments around them.'

'By my conscience, that is a warrior-like and champion-like description,' said Medb.

'It is a warrior-like and champion-like description of a people,' said Cú Roi.

'Who is that, what is that yonder?' said Ailella.

'Easy to tell: three chief warriors of Ulster there, the two Conalls and Lóegaire, that is, Conall Ánglonnach mac Iriel Glúnmáir and Conall Cernach mac Amergin and Lóegaire from Ráth Imil.'

'Here from the east and beyond,' said Crom Deróil, 'I see three dreadful unknown men at the forefront of the troop. Three linen shirts wrapped tightly about their skin; three dun-grey woolly cloaks gathered about them; three stake brooches binding the front of the cloaks; three very brown shaggy heads of hair on them; three dun-coloured bright shields with hard bronze bosses on them; three spears with broad flat heads with them; three swords with golden hilts by them. It was as the baying of a foreign hound on the attack, as at the centre of a snorting bellows, that each soldier overheard the enemy in their fort.'

'It is a savage and a heroic description,' said Medb.

'It is a description of a barbaric people,' said Cú Ruí.

'Who is that, what is that yonder?' said Ailella.

'Easy to tell,' said Cú Roi. 'Three props of war from Ulster there: Uma mac Remanfissig from Fedan Cúalnge, Errgi Echbél from Brí Errgi, Celtchair Mór mac Uithidir from Ráth Celtchair, also known as Dún Dá Lethglas.'

'Here from the east and beyond,' said Crom Deróil, 'I saw a man with large eyes, having great thighs and shoulders, exceedingly great and very tall, with a fine grey cloak around him. Seven smooth short brown cloaks about him, each shorter and lower than the next, each lower and more flowing than the next; nine men on each side; his club of iron in his hand, a furious end on it and a smooth head. Tricks and feats were laid on, so that in the twinkling of an eye the heads of nine men were felled by this furious club. At the same time they are brought back to life by the smooth head of the club.'

'It is a wonderful description,' said Medb.

'That man is described in many shapes and guises,' said Cú Ruí.

'What then, who is he?' said Ailella.

'Easy to answer,' said Cú Ruí. 'It is the Dagda mac Eithlenn, the good god of the Túatha Dé Danann. He allowed struggle and strife to co-mingle on the morning of that day on the troop, yet he was not seen by the host.'

'Here from the east and beyond,' said Crom Deróil, 'I see a strong broad-faced man, strong and dark-browed, broad of face and bright-toothed, without apparel, without dress, without weapons, without a sword's edge, but with a brown leather apron well-kneaded at the crooks of the two armpits. As stout as a big man is every single limb of him. This stone pillar outside, the Clanna Dedad could not raise up and pull away from the ground, but he did the apple feat by passing it from finger to finger. It leaves the ground as swift and as lightly as a wisp leaves a thistle.'

'It is a mighty strong description,' said Medb.

'It is a powerful description,' said Cú Roi.

'What is that, who is that yonder?' said Ailella.

'Easy to say: Trisgatail Trénfher, that is the strong man of Conchobar's house. It is he who killed twenty-seven men just by looking wrathful.'

'Here from the east and beyond,' said Crom Deróil, 'I see a fresh child-like young man, tied and in bondage; three chains around each of his feet and each of his hands. Three chains around his neck and, close by, seven great men holding each of his chains, and each is equal to seventy-seven men. He takes a powerful mighty and manly turn, and he overthrew the seventy-seven men as though they were as swift and as light as puffballs. When he perceived the odour of the enemy, when he struck the head of a man against a projecting clod in the ground or against a rock of stone, this is what that man said: 'A great turn around neither in fighting nor valour was achieved there, but it came about due to the odour of food and drink within the fort.'

A fit of shame seized the young man as he traversed a while with them in silence, until a wave of savagery overcame him.

'By my conscience,' said Medb, 'it is a deadly and intractable description.'

'Deadly and intractable he whose description it is,' said Cú Ruí.

'What is that, who is it?' said Ailella.

'Easy to tell: the son of the three warriors, as was said some time ago, that is, Uma mac Remanfisig, Errgi Echbél and Celtchair mac Uthidir. It is necessary to have so many of his host keeping guard as he goes to the territory of the enemy for the purpose of fighting for victory. He is Úanchend Arritech, and he has completed only eleven years and he has never completed a portion of food without offering it to everyone in the house.'

'Here from the east and beyond,' said Crom Deróil, 'I see an unwieldy company, one man, one man among them, with a black, close-cropped and bristly head; one great bulging bright eye in his head; a swarthy smooth blue face on him; a cloak of striped or spotted cloth wrapped around him; a brazen pin in his cloak over his front; a long bronze crook in his hand; a little bell of sweet sound along with him. He brandishes a horse switch at the troop, which causes pleasure and joy to the high king, and to all the host.'

'That is a laughable and comic description,' said Medb.

'He whose description it is, is laughable,' said Cú Ruí.

'Who is that?' said Ailella.

'Easy to answer,' said Cú Ruí. That is Róimid Rigóinmit,' said Cú Ruí, 'the king's fool, in service to Conchobar. There was nothing but sorrow at the Ulster fort, until Róimid Rigóinmit was brought there and he was seen.'

'Here from the east and beyond,' said Crom Deróil, 'I see a crimson man in his first greyness in a covered chariot above the tall horses. A wondrous much-speckled cloak about him, an ornament threaded with gold, moreover a bracelet of gold on each of his two hands, a gold ring on each of his fingers: ornamented gold weapons in his possession; nine chariots before him; and nine chariots after him, and nine chariots on either side.'

'It is a dignified and regal description,' said Medb.

'It is a dignified and regal description of that man,' said Cú Ruí.

'What is that, who is that there?' said Ailella.

'Easy to tell,' said Cú Ruí. 'Blad Briuga mac Fiachna from Tara on the Ards Peninsula, and to be sure his nine chariot drivers going about on each of the paths. He did not listen to anybody's speech to the host, only to speeches against it. Seldom do they speak to anyone but him.'

'Here from the east and beyond,' said Crom Deróil, 'I see a very great kingly troop. This one man out in front: very dark heather-like hair on him, a gentle tinge on one cheek, foaming-red the colour of the other cheek. Smooth and gentle the one, wrathful the other, a wild animal across each of his two shoulders, a white-fronted shield by his side; a sword with a white hilt by him. A great long warrior-like spear on his shoulder: when the spear ardour seized him, he bore the impact of the butt of the big spear on the palm of his hand until a measured bushel of fiery tinder sparks burst forth across the spear and the spear head, as they resisted the heat of the spear. A cauldron of very dreadful dark blood liquid is made the night before by means of druidical magic with the blood of dogs, cats and druids; the head of the spear was dipped in this poisonous liquid when its rage came on when the spear ardour seized him.'

'By my conscience, it is a dreadful description,' said Medb.

'He whose description it is is deadly,' said Cú Ruí.

'Who is there, what is that?' said Ailella.

'Dubthach Dóel Ulad there,' said Cú Ruí, 'a man who does not seek thanks from anyone; he alone of all the Ulaid is there when a foray is carried out. The swift death-dealing lance of Celtchair alone in his hand and the blood-red cauldron before it, for it would burn the spear shaft or the man who was carrying it, were it not washed in the poisonous blood of the cauldron; and it is battle that the lance prophesies.'

'Here from the east and beyond,' said Crom Deróil, 'I see another band of warriors. A sleek, ancient greyish man to the forefront of this group; a very light cloak around him, pure white borders edged with silver; a beautiful pure white shirt next to his skin; a white silver sword with rounded hilt under his cloak; a bronze baton as high as his shoulder; the sweetness of the minstrel in his voice; stately clear speech from him.'

'By my conscience, that description is both judge-like and wise,' said Medb.

'He whose description it is is judge-like and wise,' said Cú Ruí.

'What is that there, who is that?' said Ailella.

'Easy to tell: Sencha Mór mac Ailella, son of Máelchlóid from Carnmag in Ulster, a skilful man on the ground and a man who pacifies the Ulster host. The men of the world he would pacify with three virtuous words, from the rising to the setting of the splendid sun.'

'Here from the east and beyond,' said Crom Deróil, " I see the keen and comely band. A handsome young man in the forefront, curly yellow hair on him; decisions not made by the previous wiseman may be made by him.'

'It is a wise and clever description,' said Medb.

'He who made that description is clever and wise,' said Cú Ruí.

'Who is that?' said Ailella.

'Easy to tell: pleasant, fair-judging son of Sencha, son of Ailella there, and a judgement that is not made by his father cannot be upheld.'

'Here from the east and beyond,' said Crom Deróil, 'I see three dreadful tall foreigners with short shaggy hair, outlandish dun-grey garments about them, three brazen small javelins in their right hands, three iron clubs in their left hands. They do not speak to each other and they do not speak in front of the host.'

'It is a description of slavish foreigners,' said Medb.

'The people in that description are slavish and foreign,' said Cú Ruí.

'What is that, who is there?' said Ailella.

'Easy to tell,' said Cú Ruí. 'Three doormen of the royal house there, Nem and Dall and Dorcha.'

That is the description of the first group that came into the green. It is not true that the great druid invented the description that he gave.

'Is that the Ulaid yonder now?' said Medb.

'It is indeed,' said Cú Ruí.

'Was this imagined before or after or the result of a prophecy or a prediction placed before you?'

'That we do not know," said Cú Ruí.

'Is there anyone at the fort who knows?' said Medb.

'There is the ancient of the Clanna Dedad,' said Cú Ruí, 'namely Gabalglinni mac Dedad, he who is blind for thirty years and piously attending the fort.'

'Let someone go and enquire what preparations have been made for them.'

'Who will be going?' said Cú Ruí.

'Crom Deróil and Fáenglinni mac Dedad.'

They came as far as the house in which Gabalglinni was being looked after.

'Who is that?' he said.

'Crom Deróil and Fáenglinni here,' they said. 'We are inquiring whether there were prophecies or predictions as to whether the Ulaid were coming or whether anyone is attending on them or what is happening?'

'It is a long time coming to the prophecies and to the attending. This is the provision. There is an iron house and, close by, two houses of wooden palisades, and at the house of earth below are very firm slabs of iron and these are found on dead wood, and fuel and coal are packed together in the earthen house, so that it is quite full. It is prophesied that the men of Ulster should gather for one night in that house. There are seven chains of fresh iron there under the feet of my bed, provided for binding and making fast; let them be bound to the seven pillar stones on the green outside.'

Then it was that they came before the house in which were Medb and Ailella and the men of the provinces, and to them related how the Ulaid were being cared for.

'Let someone go and welcome them, somebody from you and somebody from me, O Cú Ruí,' said Medb.

'Who will go?' said Cú Ruí.

'The same pair,' said Medb, 'so that the men of Connacht are made welcome by me and the men of Munster are welcomed by you.'

'I shall recognise,' said Cú Ruí, 'that man who will answer the welcome whether in peace or in strife. For if Dubthach Dóel Ulad will answer, then they come for strife; if Sencha mac Ailella will answer, then they come in peace.'

They [Crom Deróil and Fáenglinni] went as far as the green on which the Ulaid were.

'Ever welcome, O high king of famous deeds, O noble member of the Ulaid,' said Crom Deróil, 'from Medb and from Ailella and from the men of the province of Connacht.'

'Ever welcome, O high king of Ulster, man of noble deeds,' said Fáenglinni mac Dedad, 'from Cú Ruí mac Dáire, who is in the fort yonder with the men of Munster.'

'Trustworthy with us and trustworthy before the king,' said Sencha mac Ailella, 'and the Ulaid come making neither strife nor combat, but jovial intoxication, from Dún Da Bend to Clíu Máil mac Úgaine, and it will not be an honour with them to go into the territory without spending a night in the camp.'

103

They came as far as the place where Medb and Ailella and Cú Ruí and Eochu and the men of the three provinces were. They related all to them. The poets and the musicians and the entertainers were sent to the Ulaid to perform and entertain while they were equipping themselves in their house. Messengers were sent to them saying that the best warrior of the Ulaid should make a choice about the house for them. A dispute arose among the Ulaid about that place. A hundred equally valorous warriors simultaneously arose and went for their weapons, but Sencha mac Ailella pacified them.

'Let Cú Chulainn go,' said Sencha, 'for it is for the sake of his house that you came and you are under his protection until he returns.'

Cú Chulainn arose. The Ulaid arose, rising as one man after Cú Chulainn. Cú Chulainn glanced at that house. It was the best habitable spot in the district. This latter is the iron house; there were two wooden houses around it.

Their attendants came towards them and a huge bonfire was lit for them. They divided the portions of food and drink among themselves. As night drew on, the attendants and servants stole away one by one from them until the last man closed the door after him. They put seven chains of fresh iron around the house and bound them to seven stone pillars that were outside on the green. They put one hundred and fifty smiths with smiths' bellows blowing at the fire. Three circles were made around the house. The fire was kindled from below and from above in the house until the glow of the fire came through the house from below. The host shouted out loud around the house until the Ulaid fell silent and mute. Then Bricriu said, 'What is this great glow that burns our feet? For is clearer to me a whisper than anyone else a shout: it seems to me that we are being burned from below and above, and shut in in this building.'

'This is the way we will find out,' said Triscatail Trénfher, rising and giving a blow with his foot into the iron door that was against the doorway. It did not groan, it did not creak; it did not yield to pressure.

'Not well have you prepared the feast for the Ulaid, O Cú Chulainn,' said Bricriu, 'for you have brought us into the enclosure of the enemy.'

'Not so Bricriu,' said Cú Chulainn. 'I will strike my sword Crúadín, by means of which all the Ulaid will leave here.'

Cú Chulainn thrust his sword until it reached as far as its hilt through the iron house and through the two wooden houses.

'That is the iron house,' said Cú Chulainn, 'between the two wooden houses.'

'That is worse than every trick,' said Bricriu.

[lacuna in text]

'for if my club hits them they will be killed.'

'It is worse,' said Triscoth, 'for any man who catches my wrathful look will die screaming.'

'Let me go,' said Reordae Drúth.

'Let me,' said Nia Natrebuin Chró.

'Let me,' said Dáeltenga.

'One of us shall go there,' said Dub and Rodub.

Each man arose as one.

'Do not let that arouse you,' said Sencha. 'The man whom the Ulaid may choose may be the best warrior and is the one who will go there.'

'Who is that?' said the Ulaid.

'Cú Chulainn yonder may be the best warrior and it is he who will go there.'

Then they arose and went into the liss, with Cú Chulainn before them.

'Is this sprite here the best warrior in Ulster?' said Fintan.

Thereupon Cú Chulainn leapt upwards until he was on the top of the liss, and the arms leapt onto the front bridge, so that the arm racks in which the arms were fell into the fort. They were taken to a house of oak with a vaulted roof and a door of yew three feet thick, and two hooks of iron attached to it, and a bolt of iron that the two hooks were on. The house was strewn with quilts and blankets. Crom Deróil brought the weapons with him and set them up, and the weapons of Cú Chulainn are raised above the rest.

'Heat water for them for washing,' said Ailella, and he brought ale and food to them until they were mellowed with the drink. Still Crom Deróil tended them to see what they might wish. Since they were intoxicated, Sencha struck his stick. They all heard it.

'Now give good tidings to the prince to whom you have come, for he has been magnificent. "It is not a hand in a poor field." There is plenty of ale and food. There is no need to mention that a feast will be prepared.'

'That is true,' said Dáeltenga. 'I swear by the oaths of my people that you will never reach your country, save what birds will carry off from you in their claws, but you will suffer the men of Ireland and of Scotland inhabiting your country, and carrying off your women and your valuables, and breaking the heads of your sons against stones.'

It is therefore as Fergus said in the Táin:

> Dismiss Dubtach Dáeltenga.
> Drag him behind the host;
> he did no good
> when he slew the maidens.
>
> He preferred an ill-famed and unlucky deed
> in the slaying of Fiachaig mac Conchobair;
> It was not to his greater glory
> that the slaying of Mane mac Fedelmthéo was by him.
>
> He does not contest the kingship of Ulster,
> this son of Lugdach, son of Casrubai;
> those whom he cannot kill
> he sets at loggerheads.

'Now that is not a lie,' said Dubtach. 'Look at the house, how strong it is, and at how the door is closed. Do you not see that, although ye might wish, ye have not the power to go out of it. It is a disgrace to me if outside there are not disputes about attacking us. Only the warrior yonder, the greatest in valour throughout Ulster, can find out the situation from them.'

Cú Chulainn stirred himself and leapt a warrior's salmon leap upwards, until he carried off the ridge-pole from the topmost part of the house, until it was on the ridge-pole in the other house. He saw the host below him. They formed themselves into a solid phalanx for the attack. Ailella put his back against the door to protect them. His seven sons joined hands before the door. The host broke out into the middle of the enclosure. Cú Chulainn went to the people and gave a kick to the door, so that his leg went through as far as his knee.

'If that blow were levelled at a woman,' said Dáeltenga, 'she would not be sleeping.'

Cú Chulainn gave another kick until the door-frame fell into the hearth.

'Let us come to a decision,' said Sencha.

'It will be now,' said Cú Chulainn, 'each right as due to the warriors that have been fighting nearby. See your enemies approaching.'

'What is your counsel?' said Sencha.

'Place your backs against the wall of the house and place your weapons in front of you, and let one man confer with them. Then the greater weight of the house may support you in whatever may come against you.'

'Who will address them?' said Sencha.

'They will be addressed by me,' said Triscoth. 'Any man of them who will look at me will perish.'

Their enemies were considering their plan outside.

'Question: who will be addressed and who will go first into the house?' said the young warriors outside.

'I will go,' said Lopán.

Then Lopán went into the house, nine men with him.

'That befits a warrior,' said he.

'What is befitting is a man against the enemy,' said Triscoth.

'True, true. Yonder Triscoth, speechmaker for the Ulaid; without him the speeches are not good.'

Triscoth gave him a wrathful glance, so that he fell down dead with upturned soles.

Then Fer Caille went into the house with nine men.

'That befits a warrior,' said he.

'What is befitting is a man against the enemy,' said Triscoth.

Then Triscoth gave him a wrathful glance, so that he fell down dead with upturned soles.

Then Mianach Anaidgned went into the house with nine men.

'The wounded on the floor seem deadly pale to us,' said he. Triscoth gave a glance.

'Look at me and see if I perish from it,' said Mianach.

Triscoth seized the enemy by the legs and struck him upon them repeatedly, upon three times nine men that were in the house then, so that none of them came out alive.

Then the host were summoned outside the house to seize it from the Ulaid. Then the Ulaid overturned the house so that it fell on three hundred of the host that were on the outside. One battalion closes with another. After that they were engaged in fighting until the middle of the following day. They overthrew the Ulaid, who were few in number. Ailella was looking at the dwelling house near the fort. 'Until today stories were told to me, stories of the Ulaid. There were no warriors in Ireland to equal them, so it is related to me, but today I see they are making a disgrace of themselves. It is an ancient ruling that a battle is not won without a king. However, a battle in which I am not involved will not last for long. You see that I have no control over them. It is a violation of my honour that I suffer in regard of you.'

Thereupon Cú Chulainn leapt over the troop and struck them three times. Furbaide Fer Bend mac Conchobar also struck round about them. His enemies would not strike him because of his great beauty.

'Why no slaying?' said one man. 'Is it because of this magnificent fellow? Is it not a pleasing thing he does? The golden-headed one I will slay for the slaying of my brother; I swear this by the gods of my people.'

But Furbaide struck this latter warrior with a spear and he perished from it.

After that the Érainn are defeated in the fight, so that none but a third of them escaped from it. The Ulaid then slay all in the fort, but spare Ailella and his seven sons because they were not in the battle against them. Since then Tara Lúachra has not been inhabited.

Crimthann Nia Náir of the Érainn escapes from there. He meets Riches, a female satirist, west at the river Laune. This woman was the foster-mother of Crimthann.

'Has my son been slain?' said she.

'He has,' said Crimthann.

'Come with me so that you can avenge him,' said she.

'When does this avenging stop?' said Crimthann.

'When Cú Chulainn is struck down in vengence for him," she said.

'How will that be done?' said he.

'Easy to answer, for if you use only your two hands and nothing else, you will overcome him easily.'

After that they [Crimthann and Riches] went after the host until they found Cú Chulainn at the ford before them, at Crích Uathne. Riches took her clothes off in the presence of Cú Chulainn. Cú Chulainn turned his face to the ground so that he would not see her stark nakedness.

'Seize him now,' said Riches.

'There is a man coming towards you,' said Laeg.

'Truly no,' said Cú Chulainn. 'As long as the woman is in that state, I will not rise.'

Laeg took a stone into the chariot and hurled it at the woman, so that it struck her in the hindquarters and broke her back in two; she died from the blow. Cú Chulainn arose after that to meet Crimthann and fought against him, until he brought away both his head and his weapons. Then afterwards they came with the host until they were at the fort of Cú Chulainn and they passed the night there. There they were entertained for forty nights at a lasting feast with Cú Chulainn, and after that they go from him and leave their blessings with him.

Now Ailella, came from the south to pay the Ulaid a visit. The width of his face in gold and silver was given to Ailella and seven *cumals* for each of his sons. Then he returned to his own land in peace and unity with the Ulaid. After that Conchobar was safe in his kingdom for as long as he lived.

CHAPTER 7

The Combat between Cú Chulainn and Fer Diad

Comrac Fir Dead inso

Then the men of Ireland considered who would be an equal contestant to fight Cú Chulainn early on the following morning. They all said that the fight should be with Fer Diad, son of Damáin, son of Dáire, that is, with the most courageous warrior of the Domnainn, since it was likely that they were well-matched to fight. For they had the same foster-mothers, from whom they learned their feats of valour and weaponry, namely Scáthach and Uathach and Aífe. And neither one had the advantage over the other, except for Cú Chulainn's prowess with the *gae bulga*. However, horn-skinned Fer Diad would be an equal match for the hero, fighting on the ford against him.

Then Medb and Ailella sent wise men and messengers to Fer Diad. Fer Diad refused the messengers and did not go with them, since he knew why they were there, namely to force him to contest and to fight against his friend, against his companion and against his equal, Cú Chulainn mac Sualdam. And he did not come with them. Then Medb called for the druids and the satirists and the inciters to go to Fer Diad and revile him, and for three satirists versed in the art of satire to raise three blisters on his face, of insult, of misfortune and of disgrace, should he not come to the combat, which is supposed to last for three days and three nights. Fer Diad came with them for the sake of his honour, since it was easier for him to fall in battle ardour and in valour and in feats of arms than to fall on the

110

battlefield from insult and shame. And when he reached the camp he was honoured and attended on, and drink was dispensed, so that he was intoxicated by the liquor, to the extent that he was confused and merry. And great pledges and conditions were made for a contest and a fight against Cú Chulainn, namely, a chariot and twenty-eight bondswomen and a cloak that would cover twelve men, in every single colour, together with a holding of arable land in Mag Aí without tax or tribute, without a camp or an army, without stressful encounters with sons or grandsons or great-grandsons until Doomsday. And Findabair was to be his woman, and a golden brooch that was worn by fiery Medb upon her. Then Medb addressed Fer Diad and said:

'A bracelet of great value,
together with a portion of the plains and woods,
privileges for your family
from now until Doomsday,
O Fer Diad mac Damáin.
Rise up wounding and attacking:
you will get with each breath
what is due to you
without having to seize anything from anyone.'

Fer Diad:
'I will not take anything upon myself without surety
since this warrior is not without skills in weaponry,
he who will be heavily armed against me tomorrow,
who will make a very strong effort.
Cú Chulainn, whose additional name is "gifted",
is keen with the point of a spear:
it is not easy enduring his violence
when he is under attack.'

Medb:
Warrior who will not go to the assembly,
unless his hands are holding magnificently
bridled horses.
O Fer Diad, man of valour
from a line of poets,

may you be a confidant to me,
over everybody and free of tribute.'
Fer Diad:
'I will not go without pledges
to the sport on the ford.
You must give until Doomsday
strong watertight pledges.
Unless I get these from you
you might as well offer me
the sun and the moon,
the sea and the land.'

Medb:
'What reason have you for delaying?
For you are secured by kings
and rulers, O contented one!
Here you will find room
for everything you ask,
for it is known to me that you will kill
the man who comes towards you.'

Fer Diad:
'Only if I can choose six heroes,
nothing less,
before my strength is lost
in the place where the host will be.
Grant me my request
and a vigorous battle of atonement
will be fought, between me and
the battle-hardened Cú Chulainn.'

Medb:
'Take Domnall or Cairbre
or the noted plunderer Níamán,
choose from the bards
as many as you wish,
if you take another with you
take perfect Morand,
bring with you courteous

112

Cairbre Manann
or take our own two sons.'
Fer Diad:
'O Medb of many accomplishments,
the beauty of a bride does not touch you.
It is true that you are guardian
of earthen-walled Cruachain,
with a loud voice of fierce strength.
Bring to me the much-coveted satin,
I will take gold and silver,
for such I deserve.'

Medb:
'For are you not the warrior chief?
I will bring to you a round brooch.
Rest from today until Sunday,
but no longer.
O hero in your prime and fame,
Each beautiful jewel of the Earth
will be brought to you thus,
for all will be placed before you.

And Finnabair of the heroes,
the queen of western Elga,
after the destruction of the skilled Hound,
she will await you, O Fer Diad.' A bracelet of great value.

Then Medb reached the young charioteer and Fer Diad said: 'About the contest and fight with the hero tomorrow; I would prefer if it were with anyone else rather than him.' Then Fer Diad approached the young warrior and thought to himself that, if Cú Chulainn should fall by him, he would send for the completion of pledges from the same six heroes.

Then the horse of Fergus is got and yoked to the chariot, and he came to the place where Cú Chulainn was, and he said to him privately: 'Welcome Cú Chulainn.' 'Thank you for coming father, and welcome,' said Cú Chulainn. 'As far as I'm concerned, it is not a welcome event, O foster-child,' said Fergus, 'I have come to tell you that the one who comes for the contest and the fight before you tomorrow is both sorrowful and dejected.'

'Let us hear it from you,' said Cú Chulainn. 'Your friend and comrade and foster-brother, similar to you in feats of arms, valour and deeds, is Fer Diad, son of Damáin, son of Dáire, the most courageous warrior of the Domnainn.' 'Methinks in confidence,' said Cú Chulainn, 'that the friend is not over-zealous in coming to the meeting.' 'Well then,' said Fergus, 'avoid him and take to the bed, since not everyone on this cattle raid at Cooley is able to fight and enter contest with Fer Diad mac Damáin.' 'I am here,' said Cú Chulainn, 'checking and tallying the four great provinces of Ireland from the Monday at the beginning of Hallowe'en to the beginning of spring, and there is no shame on me as I have not retired one foot from any man facing me. And it seems to me that that which is looming before me is greater than anything else.' And it is thus that Fergus spoke about the threat to Cú Chulainn, and speaking these words he approached him:

> 'O Cú Chulainn, one thing is clear,
> I see that it is timely for you to rise
> from here, before the fury of
> Fer Diad mac Damáin of red countenance.'

> Cú Chulainn:
> 'I am here moving with stealth
> and greatly disturbing the men of Ireland.
> I am not running away
> because of a contest with this one man.'

> Fergus:
> 'Violent is the wrath of this man
> shown by his blood-red sword,
> a horn-skin around him, this Fer Diad of the hosts,
> I would not insist on battle against him.'

> Cú Chulainn:
> 'Be heedful and discreet with your story,
> O Fergus of very strong armour;
> over each territory, there is dominion!
> For me, this is not an unequal contest.'

Fergus:
'Keen is the man, he fights with valour,
it is not easy to overcome him,
the strength of a hundred, his courage and honour.
Avoid his sword points, with its cutting edges.'

Cú Chulainn:
'If we might meet across the ford,
me and Fer Diad, with the usual weapons,
there would not be a parting conflict,
there would be angry sword-play.'

Fergus:
'O Cú Chulainn of the red sword,
I would, rather than seek reward,
that triumphant, proud Fer Diad
would take off eastwards.'

Fergus:
'I assembled a host in the east,
the price for my insults by the Ulaid,
they came from the province with me
champions and battle warriors.'

Cú Chulainn:
'I pledge my word to fight.
It is not an idle boast.
It is I who will triumph over
mac Damáin, son of Dáire.'

Cú Chulainn:
'If Conchobar were not with the weakness,
he would be defending hard those with the *cess*;
Medb would not have come from Mag in Scáil,
exhorting an expedition against me.'

Fergus:
'There are the deeds and the greater fighting hands
of Fer Diad mac Damáin against you.

Hard and ferocious weapons from your kinsman
will be turned against you, O Cú Chulainn.'
O Cú Chulainn.

Fergus came to the fort and the camp. Fer Diad went towards his tent
and his retinue, and he enquired of them whether Medb had gone
back on her word about his rights to the company of the six champions in the contest and fight on the morrow; or the pledges about the
contest that he alone might have to fight on the following day against
Cú Chulainn. So he went to them in case Medb had tricked him. He
told them that he would send the same six warriors to ensure that the
pledges made were fulfilled before Cú Chulainn came. Fer Diad was
neither glad nor calm nor sober with those occupying the tent that
night, but was gloomy, sad and despondent; for they knew the place
where the heroes would meet, and that each of them could make a
gap of a hundred if they came to battle, or both of them could, if they
came together. For both of them had the strength of an ox. For each
of them was his own lord. So that nothing was easy about the challenge and fight with Cú Chulainn on the Táin Bó Cuailnge.

At first Fer Diad slept heavily that night, and at the end of the
night the sleep went from him, and so did his drunkenness, and he
was concerned about the challenge and the fight that was upon him,
and he took his charioteer away to get the horses and to yoke them
to the chariot. But the charioteer kept trying to prevent him from
doing it. 'It would be better to stay rather than go there,' said the
servant. 'Be quiet, gillie,' said Fer Diad. And it is thus that he was
speaking and saying these words:

'Let us go to this meeting,
to the contest with this man,
so that we may reach the ford,
the ford upon which Badb is railing.
Let us meet Cú Chulainn,
to wound him through his powerful body
attacking it through the point of a spear,
until he is dead.'

Gillie:
'Indeed, it would be better to stay,

for it will be no smooth exchange of compliments:
if anyone has an illness
their parting will be swift.
Come to meet your Ulster foster-brother,
from whom harm will come.
Long will it be remembered:
woe to you, should you go.'

Fer Diad:
'Who thinks that I can resist this?
Discomfiture is no occupation for a champion.
As protection is not my right,
I will not resist any longer.
Be quiet about protection, O charioteer,
let us be courageous for a while about the challenge.
Strength is better than fear.
Let us go to the meeting.'

Let us go.

He took Fer Diad's horse and yoked it to the chariot before the ford where the single combat was to be; and a day did not come that was fully bright at that time. 'Good O charioteer,' said Fer Diad, 'spread the skin coverings and the cushions throughout my chariot, for I need a deep sleep, since I did not sleep at the end of the night, overcome by the problem of the fight ahead.' The gillie separated the horses and unyoked the chariot, and the pleasure of a deep fit of sleep came upon him.

Now as regards Cú Chulainn here, he did not arise until the day had brightened up, lest the men of Ireland would say that it was for fear and terror of his opponent that he had arisen early. And when the day broke, the charioteer gathered the horses and yoked them to the chariot. 'Well done, lad,' said Cú Chulainn. 'Take the horses to the fort and prepare the chariot, for the warrior we are going to meet rises early, namely Fer Diad mac Damáin son of Dáire.' 'The horses have been taken and the chariot is ready, proceed, and see that he does not disgrace you in feats of arms,' said the charioteer.

Then the striking, accomplished, battle-hardened and red-sworded Cú Chulainn mac Sualtam set off in his chariot. He was surrounded by the screams of goat-like demons, of supernatural battle bitches, of malevolent sprites of the glen and of demons of the air, and it was the Túatha Dé Danann who were causing these cries about him, and on his behalf, as it was they who were responsible for each terror, each fear and each dreaded feat in each battle and in each embattled land, and for each contest and battle that was about to happen. It was not long before the charioteer of Fer Diad heard the noise and the thunderous sound and the stamping noise coming from the clash of the shields and the meeting of the spears and the mighty blows of the swords and the clash of the helmets, and the noises made by the breastplates and the friction of the weapons, and the furious sound of the chariot feats and the loud noise of their wheels, the noise of the chariots and the clatter of the horses' hooves, and the mighty fleet of heroes and battle warriors as they approached the ford. The servant came and placed his hand upon his master. 'Well, Fer Diad,' said the gillie, 'the hosting is coming towards you, towards the ford.' And the servant said these words:

> 'I hear the sound of a chariot
> yoked with beautiful silver.
> Increasingly horrendous is the man
> behind the hard chariot wheels.
> Across Brega, across Braine,
> welcome on the way
> from the fort of yonder Baile in Bile,
> one who is triumphant with victories.
>
> It is the hound racing forth,
> it is the clean war chariot that he rides,
> it is the noble hawk of slaughter
> seizing the horses by himself.
> It is the blood-stained hero,
> it is the dark red demon.
> Is it known that he will not attack
> the ramparts or the fort?
>
> Woe to the assembly on the hill
> who face the well-proportioned hound.
> He will cut down the mercenaries,
> the hound with a headband.

It is the Hound of Emain Macha,
the hound who is shapely in each colour,
the perfect hound, the battle hound.
I hear the sound.'

                                 Let us hear.

'Well, O charioteer,' said Fer Diad, 'why did you praise that man who came from the house? You were almost giving him too much praise, and Ailella and Medb will fulfil their pledges to me when this man comes and fights with me. For because of the reward the injury to him will be swift. And assistance is timely.' And with these words he answered his gillie:

'Help is timely.
Be quietly protective rather than extolling,
deeds are not carried out asleep,
since Doomsday is not far off.
If I see the hero from Cooley,
then from motives of ambition,
and because of the reward,
I will despatch him fast.'

Gillie:
'If I see the hero from Cooley,
I know that, for reasons of ambition,
he will not run away from us
but rather will come towards us,
he runs and is not slow;
although he is wise, he is not grudging,
more like water hurtling down a precipitous cliff
than sudden thunder.'

Fer Diad:
'It is almost an excuse
for giving him more praise,
so why did you elevate that man
coming from the house?
Just now they are proclaiming
that he is about to rise up.

He will not depart from the attack,
except like a decaying churl.'

It was not long before Fer Diad's charioteer saw a five-pointed, four-wheeled chariot moving swiftly and astutely, with a green awning and with a dry, open-mouthed box, and the hero's horses, beautiful and strong, with long ears, smooth-bellied, broad-breasted, lively-hearted, high-groined, broad-hoofed, with slender flanks, very strong and violent in attack. The grey horse [Liath Macha], wide in the haunch, leaping like a lynx, with a flowing mane, was one of the horses yoked to that chariot. The black horse [Dub of Sainglenn], with plaited hair, well-running, broad-backed, was the other horse yoked to the chariot. Thus it was like the feathers of a hawk, nest-building against a hard wind, rather than the gust of a spring wind in March, their manes flowing across the meadow, or like a wild stag when first moved from his resting place, the two horses of Cú Chulainn about the chariot. Swiftly are they driven to the killing stone, swiftly the shaking troop are taken to the place.

And then Cú Chulainn reached the ford. Fer Diad remained over at the southern side of the ford. Cú Chulainn settled over at the northern side. Fer Diad welcomed Cú Chulainn: 'Welcome is your coming, O Cú Chulainn,' said Fer Diad. 'Fitting to me is the welcome up to this time,' said Cú Chulainn, 'but beyond today it is not fitting. And Fer Diad,' said Cú Chulainn, 'is it not fitting for you to come here to me, as it is you who have sent into flight my women, my sons and my children, my horse and my horses, my flocks, my herd and my property?' 'Well, Cú Chulainn,' said Fer Diad, 'what have you brought to this contest and fight? For when we were at Scáthach's and Uathach's and with Aífe, you were my alert attendant at arms, preparing my spears and making my bed.' 'Well, that is true indeed,' said Cú Chulainn. 'In my youthfulness at night I was carrying out your wishes, and that is not at all how you would describe it today, for there is no champion that is not a match for you today.'

And then each of them in a vivid way revoked his friendship with the other. And Fer Diad chanted these words and Cú Chulainn responded.

'What has brought you here O Hound,
to fight with a new champion?

There will be hard red gore
above the breath of your horse.
Pity your journey:
you will reach the rampart as arranged,
sparkling before the tryst
as though it was before your house.'
Cú Chulainn:
'I have gone before young warriors,
like a furious boar among flocks,
through a hundred battles,
rebuking them on the wet slopes;
testing your anger in combat
at this first place
will show you that it is an armed attack
that you will be defending against
until the finish.'

Fer Diad:
'I am not ashamed to be here with you.
It is I who have been mocked,
since I have come all the way
into the presence of the Ulaid,
into the company, O champion,
and it is I who will bring a loss to them.'

Cú Chulainn:
'Who determines where we shall meet?
Shall we groan over corpses?
Whom shall we follow before we reach
the ford of combat?
With our hard swords
Rather than our red spear points,
smiting before the host
when the time comes.'

Fer Diad:
'Before sunset, before night,
before the new day breaks forth,
the challenge will be taken to you

facing the mountain range;
the fight will not be bloodless.
The Ulaid are screaming at you,
as they are left unguarded.
It is wrong that they are being subjected
to the spectres coming to them.'
Cú Chulainn:
'If I catch you at an unguarded moment,
then the end of your life will have come.
The reason will not be from gentleness,
but from practising on a hard sword edge.
Great will be the deeds
each time this pair will meet,
as from today until eternity
you will be bereft of your leaders.'

Fer Diad:
'Be mindful of a warning,
you who are most boastful upon the Earth,
a contest where no quarter is given,
where there are no protectors.
It is known to me
that home is where the affection of the bird lies.
You are a gilly who excites
without valour, without vigour.'

Cú Chulainn:
'We were with Scáthach,
where we learnt the craft of arms,
where together we rode about
and traversed through each camp.
You, my heart's companion,
you, my kith and kin,
I had not realised before, beloved,
how sorrowful your loss would be.'

Fer Diad:
'Let you leave honour aside
so that we may be battling.

Before the cock crows
your head will be on a stake.
O Cú Chulainn from Cooley,
frenzy and affliction have taken hold of you,
since each tide of woe
stretches before you.'

'Well, O Fer Diad,' said Cú Chulainn, 'it is not proper that you should come to challenge and fight with me, through the incitement of Ailella and Medb, for those who came neither took triumph nor advantage from it. And these tidings reached me, and I will bring neither victory nor glory to you, for you will fall by me.' It is thus he was speaking and saying these words, and Fer Diad listened to him:

'Do not come to me O mature warrior,
O Fer Diad mac Damáin.
It is I who will overthrow you
while you are mocked by the host.

Do not come to me unprepared,
for it is by me your grave is to be.
Take my word for it
my fighting will be worthy of a warrior.

Regardless of many feats,
the purple horn-skinned one will fall.
The maiden who silently hears this boasting
will not be with you, son of Damáin.

Findabair, daughter of Medb,
of excellent form,
the daughter of beautiful shape,
you will not co-habit with her.

Findabair, daughter of the king,
truly it is said,
the one whom she deceived to the host
and ruined is one such as thee.

Do not break an oath in ignorance,
do not break loyalty nor friendship.
Do not break a pledge nor renege on a boast,
do not come to me, O seasoned warrior.

Fifty warriors were promised her.
It was a foolish gathering.
By me they went to their graves,
borne on a spear shaft.

Although Fer Báeth was judged high-spirited,
he was a brave hero at home.
In a short time his fire was extinguished,
for he was killed from one shot.

Srubdaire, bitter the erosion of his valour,
for whom a hundred women had secret longing.
Great his fame for a while;
neither gold nor prayer protected him.

If the woman were to be betrothed to me,
if the fair one of the province were to smile at me,
would not the bosoms blush
from south to north and from west to east?'

'So, Fer Diad,' said Cú Chulainn, 'it is not right that you should come to challenge me. For we were under Scáthach and Uathach and Aífe, and together we set out on each battle and each battlefield, for each challenge and each fight, and through each wood and wilderness, through each secret and remote place.' And it is thus he was speaking and he said these words:

'We were heart companions,
we were companions of the forest,
we were friends who shared the same bed,
where we slept the heavy sleep.
Sharing severe conflict
on the borders of the enemy
we rode about together.

We set out through each wood
while under the instruction of Scáthach.'

'O Cú Chulainn, of noble feats,' said Fer Diad:

'We practised the same arts,
listened to stories of our friendship,
shook when first wounded,
remembered our fosterage.
O Cúa, it is of no avail to you,
O Cúa, there is no help for you.'

'For long we are thus,' said Fer Diad, 'and why am I going in battle array today to Cú Chulainn?' 'You will have your choice of weapons throughout the day today,' said Cú Chulainn, 'since you reached the ford first.' 'Do you remember,' said Fer Diad, 'the choice of weapons we made when we were with Scáthach and Uathach and Aífe?' 'I do indeed,' said Cú Chulainn, ' but now let us proceed.'

They went for their choice of weapons then. They seized their emblematic shields of feats for their eight edge feats, and their eight small light javelins, and their eight ivory-hilted swords, and their eight spears of combat. They rode out towards each other, on a fine pleasant day, and they did not cast a weapon that did not strike. They started throwing these weapons at one another from dawn to midday, so that they blunted the edges and bosses of their shields with mighty feats. There was an excellence in the casting of weapons and an excellence in defence, so that they were neither bloodstained nor bloodied before they finished fighting. 'Let us finish fighting now, O Cú Chulainn,' said Fer Diad, 'since the fight so far is indecisive.' 'Indeed, for it is time to finish,' said Cú Chulainn. Then they ceased, and placed their weapons into the hands of their charioteers.

'What weapons shall we choose henceforth, O Cú Chulainn?' said Fer Diad. 'Let you choose the weapons from now on, as you were the first to arrive at the ford,' said Cú Chulainn. 'Let us go bearing the smooth hard spears of polished handiwork, with their thongs of tight flax at their ends. 'Let us go indeed,' said Cú Chulainn. Then they took their hard shields of great strength upon them. They went with their smooth hard spears of polished handiwork, with their thongs of tight flax at their ends. They cast their spears at one another from midday until the evening sunset. There was a great skill in defence and in the mutual casting of weapons, so that each of them was bloodied and bloodstained and cut open before they ceased fighting. 'Cease now, O Cú Chulainn,' said Fer Diad. 'Indeed we will if the time has come,' said Cú Chulainn. Their weapons were given to their charioteers.

Later on they came seeking each other and placed their arms around each other's neck, and gave each other three kisses. The horses were unyoked and the charioteers gathered around the hearth that night. And beds of fresh rushes were made by the charioteers and pillows of grass placed against each wounded man. The physicians came with their cures and remedies, and placed healing herbs and healing omens on their sores and cuts, and on their limbs and on their mighty wounds. Each herb, healing plant and omen was placed on the sores and wounded joints and on the many cuts of Cú Chulainn, and conveyed westwards across the ford and shared with Fer Diad; the men of Ireland said that Fer Diad himself might have fallen as he had given himself an excess of medicaments. Every kind of food and pleasantly intoxicating drink was brought from the men of Ireland to Fer Diad, and was conveyed northwards across the ford for sharing with Cú Chulainn, since Fer Diad had more hereditary suppliers of refreshments than Cú Chulainn. By supplying Fer Diad in this way the hospitallers warded off Cú Chulainn. Moreover, the hospitallers from Brega supplied Cú Chulainn. They came to converse with him by the smoke at night.

They settled down for the night then. They arose the next morning and came to the ford of the combat. 'What weapons shall we choose today, O Fer Diad?' said Cú Chulainn. 'Let you choose the weapons for today,' said Fer Diad, 'since I chose them yesterday.' 'Let us go now,' said Cú Chulainn, 'and choose the great spear with the broad blade today, since we can hurl ourselves into the fight at closer range today than yesterday, when we were only casting about. Seize the horses and yoke them to the chariot, so that we may wage battle with the horses and the chariots today.' 'Indeed, let us go,' said Fer Diad. Then they seized the two broad shields and went for their great broad-bladed spears. Then they seized their weapons, and pierced and wounded by striking and smashing at each other from early morning sunrise to evening sunset. It was customary for birds in flight to feed on the bodies of mortals: thus they would go by the bodies, taking portions of blood and flesh from the sores and wounds while flying through the mist and the air. When evening came their horses were tired and their charioteers were wearied, and so were the champions and heroes themselves. 'Let us quit at that now, O Fer Diad,' said Cú Chulainn, 'since the horses are weary and the charioteers are jaded, and everyone is exhausted; moreover, what person would not be exhausted?' And it is thus that he was speaking and he said these words:

> 'There is no obligation on us
> to be swaying in chariots,
> or to be struggling like giants on this undertaking,
> we are bound to be weary
> from this battle clamour.'

'Indeed, let us desist, if the time has come,' said Fer Diad. They quit then and placed their weapons into the hands of their charioteers, and approached each other. They embraced each other and gave one another three kisses. Their horses went to the meadow and their charioteers to the fire. Their charioteers made beds of fresh rushes for them and placed pillows of grass against the wounded. The physicians came, and guarded over, observed and took care of them during the night, since they were unable to rise on account of their sores and inflictions, their cuts and their many wounds. Spells, incantations and charms were uttered over them, in order to prevent the blood from flowing and clotting. Each spell and charm and incantation was placed over the wounds and sores of Cú Chulainn, and delivered to the west side of the ford and shared with Fer Diad. Each food and beneficial and intoxicating drink was brought from the men of Ireland to Fer Diad, and was sent northwards across the ford for sharing with Cú Chulainn, for more public hospitallers supplied Fer Diad than Cú Chulainn, since all the hospitallers of the men of Ireland supplied Fer Diad: they were averting trouble from Cú Chulainn. The hospitallers of Brega supplied Cú Chulainn. They came to converse with him at night. They settled down for the night then. They arose early the next morning and came to the ford of the contest. 'Cú Chulainn looks destructive and warrior-like today,' said Fer Diad. 'It is evil you look today,' said Cú Chulainn. 'Your hair has grown darker and your eye has become restless, and your appearance and form have changed.' 'There is neither fear nor anxiety on me today,' said Fer Diad, 'since there is not a warrior in Ireland today that I am not equal to.' And Cú Chulainn was lamenting and complaining, and he said these words in answer to Fer Diad:

'O Fer Diad, if it is you
it is doomed you are,
to come at a woman's bidding
to fight with your foster-brother.'

Fer Diad:
'O Cú Chulainn, perfectly wise,
O true champion, true hero,
it is destined for one to come
to the sod where one's grave is to be.'

Cú Chulainn:
'Findabair, daughter of Medb,
of lovely shape,
was given to you not to love,
but as a test of your royal strength.'

Fer Diad:
'Proving my strength for a long while,
O Cú, by fair play.
Of one more courageous I have not heard,
nor till today have I found.'

Cú Chulainn:
'It is you who caused us to be here,
O son of Damáin mac Dáre,
coming at a woman's bidding
to cross swords with your foster-brother.'

Fer Diad:
'If you and I were to leave this fight,
foster-brothers though we are, Fair Hound,
where would my word and honour be
with Ailella and Medb of Cruachain?'

Cú Chulainn:
'Food has not passed his lips,
nor has he been conceived,
the offspring of blameless king or queen
for whom I would have done harm.'

Fer Diad:
'O Cú Chulainn of piercing fury,
it is not you but Medb who has betrayed us.
Fame and triumph will be yours;
not on you is there any fault.'

Cú Chulainn:
'A clot of blood is my fair heart,
I am close to separation from my soul;
It is not an equal contest for me to fight with you,
O Fer Diad of numerous deeds.'

'If you are to suffer more on my account,' said Fer Diad, 'then what weapons shall we choose for the feat of arms today?' 'Let you choose the weapons for today,' said Cú Chulainn, 'since I chose them on the day that has gone by.' 'Let us go today and trade strong blows with our heavy swords, for the fight will consist of cutting and hacking today, rather than the mutual casting [of spears] of yesterday,' said Fer Diad. 'Indeed, let us go then,' said Cú Chulainn. Then they seized their great broad shields. And they went for their heavy swords for dealing heavy blows.

Then they began striking and cutting and hewing down and smiting each other, and they were equal in the way they came at each other, cutting one another on the shoulders and thighs with the flat tops of their blades. They were striking one another in this way from dawn to late evening. 'Let us quit at that, O Cú Chulainn,' said Fer Diad. 'Indeed it is necessary for us to quit now,' said Cú Chulainn. So they quit. They placed their weapons in the arms of their charioteers. The fighting was merry, easy, grievous and well-spirited.

Their separation was unfortunate, very sad and full of grief that night. That night their horses were not in the same meadow and their charioteers were not around the same fire.

They separated that night then. Fer Diad arose early the following morning and came alone to the ford of the battle, for he knew that there would be an outcome of the battle and that only one of them would come from it, or that neither of them would come from it. Then he put on his battle dress for the challenge and combat, before Cú Chulainn arrived seeking him. The following was what his battle dress consisted of: an apron or girdle of fine-textured satin with a hem of speckled gold against his fair white skin; a girdle of well-sewn brown leather he put on over it; and a great girdle with precious stones the size of millstones was put on over that. He put on an apron of strong deep molten iron with precious stones the size of millstones, in fear and apprehension of the *gae bulga*.

He put on his crested helmet for battle: there were forty studded gems adorning it, inlaid with red enamel and crystal and carbuncle stones and alive with a loop of bright stones in front of it. He took his fierce, angry, smiting spear in his right hand. He took his curved war sword with its hilt of gold and ending in a knob of red gold. On the curve of his back he took his great shield: there were fifty bosses on the shield with a boar displayed on each boss; there was a great boss besides of red gold at the centre of the shield. Fer Diad performed many brilliant and wonderfully varied feats that day, which he had not learned as a student from any other place, not from his foster-mother or foster-father, or from Scáthach or from Uathach or from Aífe, but was performing them that day as he faced Cú Chulainn.

Later Cú Chulainn reached the ford and he saw the many wonderful and varied feats being performed by Fer Diad. 'I see, master Laeg,' said Cú Chulainn, ' Fer Diad on high, performing many illustrious feats, and soon I will take on those feats by myself. Therefore it is necessary, if things go against me today, that I am being incited and reviled by sayings and boastings about my integrity and anger. For if things go well, the sayings may be of praise and exhortation and of excellence, and I will take heed of these boasts.' 'Indeed, it will be necessary to do that, O Cúcan,' said Laeg.

Then Cú Chulainn put on his battle-dress for the duel, and performed many scintillating feats that day, many of which as a student he had never learned from either Scáthach or Uathach or Aífe.

Fer Diad saw these feats and he knew that he would have to come to grips with them in time. 'What weapons shall we use, O Fer

Diad?' said Cú Chulainn. 'Let you choose the weapons for today,' said Fer Diad. 'Now let us go to the games at the ford,' said Cú Chulainn. 'Indeed, let us go,' said Fer Diad. Fer Diad was saying and telling himself that it would be more difficult for him if he should go, since he knew that Cú Chulainn would overcome him and every warrior and hero whom he encountered at the battle ford.

Great indeed was the feat that would be performed at the ford that day, by the warriors, by the two heroes who arose in the west of Europe, two bright torches of the valorous Gael, whose two arms serve as guarantor and conqueror and reward in the northwestern part of the world; two torches of the Gael and two key defenders, here to fight against one another as long as they should live, as a consequence of the dissension and incitement sown by Ailella and Medb. They began to cast at one another using their feats from dawn until midday. When midday came, the warriors grew fierce and fiercely they attacked one another.

Then Cú Chulainn proceeded to the edge of the ford, to where the bossed shield of Fer Diad mac Damáin was, and pursued him, hitting him over the rim of his shield at his head. It is then that Fer Diad struck the shield with his left elbow, so that Cú Chulainn was thrown from there like a bird, over the edge of the ford. Cú Chulainn proceeded towards the border of the ford again, to the embossed shield of Fer Diad mac Damáin. He went for his head, hitting the rim of the shield from above. Fer Diad struck his left knee against the shield, so that Cú Chulainn fell like a little boy over the edge of the ford. Laeg noticed this. 'Well, well,' said Laeg, 'the warrior put you down as a mother would her son, as foam is poured out of a pool of water, as a mill grinds fine malt. He has cut you as an axe cuts the bole of an oak. He has bound you as the woodbine binds the tree, he has attacked in the way a hawk attacks a small bird, yet there is none to equal you, either in war-like fury or in craft of arms, from now until Doomsday, you little demon,' said Laeg.

Then Cú Chulainn arose as quickly as the wind, with the swiftness of a swallow, with the fury of a dragon, and with three powerful leaps was upon the battle shield of Fer Diad mac Damáin, pursuing him and hitting his head over the rim of the shield. The warrior shook his shield, so that Cú Chulainn was thrown from it and landed in the centre of the ford. Then Cú Chulainn arose with the speed of the wind, with the swiftness of a swallow and with the fury of a dragon, like a cloud in the air, and in a third of the time he was upon the battle shield of Fer Diad mac Damáin, bringing up his head over the rim of the shield in order to strike. Then the battle warrior shook his shield, so that Cú Chulainn was thrown from it into the centre of the ford, as though he had jumped into it. Then Cú Chulainn performed his first contortion, which consisted of a swelling up like a bag being breathed into, so that his body made a terrible arch of many wonderful colours, so that he was the size of one of the Fomorians, the great courageous warriors from the sea, over the head of Fer Diad.

They became immersed in a close encounter, so that they struck at the upper part of their heads and at the lower part of their legs and at the middle of their arms, over the rim and the boss of their shields. It was this close combat that led to the cutting and splitting of the shields from the rim to the boss. They engaged in close combat, so that their spears were twisted and bent from tip to rivet. It was while they were in close combat that the goat spirits and the wonderful white preternatural demons of the air started screeching on the rims of their shields and on the hilts of their swords and on the shafts of their spears. And it was while they were in close combat that they swept away the river out of its bed and out of its course, so that a king or queen could have reclined in the centre of the ford, for not a drop of water was to be had, unless it were poured forth from the trampling and the subduing that was being carried out by the two heroes and the two warriors over at the centre of the ford. It was during this close combat that the horses of the Gael broke away in terror and fright and fury, so that they broke their long spancels and fetters, their bridles and halters, and the women and the boys and the children, and the cowards and the madmen among the men of Ireland, broke out by the southwest camp. They performed the edge feat on the swords then before everyone.

Then, at an unguarded moment, Fer Diad reached for his ivory-hilted sword and struck Cú Chulainn on his chest, so that blood seeped into his leather girdle, and the ford was reddened with the gore from the body of the battle hero. Cú Chulainn did not have much time before Fer Diad struck him with strong blows and quick strokes against the legs, and with beatings against the middle of his body. He entreated Laeg mac Riangabra to send the *gae bulga* downstream; and he caught it in the space between his toes. It was customary for him to take the *gae bulga* with him when approaching a man, and to have thirty loose heads as well, and once it pierced the body of a man it could not be extracted from it. And Fer Diad heard the *gae bulga* being discussed, so that he made a protective sweep with his shield down to his hindquarters in order to protect his body. Then Cú Chulainn released the hard-spiked javelin from the palm of his hand across the rim of the shield and over the breast-piece of the horned skin, so that on the further side it caused pain to the heart in his chest. Then Fer Diad took the blow with his protecting shield and placed it over his body in order to help him from the onslaught. Then the gilly prepared the *gae bulga* and Cú Chulainn placed it in the space between his feet, and it shot a distance from under Fer Diad and it went well through the stout leather apron, breaking through the iron, so that it broke the precious stones, each the size of a millstone, and went into his body through his anus, and each joint and each limb was smashed by the barbs. 'That's enough for me now,' said Fer Diad to his friend, 'for all is changed by that strong man I see to my right, and it was not right that I should fall by your hand.' And while he was speaking he said these words:

'O hound of great feats,
it was not fitting that you should wound me,
your hand is not at fault
for spilling my blood.

Indeed one is dismembered
when one reaches the gap of betrayal.
It grieves my voice, alas
that I should end in ruin.

My mangled ribs burst out,
as does the gore from my heart.
It is not a twisted boast
to have fallen by you,
O hound.'

After this Cú Chulainn approached Fer Diad and put his two arms around him, and took his weapons, his clothing and battle dress northwards across the ford, so that he was at the northern side of the ford in triumph, and not at the back by the men of Ireland. Then Cú Chulainn lowered Fer Diad onto the ground and fell into a faint. Laeg saw this happening, and then all the men of Ireland arose and approached him. 'Well, O Cúcan,' said Laeg, 'rise up now, show the men of Ireland who are approaching that there is none who is a match for you, by whom fell Fer Diad mac Damáin, son of Dáire.' 'Why get up when one such as this fell by me?' And it was thus that he was talking to his charioteer and saying these words, and Laeg answered Cú Chulainn:

> Laeg:
> 'Rise up, O hound of battle
> for your courage has been justified,
> you the ruin of Fer Diad of the hosts;
> the god of doom is hard on those who do combat.'

> Cú Chulainn:
> 'What is courage to me?
> Hemmed in as I am by death and sorrow
> for what I have done,
> and the body I have rent.'

> Laeg:
> 'You should not be lamenting,
> but rather exulting,
> for he has left the red spear in you,
> and you lamenting, wounded and spilling blood.'

> Cú Chulainn:
> 'If he had struck my leg
> or severed my arm [what then]?
> Alas for Fer Diad the horseman,
> mangled now and forever.'

> Laeg:
> 'Better for the daughters of the Red Branch
> what has been done,
> he to perish, you to survive:
> your lasting separation would be a great loss to them.'

Cú Chulainn:
'From the day that I came from Cooley
after radiant Medb,
my fame is known to man
through death and destruction.'

Laeg:
'You did not sleep peacefully
after the great raid.
Few and slow was the company
that rose with you in the early morning.'

Rise up O hound.

Cú Chulainn began lamenting and bewailing Fer Diad then, and he said these words: 'Well, Fer Diad, it is a pity that you were not informed by someone who knew of my feats in battle and valour before coming to this duel of skill. It is a pity that Laeg mac Riangabra did not put you to shame from the fact of our being foster-brothers. It is a pity that you did not accept the genuine advice of Fergus. It is a pity that you did not avail of the advice of beloved Conall, the triumphant and exultant battle lord, about your foster brother. For these men know that no one will be born among the Connachta whose feats will equal mine, from now until Doomsday. These men also know of the wheelings and dealings, of the broken pledges of the fair-headed woman from Connacht. These men know of my skills with the shield between the rim and the boss, with the spear and the sword, with all types of board games, with the horse and the chariot. No more will a warrior's hand hack the cloud-coloured flesh of the champion Fer Diad; no more will the gap of red-mouthed Badb bellow to the sound of speckled-shadowed shields. No one in Cruachain will be my equal from now until the end of time, O son of Damáin of red appearance,' said Cú Chulainn. Then Cú Chulainn rose and bent over Fer Diad. 'O Fer Diad,' said Cú Chulainn, 'it is great the destruction and the abandonment that has taken hold of the men of Ireland, having taken part in a contest of battle strength with me. For it is not an even contest against me on this cattle raid of Cooley.'

It is thus that he was speaking and he said these words:

'O Fer Diad, destruction has blotted your fame.
Sad our last meeting,
you to die, I to survive;
sad indeed our separation.'

If we were over yonder as before,
with Scáthach the pre-eminent nurse of warriors,
we would be boasting our spoils,
not destroying our friendship.

Dear to me your noble blushes,
dear to me your beautiful shape in battle,
dear to me your bright blue-green eye,
beloved your bearing and your speech.

He has not sought shelter, but skin-splitting combat,
he does not place anger before virility,
he does not sling his shield on his broad back,
one who has practised with you, O red son of Damáin.

It has not happened,
since the only son of Aífe fell by me,
that I have found here, O Fer Diad,
a warrior to equal your battle fury.

Findabair, daughter of Medb,
excellent her shape,
what was shown to you
was a mere illusion, O Fer Diad.'
O Fer Diad.

Cú Chulainn began looking at Fer Diad then. 'Well, my friend Laeg,' said he, 'take off Fer Diad's weapons and his clothing now, so that I can see the brooch that was made for this contest and battle duel.' Laeg came and took the arms and clothes from Fer Diad, and showed him the brooch, and he began lamenting and bewailing, and he said these words:

'Pity the golden brooch,
O Fer Diad of the warrior bands,
of lasting blows,
victorious was your arm.

Your thick curly yellow hair
a beautiful treasure,
your girdle of leafy ornament
around you, until your death.

Beloved foster-brother
with a clear straight eye,
your shield of edged gold,
worthy player of the treasured board game.

To fall by my hand,
I realise it was not right,
it was not a fair match;
pity the golden brooch.
Pity.

'Well, master Laeg,' said Cú Chulainn, 'go to defeated Fer Diad himself and cut the *gae bulga* from him, since I am useless without it.' Laeg went to the mangled body of Fer Diad and cut the *gae bulga* from him, and when Cú Chulainn saw the bloody weapon before Fer Diad's side he said these words:

'O Fer Diad, alas for our tryst,
behold you from ruddy to bloodless.
I without weapons washed,
you on a layer of gore.

If we were east [in Scotland],
with Scáthach and Uathach,
there would be neither whitened lips
between us, nor weapons of conflict.

Scáthach spoke sharply
with a strong message of warning:

to rise up in close order for combat
against Germán Garbglas.

I said before Fer Diad
and Lugaid of noble bearing,
and before fair mac Baetain,
to come to the camp against Germán.
We came to the battle rock
from the lake shore of Loch Lindformait.
I dispensed with four hundred
from the Isles of Misery.

I was with Fer Diad in combat
at the door of the fort of Germán.
Rind mac Níuil was killed by me,
Ruad mac Forníuil by him.

Fer Báeth killed
Bláth mac Colba of the red sword by the shore;
Lugaid, a swift and surly man,
killed Mugairne from the Tyrrhenian Sea.

Four times fifty were killed going yonder
by vigorous manly exploits.
Fer Diad killed the gloomy band
of Dam Dreman and Dam Dilenn.

We ravaged the camp of shrewd Germán
above the expansive and broad-speckled pool,
alive I brought Germán with us,
to Scáthach of the broad shield.

Our renowned instructress
bound us to a blood pact of unity,
so that anger would not come between us
on fair Elga.

Alas for the morning battle
that left the son of Damáin weak,

woe for a special friend
when a drink of red blood is poured for him.

If I had seen you die
among the warlike Greeks,
I would not have lived after you,
we would have died together.
Alas that it has come to this
for the foster-sons of Scáthach,
I covered in rough bloody wounds,
you without a chariot.

Alas that it has come to this
for the foster-sons of Scáthach,
I covered in bloody wounds,
you quite dead.

Alas that it has come to this
for the foster-sons of Scáthach,
you dead, I alive, defiant.
Battle fury brings out the warrior spirit.
O Fer Diad.'

'Well, O Cúcan,' said Laeg, 'let us leave the ford now, for we are here too long.' 'We will leave in our own good time, O master Laeg,' said Cú Chulainn, 'for each contest and each combat that I have taken part in is as a game or a prank compared to the fight with Fer Diad.' Thus as he was speaking he began to say these words:

'Play and delight was all,
until Fer Diad reached the ford.
Yonder wandering and learning
of strength and honesty,
yonder our good foster-mother
offering wholesomeness to each.

Play and delight was all
until Fer Diad reached the ford.
Yonder we had special training

in the customary weaponry,
where Scáthach brought two shields
to me and to Fer Diad.

Play and delight was all
until Fer Diad reached the ford.
Beloved the golden pillar
that I laid low by the ford:
he was courageous above all,
he was the strength of his people.

Play and delight was all
until Fer Diad reached the ford.
Lion-like, fierce and mighty,
reckless and doomed like a swollen wave.

Play and delight was all
until Fer Diad reached the ford.
I thought that beloved Fer Diad
would after me have immortal life.
Yesterday he was as big as a mountain
today a mere shadow.
Through the countless plunderings
they fell by my hand,
the best of cattle, men and horses,
fiercely I slew them on every side.

It was a massive host
that came from hard Cruachain:
I killed at rough sport
more than a third and less than a half.

Never has such bloody battle occurred,
nor has Banba ever nurtured
out of land or sea
the son of a king of greater fame.

Play and delight.

The death of Fer Diad as far as this.

CHAPTER 8

The Death of Cú Chulainn

Oided Con Culainn

Now the Ulaid came to Emain Macha, many and in good spirits. Cú Chulainn came to Dún Delca after victorious triumph and boasting against the men of Ireland, at the battle of Finncora and at the battle of Ros na Ríg on the Boyne and at the perilous battle of Gáirech. Although great heroes and warriors, kings and chiefs of the men of Ireland fell by Cú Chulainn, his exploits against the hosts of the Táin Bó Cuailnge and their disgrace was greater, or his deeds against the Clan Calitín, and his twenty-seven sons who fell by him. There was no question of death or slaughter by the Ulaid, since they fell by him [Cú Chulainn]; for since Calitín left his wife and female companions, and she pregnant, after him, and when Calitín died his wife's pregnancy came to an end and she gave birth, she bore three sons and three daughters. Medb came towards them, and it was noticed that they were mute and simple, and blind in their left eyes. And they were well-educated by Medb until they were capable of acting as adults. And Medb said to them:

'Do you know who killed your father?' said she. 'We do,' they said, 'it was Cú Chulainn, son of Sualtam, who killed him, and we will require your help in killing him.' 'That is true,' said she, 'and now you are going throughout the world learning your skills,' said Medb, 'seeking druids and enlightenment, and learning magical arts.'

They travelled to Scotland and were there for a year, and then they went to the Saxons and were there for a year. Then they resorted to sorcery and devil-craft, and they went to Babylon; thus they sought druids of the world exercising their craft. And they reached the densely populated borders of the Underworld and they spent a year there. And Bolcán the smith made arms for them, namely three swords, three knifes and three spears.

'There are your arms, O Clan Calitín,' said Bolcán, 'and you will go with them and kill three kings with the three hardy sharp-bladed spears, namely the warrior kings of Ireland, Cú Chulainn son of Sualtam, and the horse king of Ireland, the Liath Macha, and the servant of the king of Ireland, Laeg mac Riangabra, for in truth these are the most venomous spears and misfortune is carried on their tips.'

The Clan Calitín rose up from the Underworld and came towards the clouds of the blustery winds, so that they arrived at the green of Cruachain in Connacht, and Medb rose early on the morrow from her sunny chamber made of glass, and she saw the six partially blinded, very strong, wondrous and abominable ones out on the green. She put her five fold purple cloak around her and came out on the green, and recognised the Clan Calitín there, and the men were kind and welcoming to them, and they sat among them, and they were asked about their adventures and their wanderings from beginning to end.

'Did you learn well?' said Medb. 'We did,' they said, 'for we engaged in mighty and extensive battles with the aid of sprigs of sanicle, and were agitated by druidic fungus among the foliage of oak groves.'

Then Medb took them with her to the house at Cruachain and attended to them and prepared a feast for them there, and brought food and old companions to them, eventually they were confused and merry with drinking.

They were three days and three nights arranging the festivities at Cruachain. It is there that the huge and vast host was summoned to Ailella and Medb from the four great provinces of Ireland, to Cruachain. They sent learned men and messengers in search of Lugaid, son of Cúroi mac Dáire, and they brought him towards Cruachain, and Lugaid and Medb were conversing together. 'Do you know, O Lugaid, who murdered your father?' said Medb. 'I do,' said Lugaid, 'it was Cú Chulainn who killed him.'

'That is true,' said Medb, 'and now the Clan Calitín have come to us, having visited the world, and in pursuit of learning, with the intention that Cú Chulainn should fall before them. It is probable that there is not a freeman, or a high king or a tribal chief, or a landlord with a hundred cows on his homestead, nor a stranger nor a mercenary, nor a lord from one of the strong provinces of the four provinces of Ireland that was not against him, there was not a father nor a brother nor a friend nor a son-in-law nor a foster-brother that did not fall by Cú Chulainn at the great battle of the Táin Bó Cuailnge. One should be aware of damage done to the great host, so that you should seek to have your wrongs avenged on him.'

Lugaid pledged an expedition then to accomplish this and he came solemnly to the kings of Munster to muster an army. They sent learned men and messengers to the many warriors of Leinster, and Mac Niad mac Finn and Conchobar mac Rosa came, and the kings of Leinster, seeking a meeting with Medb.

'O son of Niad and Conchobar,' said Medb, 'have you heard that the Clan Calitín have come to Ireland?' 'We have not,' said Mac Niad. 'They came,' said Medb, 'fully skilled in sorcery, and do you know who killed their fathers?' said Medb. 'We know that it was Cú Chulainn who killed them.' Medb sent other men for Erc mac Cairbre and they sought him out. 'O Erc,' said Medb, 'do you know who killed your father, and the father of each champion and warrior of the Meath men?' 'Cú Chulainn killed my father,' said Erc, 'at the battle of Ros na Ríg.' 'That is true,' said Medb, 'and may the army with you avenge your scars and wounds on Cú Chulainn.' 'That this army will do,' said Erc. And following their conversation Medb bound him to his word in the company of the army. Subsequently, Conchobar and Mac Niad and Erc, son of Cairbre, left with one accord. And they visited the forts and homesteads of the four provinces of Ireland, and when the time came they left, and when they came they gathered and collected warriors for Cruachain, and they were three days and three nights there.

And the host rose up and across Mag Finn, a place where Finn mac Lonchraos fell by Cú Chulainn. And they came to the Black Country, a place where Dub mac Lonchraos fell by Cú Chulainn, and they came to Senáth and towards the place called Athlone. And weariness grew on the men of Ireland, and they camped there that night. And on the morrow they moved, and came to Glen Eóin and to Glen Mór and to Crinnloch and to the place called Loch Luatha then. And they camped the night there. And the next day they travelled until they reached green-sided Telltown, and they camped there, and they rounded the plain of Brega and the plain of Meath, and the territory of Tetha in Westmeath and Telltown, and the territory of Cnogba and of Cerma and Cooley. And Conchobar and the Ulaid heard about the regions destroyed by fire and those that were harassed by

143

the large armies of Medb and those of Munster, and by the warriors of Leinster and by the champions of Connacht. It is probable that Medb left Fergus and Cormac, the black exiles from Ulster, without a word about the expedition. For she was sure that Cú Chulainn would not come against the men of Ireland, due to the treachery of Fergus and the black exiles.

And the *Cess Noínden* or wasting sickness fell on the Ulaid at that time. 'Where is Lebarcham?' said Conchobar. 'I am here,' said Lebarcham. 'Go to Cú Chulainn and bring him to me. Make sure that the expedition is made with stealth, and leave Dún Delca and the plain of Mag Muirthemne, and come to Emain, and wait for me while I assemble my company in the presence of Geanann and Cathbad and Amergin and Ferceirtne, and the poets besides. For if I can go safely by concealing the chaos of the war that is raging with Medb and if I can control the enemy, then all the men of Ireland will fall by us and by Conall, and by the army that we will bring towards them. And fear will not be permitted and the fear of the champion Conall was placed on them, and no messengers came from the fifth province. No sooner were they at the borders of Brega and Meath than they slaughtered those from that province. And he escaped this time from the treachery of Medb and the evil druids, and the invasion of the Clan Calitín and the wickedness of Ailella mac Magach, and faced alone the mighty power of four provinces on one plain. Probably after the killing of Finn mac Rosa at the battle of Finnchora, this Finn was the king of Leinster, and it is he who killed Fraech mac Fidaig, a fierce and powerful, brave king of the smiths. Besides with him fell Derg, son of Cúroi mac Dáire, and a throng of Munster nobles about him, and was put with him alongside the dead bodies on the battlefield at Brega and Meath. After that they all fell; a story of death was each story. There was the death of Cúroi mac Dáire, a high king of the world and a strong king of the two provinces of Munster, and a defender of the land. Besides him were killed Ferceirtne and Fiamain Mór and Fiamain Mál, Li and Lugaid, Loch and Lochbuin, together with the great Munster slaughter. That account, as is proper, was given by Cathbad and his foster-brothers, with my blessings and the blessings of all the Ulaid: avoid it at your peril.'

Then Lebarcham came nimbly with a message from the high king of Ulster, and she came to where Cú Chulainn was, and on that day

Cú Chulainn was between Ochaine and the sea, watching a flock of birds, for on that day there were many birds flying overhead; they all went safely above him. It is there that Lebarcham came into the company of Cú Chulainn, and Cú Chulainn bade her welcome.

'It is sincere with us, that welcome,' said Lebarcham, and it is thus she was, and words dripping from her tongue and her eyes fluttering, and her lips beautifully shaped, and Cú Chulainn asks her about her news. It was then Lebarcham tells everything that was not told to him: 'The good people and the nobles, the women folk and the assembly of women, all the *ollaves* of Ulster beg and entreat you to help us escape the noise of the great army of the men of Ireland, and the invasion of Dún Delca and the plain of Muirthemne, without going so far as to engage in combat on your own.'

'Then he will go,' said Laeg mac Riangabra, 'because Emer is the daughter of Fergal Manach.' And Cú Chulainn left before them for Dún Delca and brought Emer towards the green there, and a council was held, and this is the meeting that brought Emer and Laeg and the good people of Ulster to it. The council decided to go to Conchobar and Cathbad and the Ulaid at Emain Macha, because it was there that the people of Ulster were with the *Cess Noínden* about Conchobar. And it was then that a decision was fixed with Cú Chulainn, lest he withdraw from it; for Mag Muirthemne and Dún Delca and the region of Cooley had never been evacuated before since he had first occupied it as a chief until this very moment. He lifted Emer into the chariot and evacuated the fort hastily with them, and escaped with the flocks and headed northwards to Sliab Cuilinn in Ulster. Then Cú Chulainn came to Emain Macha, and unyoked the horse and the chariot, and put the Liath Macha and the Dub Sainglend into the 'tethering field', and then Cú Chulainn went into the *grianán* [sun house].

Conchobar heard that Cú Chulainn had come to the fort, and the female retinue and the assembly of women also heard it, and there arose great mirth and merriment, delightful and pleasant, and a merry, gay clamour out of the well-lighted banqueting hall of Emain; and in the distance the destruction was heard. And Conchobar said before the poets and *ollaves* of all Emain, besides the women of the province, that Cú Chulainn would be well-advised to keep a constant vigilance at this time. 'Indeed, he will bear the burden of the warrior rather than refuse what is necessary regardless of the consequences, during day or night. Since it is the spear of promise that over the years was used by Medb and by the men of Ireland, and by the powerful Clan Calitín, that will doubtless kill him, so use your sense and skills to comprehend this. For if he falls on this journey, we all fall, and the good fortune and the defence of the province will collapse for ever after that.' 'That is true,' said Cathbad and all the others. 'And we shall go and seek him, and see if there is anything to gain by intervention,' said Genann. And the poets and women went into the sun house where Cú Chulainn and Emer were, and Emer gave him three kisses, and the poets and the women and the musicians and those from the arts and the crafts sat down around him, and there was merriment and entertainment and games and music and sport in his presence, to soothe him until he should follow his destiny.

As for the men of Ireland, they came to Áth Alad on Muirthemne and they set camp there, and they left the advance guard, with their broad enemy blades with them, on the slopes of the surrounding territories, and they ravaged and destroyed Mag Muirthemne and Dún Delca, and the meadow of Conall as far as Áth Alad on fair Mag Muirthemne, with great plundering. It is then that the Clan Calitín was brought to the men of Ireland. 'You promised, O Clan Calitín', said Medb, 'to bring Cú Chulainn to the men of Ireland by the end of three days and three nights.' 'If we promise it, we will fulfil it without doubt.'

It is then that the three maimed and partially blinded daughters of Calitín rose up, three begging scaldcrows there, three black, hateful, ill-coloured, devilish witches there, and they moved solemnly, barely visible, with a gust of wind and in good cheer, they will reach Emain without doubt, and the three aged, ugly spectres will sit on the green at Emain, and they will alight on the very green lawn, eating all about them, they will transform themselves into warrior troops as great as armies, the troops will be formed from the sprigs of the *sanais* plant, and from the fungus and foliage of the beautifully coloured oak wood. And Cú Chulainn heard the shouts of war [lacuna in text] and the standing stones being desecrated and the swift destruction in the camp.

As Cú Chulainn was on guard that day, Genann, son of Cathbad, saw him out on the green and he saw the soldiers mercilessly crushing each other. He was deeply upset and enraged and incensed with the frantic activity there, and he put his left hand under himself to stop him rising, and Genann put his two powerful hands on him to stop him rising and to sit him down. 'It is a pity,' said Cú Chulainn, 'that I would prefer to the gold of the world or the nobles of the land to die before this disgrace [lacuna in text] over yonder. For it brings to mind the old saying: 'fame outlasts life.' 'Forget that over there,' said Genann Gruadsolus, 'since it is nothing but a false host of fairies that is there, and the sound of the troublesome druids and the shape-changing Clan Calitín, there only to disturb and frustrate.' Cú Chulainn looked out again and saw the great standing stone out on the plain, and the second time he looked out he saw the horses of Manannán mac Lir on the green. And there was a taboo placed on one who saw that, and it seemed to him that he heard the harp of the son of Manannán playing soothingly and plaintively. And there was a taboo placed on those who heard that music, and to return there would surely violate his taboos and break his power, and thus he came to the region of his triumphs.

And it is there Badb, the daughter of Calitín, came and she came in the form of a scaldcrow over the sun house in which Cú Chulainn was, and she said magical words, which were directed to him there. The host shouted out on the green again when Badb came towards them, and Cú Chulainn heard the shouting around Badb and said: 'It is a pity for me to be listening to this noise here, O Genann Gruadsolus,' said Cú Chulainn, 'and should I allow the troop to approach me or should I scatter their shadowy spectral shield hosts? For if they overcome my strength with loud noise, and if these foolish witches disturb my soul and with sorcery dissolve my strength and my courage, the music of the harp that I heard a while ago in memory and in my senses will now cause me to violate my taboos. And if my strength and vigour are taken from me, the beautiful fair-skinned women from the province will be under the heroes from Connacht and Munster and Leinster, and the champions of Meath, who will be burning and destroying the territory of Cooley and the Plain of Muirthemne. For I have violated all my taboos and the signs are that my life has run its course.'

'Leave all that behind you,' said Genann Gruadsolus to Cú Chulainn. 'Take no notice of them, nor heed the screams or cries of false destruction from the fairy hills, nor the painful and deceitful tricks of the Clan Calitín full of drunkenness and destruction. For they are seven years seeking druidic spells throughout the world in order that you may fall by them, and by the weaponry they have taken with them and with the great power of the four great provinces of Ireland, readily set against you on Mag Muirthemne. Beware of them for three days from today and their magic will be reduced to nothing, and the power of the warriors will rise and help you, and Conall will come without doubt out of the territory of the Cruthin with help and support. If you need my advice, then this is it, namely, without waiting for the treacherous arts or the unreal cold-hearted bodies of the Calitín, go back from the weak and those in decline, and let it be told and related throughout the world how you were forever victorious.'

And Cú Chulainn seized his weapon on account of this advice, both for his honour and for his valour, although he should come to the end of his life. And beautiful, sweet music was sung for him by noble and illustrious artists, and there were women carousing and playing board games, and there was mirth and merriment around him on all sides.

The Clan Calitín departed and Cú Chulainn did not do battle with them that day. And they came to the camp of the men of Ireland, and the men of Ireland asked them for tidings of Cú Chulainn. 'He avoided us today,' said the Clan Calitín, 'but tomorrow we will take him with us.' They remained the night there, and the following morning the three Calitín rose early. The spectres kept watch then, and the one-handed, half-blind, bare-legged and yellow-cheeked sprites and the three ugly shaped, terrible coloured witches moved quickly on the back of the swift wind until they reached the green at Emain, and there they descended, transforming bloody battles into vistas of the oak forest and greatly waging wars [with exhortations and screams] terrible and horrendous to hear, and causing panic across the borderlands.

It is at the borders that Cú Chulainn kept guard that day for the daughters of the king and chief of Ulster, and for his own mistress Níam, daughter of Celtchar mac Uithechair. The women held a meeting on that day to see how Cú Chulainn could be protected, and they decided to bring Cú Chulainn with them to the Valley of the Deaf. For there was a fortress in that black glen, and a gathering of deceiving women came with them to that place, and the scaldcrows were listening to any disturbance rather than screeching, the witches were destroying and challenging at the head of the enemy. And Níam the daughter of Celtchair approached and said: 'O dear boy, the Ulaid and Conchobar brought us here today for your protection. Come with me and the womenfolk and let us go as far as my fort for drinking and pleasure, since there is drink there and you will be safe drinking.' And he came out from the sun house and they brought him with them to the Valley of the Deaf. And once he saw it, he recognized it as the Valley of the Deaf. 'That is unfortunate,' said Cú Chulainn, 'for the Valley of the Deaf this is, and you will not be here forever.' And it is not for long that he is.

At that time the Clan Calitín were influencing the battle greatly all along the border. The raiders plundered both along the pathways and throughout, with one battle cry and battle signal, so that the three bewildered the soldiers at that great battle. 'Woe for that, that my expedition and my journey with the women should be injurious and dangerous to me, deprived of my arms, my horse and my armour, so that I fail to hold back the plunder and the battles, and to protect the province.'

He came to Emain. 'Get my horse and prepare my chariot, so that I can approach the men of Ireland.' 'You have given me your word,' said Níam, 'that you would not approach the men of Ireland, nor have I given you permission to do so.' 'If I have given it, I will not go,' said he. And they came out from that place, and the eldest of the sons of Calitín went above the sun house. Cú Chulainn arose, and Níam placed his hands under him and the palms of his hands towards him, and sat him down. 'Wait for me,' said Níam, 'and fulfil your pledge.' Cú Chulainn sat down regretfully and the Clan Calitín departed, since they saw Cú Chulainn staying still, and they came to the camp of the men of Ireland. 'Did you bring Cú Chulainn with you?' 'We did not,' they said. 'If we do not bring him tomorrow to you, he will carry six heads from us.' They pitched down for the night there.

As for Conchobar, Cathbad and Gruadsolus and all the druids approached him the following morning, and Conchobar asked what protection there would be for Cú Chulainn on that day.

'We do not know,' they all said. 'Find out,' said Conchobar. 'Take ye to the Valley of the Deaf today, since it is said that that is where he is: since all the men of Ireland were around there, and

149

with the battle cries high above them, nobody will hear anyone in the glen. And with the same cries coming from the valley nobody will hear them coming out from the valley. Be mindful then that it is right to take Cú Chulainn away with you from that glen, and to protect him in a prudent and a skilful way, until he may see his strength and his luck and his fortune returning, and until Conall may see the borders with great numbers of the Cruthin coming to help. 'O high king,' said Níam, 'he did not accept the obligations from me or from all the women to go into that valley, even though we pleaded with him all day long.' Cathbad and Geanann Gruadsolus rose, as did all the poets and the women side by side with Emer, and went to him, and he was taken into the valley, and a pleasurable time was had with drinking and merriment, so that he would not hear the incitement of the army with all the confusion. 'I will not go with them into the glen,' said Emer, 'but let Níam arise with my blessings, for it is difficult for him to refuse her.' And this advice decided their course of action.

And women and youth and poets and *ollaves* came throughout the province, and approached him, and Cobtach Ceólbinn the harper approached him playing music to him, and Ferceirtne the poet was with them guarding him, and Cathbad came and bent over him and prayed, and he went there with the rest, and he gave him three fervent and diligent kisses. 'O dear son,' said Cathbad, 'come with me today to drink at my feast, and the women and all the poets will come with us, and it is taboo for you to refuse or avoid the feast.' 'It is a pity then,' said Cú Chulainn, 'for it is not good to be mentioning drink or merriment to me now, and four of the great provinces of Ireland are burning and plundering the fifth part, and Ulster in the grip of debility [*Cess Noínden*], and Conall on the borders of the foreigner. And the men of Ireland are rebuking and shaming me, and what is there to say but that I should be taking my leave of you? And that is that; if it were not for you and Conchobar and Genann and the poets, I would go and scatter the enemy at the borders, so that there would be more dead than alive.' And Emer and all the women began pleading, and this is what she said: 'O Cúcán,' said she, 'you have prevented yourself from taking either a journey or an expedition until this very moment. Do as I say, O first love, O first love in courting from all the men in the world, favourite of the womenfolk, and of the poets of the world and all the rest of Ireland, go with

Cathbad and Genann, and with Níam daughter of Celtchair, and drink at the feast where Cathbad is waiting.'

And Níam turned her face to his and entreated him in a subtle sweet voice, and he rose with them reluctantly, and they came to the valley.

'Alas,' said Cú Chulainn, 'long have I attempted to avoid this glen, for I have not come to a place before more horrid than this, and the men of Ireland are saying that I am avoiding them by coming here,' said Cú Chulainn. And they came to the great hostel of the king with Cathbad. They unyoked the Liath Macha and the Dub Sainglend at the bottom of the glen, and Cú Chulainn sat down, and Ferceirtne and all the poets sat on one side, and close by the singers performed for them. And they ate and drank to festive music, and there was mirth and merriment in abundance. And that is as far as that.

As for the Clan Calitín, their story is well-known. The three peak-handed daughters of Calitín came to the green at Emain, and went to where they saw Cú Chulainn the previous night, but they did not find him there. When they did not find him they searched all Emain and still did not find him. And they wondered whether Cú Chulainn was in the company of Emer or Conchobar, or the champions of the province besides. And they clearly understood that it was the power of Cathbad that was concealing him. They rose in an airy birdlike way and they visited the province, asking about him, and they arrived above the Valley of the Deaf, and they saw the Liath Macha and the Dub Sainglend at ease at the bottom of the glen, and Laeg mac Riangabra nearby, guarding them, so they perceived that Cú Chulainn was in the glen, for they heard the sound of the music from the poets that were with Cú Chulainn. The Clan Calitín gathered hooded thistles with sharp plumage there, and small bellied mushrooms with light tops, and decaying foliage that flies about the wood, and thus created an illusion of many young armour-clad soldiers, so that there was not a knoll or a hill in the glen that was not full of soldiers in both troops and battalions, and of standing stones that resounded from the poisonous mists to the walls of the firmament with the ugly and swiftly savage cries that rose above the Clan Calitín, who were wounding and plundering, burning and wailing, and the loud clamour of the trumpet and horn was heard everywhere; such was the supernatural power of the Clan Calitín. And because the women heard the lasting cries there, they

151

made other large cries against them, and because they sounded the same, Cú Chulainn heard the cries as though they were coming from the one place. 'Alas,' said Cú Chulainn, 'it is great the cries I hear from the men of Ireland, plundering across the province, and they have come to the scene of my victories and to the province whose greatness is over forever.' 'Leave all that behind,' said Cathbad. 'It is nothing but the whistling noise of an illusory host moving about, the shape-changing Clan Calitín coming towards you, and it is nothing but the false sights and sounds of magic moving there, so do not pay any attention to them.' And they enjoy themselves for a while with drink and entertainment until they hear the great cries being made outside by the Clan Calitín again. And because of what they heard while guarding Cú Chulainn, they lifted their own voices with both contentious and mocking cries about Cú Chulainn, and the Clan Calitín was worn out at last, and was not pursued with spells by Cathbad and the women.

'Wait here and bring the battle to a head,' said Badb, the daughter of Calitín, to her two sisters, 'for I will come into the glen when death will take Cú Chulainn.' And they went before her bringing false shame to the hostel, and she went with the appearance of a woman to the women of Níam inside the hostel, and called the mistress of Cú Chulainn out. And a great multitude of women came out with the lady, and for a long while Badb brought forth magic and deceiving spells in that hostel, and a fog of confusion and bewilderment enveloped them throughout the valley, and a druidic mist was put between them and the hostel, and she came by them knowing that Níam had begged Cú Chulainn not to go seeking the men of Ireland, nor had she given him permission to do so. And Badb took on the appearance of Níam and came to where Cú Chulainn was, and called out before the approaching host. 'O life, O champion, O warrior, O Cúcán,' said she, 'Dún Delca is burning, and Mag Muirthemne and the meadow of Conall, and the whole province is being plundered, and the army has come to Emain, and it falls on me to get the good people of the province to stop the attack and not to allow the borderlands to be avenged, and to stop the army. And still I know that truly Conall will kill me for not protecting the province and for allowing the men of Ireland to advance.' 'Alas then, O Níam,' said Cú Chulainn, 'for it is difficult to resist the women after that, and I suppose that you would not give me permission to own all the gold or all the riches in the world, but want me to meet with suffering and injury by facing all the men of Ireland. I shall go then,' said Cú Chulainn.

And Cú Chulainn rose suddenly with that advice, and as he was rising it happened that he was pricked on his left foot, so that he sat down. And he arose again, startled by the injury, which shamed him. For the golden pin that was in his cloak on the ridge-pole of the white hostel fell down and went through his foot until it reached the ground. 'It is true,' said Cú Chulainn, 'it is an enemy pin, for it is not an enemy cloak, and it is giving a warning to me.'

Cú Chulainn came out of the hostel then, and ordered Laeg to take the horses and prepare the chariots. And Cathbad and Genann Gruadsolus rose, and all the women after them, and they lifted all their hands and knew nothing until they had come from that glen, and Cú Chulainn left and inspected every part of the province. And Badb left them after this, and they lifted their voices aloud so that their voices were great and terrible. And Cú Chulainn heard it, and it is great the spectres, terrible and wonderful, that were manifest, and he had never seen their like before, and it was there at that time that he violated all his *geasa*. Cathbad then took it upon himself to appease everybody and said the following words: 'O dear son,' said he, 'for my sake today, do not go and meet with the men of Ireland and thus you will prevent the evil magic of the Clan Calitín.' 'O dear foster-father,' said Cú Chulainn, 'the end of my life has come, and I have violated my *geasa*, and Níam has consented to go with me to meet with the men of Ireland, and I will go there, with your permission.' Níam seized Cú Chulainn and said: 'Alas, Cúcán, as true as there is gold in the ground, I would not have given permission to you to go, and it is not I but Badb, the daughter of Calitín, who deceived you by taking my form and appearing as me, O friend, O dear love.' And Cú Chulainn did not believe anything that was said, and he summoned Laeg to get the horses, arrange the chariot and prepare the weaponry.

Laeg came before him with the horses harnessed and no one ever saw a more reluctant man than he preparing to go on an expedition. And the Liath Macha was not with him, so he shook the reins against her and brought her out, and when they heard the horses there they retreated before them. And the Liath Macha goes around three times, and it is furious and fierce.

'It is true,' said Laeg, 'if it is a bad omen for you there, it is a bad omen for me, and the same happiness and misfortune for both of us, and it was seldom until now that you did not face the reins and that you came against me.' And Laeg was addressing the Liath Macha. The Liath Macha was not before Laeg after that, and Laeg came and approached Cú Chulainn, and told him that the Liath Macha was not with him. Cú Chulainn rose and seized the Liath Macha, but the horse would not come to him, and it was as large as a great warrior's fist, the dark tears of blood that were flowing down its cheeks, and Laeg came to its other side. 'O Liath Macha,' said Laeg, 'it is rightly just that you comply with me today more than any other day regardless of whatever your feelings were before.' The Liath Macha came before Laeg then, and they got the Dub Sainglend and yoked the chariot to them, and they got and prepared and arranged the weaponry and arms and the many sword-blades. And Cú Chulainn put his battle cloak next to his skin and performed the wheel feat and the high feat, the sword-edge feat and the apple feat, the javelin feat and the galloping feat, and all the other skills as well. And he leapt into his chariot without further ado, and his arms and battle weaponry fell under his feet in the chariot, and they came out of their fittings, and out of the places from whence they would strike, and great were the evil omens that were with him then.

And he came, his head in front of him, facing the road, and they came to Emain Macha, and it was not long until Cú Chulainn was shown the site of the great battles on the green at Emain, and he saw the broad plains full of depleted foot soldiers of many leaders, and a hundred troops, and a multitude of weapons and horses and armour, and close by he heard terrible shrieking, which was getting louder, and fires that were extending and the fortress of Conchoban ruined completely, and it appeared to him that there was neither a hill nor a hillock around Emain that was not full of battle-wounded. The sun house of Emer was shown in ruins and the house of the Craeb Ruad ablaze, and all Emain alight with burning, all red, red. 'Alas then, O Cathbad,' said Cú Chulainn, 'that you should be trying to stop me. It is great now the plunder and the damage and the sudden destruction throughout the Plain of Macha and the meadow of Emain, and the province in general.' Cathbad answered then and said: 'O dear son,' said he, 'it is great the confusion and anger that the weary and exhausted army brings, for it is a disturbing story; it is you who are bewildered and enchanted by a phantom host. For there is neither a single person nor a multitude there, but grass and leaves.' And he did not believe one single word of Cathbad's until they reached Emain, where the women were lamenting and shrieking before and after him.

And he came as far the sun house where Emer was, and Emer came out towards him and they spoke, and he dismounted and went into the sun house. 'I will do nothing at all, young woman,' said Cú Chulainn, 'until I go and approach the four great provinces of Ireland that are at Mag Muirthemne, to avenge the plundering and the wrong doing and the injustice that they have inflicted on me, and on the whole of the province, and it was shown to me that this place was until now full of the hosts of the men of Ireland, burning and scorching the land.'

'Indeed,' said the lady, 'they are nothing but the phantoms of sorcery there. And do you give them neither heed nor attention.' 'I am pledged for what my life is worth to journey on until I reach the camp of the men of Ireland.' And when the women heard this they began a piteous mournful wail, and Cú Chulainn bade farewell to his queen and to all the women.

And he came to bid farewell to his mother at Dún Deichtine, with Cathbad and the poets zealously following him. And he came to the green within the dwelling, and Deichtine approached him and noticed that it was a pleasant gathering that had come with him, and gave him a drinking vessel for his safety. And a drink from this vessel would bring him victory, whether he would be facing the road or travelling, but the vessel was full of blood. 'Alas, Deichtine,' said Cú Chulainn, 'no wonder that I have betrayed everyone when I have taken the vessel of very red blood that you approached me with.' And Deichtine got the vessel again and filled it, and took it to him, and it turned to blood when he went to drink it. Three times the queen filled the cup and three times the liquid turned to blood, at each time when she placed it before him, and Cú Chulainn became angry with the vessel and he crushed it under a standing stone. And Tulach in Bálláin is still the name of that hill, and Cairthi in Bálláin is still the name of that standing stone. 'It is true, O woman,' said Cú Chulainn, 'that you are not guilty, but my *geasa* are violated and my life is going from me, for I will not come out alive from this expedition against the men of Ireland.' Deichtine and

Cathbad were praying for his life by asking Conall to come to the territory of the strangers, to help in the face of the evil omens. 'I have no life,' said Cú Chulainn 'since my hour and my time have come, yet I will not betray my fame nor my lasting triumph by lies at the end of my life, and battle has not been shunned by me nor courage in battle, from the time I first took a weapon in my hand up to this day. I will not exert myself now since lasting fame will follow the end of my life.'

Cú Chulainn came before the meadow at Emain, and the daughters of the green and all the chiefs there lifted up their voices, yelling their misfortunes and sorrow, and lamenting their grief in his memory, and at last Cathbad came out from the place. When they quickly reached the fort, it then happened that a beautiful, white-bodied and well-proportioned maiden appeared before the Ford of the Watch on the plain of Emain, and she was moaning and lamenting, and cutting and attacking and squeezing the purple spoils [of the dead], and becoming furious at the outer edge of the ford. 'See over yonder, O Cúcán,' said Cathbad. 'That is the daughter of Badb, and is she not washing the spoils from the champions? She is sorrowful and moaning in lasting sighs as she foretells of the fall; when you will fall as a result of Medb's wiles and the sorcery of the Calitín. For this reason, my dear foster-child, it would be wise for you to wait,' said Cathbad. 'Good O beloved foster-father,' said Cú Chulainn, 'do not follow me anymore, since I will not be remaining here, but will be going to seek vengeance on the four high provinces of Ireland that have come and plundered my territory, and burned my fortress, even if it is Badb who is washing the spoils from our warrior dead. Great were the spoils and weapons of those slain that were bathed in blood, so that the stream-pool is a mass of red blood from the swords and lances from that conflict. Although you are reluctant to allow me to meet death and destruction, and face the enemy who is menacing me, I am even more reluctant to have my side pierced and my body hacked. It is better that I should learn of my fall from myself than from you,' said Cú Chulainn, 'so do not prevent my way nor my journey any more. Since I have come to my death and set out on my journey towards the end of my life, health to you as I approach the Ulaid and Conchobar, and bring my blessings to Emer, for I will never reach her until Doomsday: sorrowful our separation and painful to be apart. Although it is with reluctance that today we are leaving Emain, it is great that the day has come and Laeg can walk booty-laden from the distant borderlands of the neighbouring race.'

After this Cú Chulainn turned and faced Emain again, and looked over the place, and he listened to the heavy shrieks of the women-folk and the assembly of women, and he was shown an assembly of angels above Ráth Soilech [the earthen fort of willows] in what today is called Ard Macha [Armagh], and between Heaven and Earth the sky was full of musical performers, all above the ring fort, and his soul was greatly pacified by this, by all that he saw, he was heartened by all this, namely the loving music that he heard, and Cú Chulainn told all this to Cathbad [the visions that were shown to him], 'and these are different visions from the phantoms I saw a while ago that were horrid and very ugly, as I approached Emain.'

And he came to Áth na Foraire by Sliab Fúait and he saw smoke from one side, and he came in order to approach it, and it seemed to him that there was a multitude of the men of Ireland there and they were plundering the province there. 'O Laeg,' said Cú Chulainn, 'prick the horses there with your goad, so that we can go and see what made the fire there.' They came and approached the hateful multi-tude that were making the smoke, and they saw who was making the fires, namely the hereditary enemy, the frenzy-stricken hags, the Clan Calitín. And easily known, the six of them, by their appearance: each hag had one great red eye, broad and black in her forehead, and each hag had one sinewy hand with long nails in front of her body, and one foot crooked and leather-like, slender and ugly; their lower parts were like vultures, and overcoming the weight of their plump sides, their jet-black hard-hooded hides, their heads like bucks and rams, their feet like cranes and barnacle geese, their bones white, their sharp-pointed horns in fetters, which dangled beside each ancient rough hide; and the cooking hearth with little pieces of calf of the leg in it and wild meat from the red-tipped sharp points of the quicken tree; and he saw there the destructive work of the witches, and he put on the left plank of the chariot and came out along the way. As Badb saw this, she took a sharp spit and threw it straight against him, rebuking him as he approached, and it hit Cú Chulainn's head, and Cú Chulainn seized the spear and was bent over as a result of Badb's assault, and a drop of keen blood fell from his head as well as from one of his sides that was pierced by the spear. This is what happened to the champion warrior, whose horse, the Liath Macha, was also injured. It was this wounding that left him without half his strength and with his courage impaired. And he cast a shot sadly yet resolutely from him towards the approaching Badb, the hero threw the dart athwart through her body, it was thus that she went to the men of Ireland, with the spear through her.

Cú Chulainn was weary and morose after that casting. 'Alas,' said Cú Chulainn, 'my strength has been halved and my vigour has been taken from me, and if it were not for the Clan Calitín hacking at everything a great many of the men of Ireland would fall at the mustering for battle. Hold back the horses, O Laeg,' said Cú Chulainn, 'since pestilence and heavy clouds of poison are coming towards me.' 'I will do that,' said Laeg, 'for when we returned with fortune and wealth from our expedition, no ale would suffice unless there was an abundance of it, and these were all the victories and foreign fortunes until this very moment, and you will not kill men but women, and besides you would kill neither men nor women, were it not that you killed them by sorcery, and you would not have killed Cúroi mac Dáire, if Blathnat had not deceived you.'

It is then that Cú Chulainn came and approached the men of Ireland, and the men of Ireland heard Cú Chulainn approaching, and they were asking was the honour of one man better than the honour of six, and Cú Cuillesc the satirist asked Cú Chulainn about the spear he was carrying, and Cú Cuillesc came towards Cú Chulainn with three times nine poets asking about the spear that was before him, and Cú Chulainn bade them welcome with caution. 'I came seeking your spear,' said Cú Cuillesc. 'I swear,' said Cú Chulainn, 'that never has one risen up before, and woe to them that come seeking my sword while I am in the company of the men of Ireland. As to the manner in which I carry my spear to you,' said Cú Chulainn, 'is it the point of the spear I carry before me or is it the shaft?' 'Neither of the two,' said Cú Cuillesc, 'but give it over to me.'

He sent the thick heavy lance towards them, and it killed Cú Cuillesc and three times nine men with her. 'Alas then,' said Cú Chulainn, 'that my honour should return after I felled Cú Cuillesc and three times nine men with the poison of my lance, and let us hurl darts at the horses, so that we may come onto the host from one place and let us not delay.' 'Do not hurl at all,' said Laeg, 'but take your spear with me.' 'I may not take it at all,' said Cú Chulainn, 'for I have not gone after this prize that I have taken before and I will not go after that yonder.' And Laeg dismounted and took the spears, and they came before the men of Ireland.

And Lugaid mac Con Rí heard Cú Chulainn approaching the men of Ireland and said, 'I shall go and look at the father yonder to see what is to be said, to confirm if he has come to the men of Ireland.' Lugaid came before him to look at the form and shape of Cú Chulainn and gave his description out loud to the men of Ireland: 'I see coming towards you,' said he, 'a chariot, calm, swift and of white bronze, approaching swiftly, and with vigour and cunning, and with a green awning, and with chariot shafts of white copper, with very clean wheels, a chariot with a gaping jaw; the body of the chariot wall tall and beautiful going directly, squeaking and furious; that hero as swift as a deer or a weasel or as fast as a whirlwind from the cold days of spring that comes across the meadow or the mountain plains; and it is crafty, swift, impetuous and sturdy horses, which are tall, haughty and beautiful, that I see coming towards you,' said Lugaid. 'One of the two horses coming towards you, namely the grey, of great vigour and with great leaping, impetuously spreading large sods with its four great hooves, and blazing red tinder sparks issuing in a blaze from its bridle bit. The other horse truly slender-footed, light-headed black feet, having hair plaited and well-running, slender, brave and with slender ankles, bent legs, and a long head covered with an inlaid jet-black hood. Dark fair the youth, purple-coloured the presence of the young warrior, as if it were rose-coloured the complexion of his head; a satin hood with a headband of precious stones above his face, worn as a protection against bad weather and against the heat of the sun; a silver rod in his hand, to lead on the horses and to give them direction, except that the young warrior desires direction.'

It is then that Lugaid approached the men of Ireland. 'Let ye arise,' said he.

Cú Chulainn approached them and said: 'Arise, men of Ireland, it is Cú Chulainn, triumphant, victorious in battle, exultant and red-sworded, who is approaching you. The host will be smitten, and the scaldcrow and the enemy will be broken by the spears of the Ulaid. Woe to women, woe to boys, woe to the common people, woe to the sea, woe to the country where grief comes and is found in the kingdom on the backs of the entire retinue; before robbery comes, and plundering begins. Welcome to each and all of the rising host.'

It is then the four great provinces of Ireland rose up with a loud roar, their shining shields well-arranged and with their rich, well-made armour, and formed in a great war phalanx awaiting Cú Chulainn. Medb arose early that morning, and she seized the poisonous weapons that the Clan Calitín had taken with them from the Underworld in order that Cú Chulainn should be killed. She divided the weapons among them: she gave a spear to Lugaid mac Con Rí and a spear to Mac Nia mac Finn and a spear to Erc mac Cairbre. 'Here are,' said she, 'the three poisonous spears that are destined to kill Cú Chulainn. Take them, and avenge your fathers with them.'

It is then that Cú Chulainn saw the men of Ireland by him. 'O gilly,' said he, 'release the spikes on the horses and turn the left board of the chariot towards the enemy.' And in this manner Cú Chulainn came around the men of Ireland.

Then great distortions and rage possessed the kingly warrior, that is, they enveloped Cú Chulainn, and he turned into a many-sided, unknown spectre, and his haunches shook as if they were trees before a stream, as though he were a swift, soft reed in the midst of a stream, with each limb and each joint and each member moving from head to toe. And he utters a cry of wrath that comes from the centre of his body. They came on their heels, by the calf of their legs and by the hollow of their knees, until they were beyond him, and their warrior fists were immense and numerous and as large as turnips. And they rose up as though their head muscles were yoked to their necks, as though the heads of these youths of a fair age were large as a huge bare mountain. And he contorted his face and aspect, so that he swallowed one of his eyes into his head, in such a way that a crane could hardly have reached to peck it from his wild cheeks from on top of his skull. They came, their lungs and livers fluttering as though they were hostages on the tops of spears. And from the upper part of the chariot against the roof a blow is struck that would fell a lion equal to the size of a ram, and numerous glowing fires blazed from his teeth and from his neck. The swelling sound of torment was heard from his chest like the yelling of a hound of battle standing by its prey or like a lion going under a bear. Shining Badb was seen and the shower-clouds of the heavens and the tinder-sparks burning flaming red, kindling and gleaming above them. His hair was curling from his head like glorious branches of well-trimmed hedges, and he shakes two apple trees full

of fruit above his head, and the apples do not reach the ground yonder and each apple stops at the top of each single hair that rises
above the hair on his head. A beam of magic fire springs from above
his head and above the high thick forehead that is the measure of
the young warrior. Like the thick tall mast of a great large ship, rising straight on the waves of dark blood, like a tree trunk rising
straight up to his head and the crown of his head; dark laments of
sorcery are made, lamenting the kingly hostel, the royal feasts, when
the king came for entertainment in the winter evenings.

Then the hero rose from the sickle chariot with his weaponry
made of iron, with his slender sharp-edged sword, with the sickles
and hooks and small spikes with sharp points that were attached to
each wheel rim of the chariot, and that mangled each limb and each
joint and each member, from head to foot, of those that came within its reach, impaled on the fast-moving spits; while attempting to
ward off the contrivance, they were held by ropes and cords to the
wheels, where their heads and flesh and bones and necks were sliced
into pieces. And then he performed a hundred thunder feats on the
chariot, and then two and three and four hundred thunder feats,
and he stopped at five hundred thunder feats, for that was the number of the foe, and the enemy and the stranger whom he was obliged
to fell in combat, and as a champion to avenge the evil and wrong
doing on the men of Ireland. Then he took a heavy course upon the
chariot that was quite a distance from the fort and the fortified area,
so far that the iron wheels of the chariot went down into the earth
outside, until eventually rising up with the dykes and the pillar
stones and the sea gravel outside, until they were of equal height
against them. It is then that he came about the four great provinces
of Ireland, so that he came flying past them rather than shunning
them, and eventually arrived at the place where they were all assembled. He comes to them to the centre of where they are assembled
and after this he took the attack before the enemy. He threw down
a great hedge of hazel from the enemy and the foe, and from the
stranger around about the battle, so that it fell, sole against sole,
elbow against elbow, hand against hand and wrist against wrist, so
that there was a pool of very red blood upon each shot from where
they had set out; it was in front of a hound and a horse and a man
that the great rout of Mag Muirthemne began that night. Anyhow,
it is impossible to tell or to declare the total number of kings and

chiefs that fell by him, the heroes and the warriors, and the gap of a hundred in the ranks, besides the mercenaries and the field of slaughter, and the young lords and the useless plebeians of the men of Ireland. And not one in three of the soldiers of the men of Ireland escaped from him without a lump or without a mark or without defeat, or without a leg or a shin or half a head or one of their eyes, or without a lasting blemish forever on him.

He went safely from them that night without red upon him, neither on his charioteer nor on his horses, and he came to the western side of the host, and cast a sling towards it. 'Well, my dear Laeg,' said Cú Chulainn, 'bring stones and rocks to me and approach the host so that you cast them at them.' And Laeg took a very powerful bulky load of stones towards them. Then he grabbed them and flung them at the host. After this he threw the rocks one after the other above the host, so that the fixed and solid stones were broken up for throwing then; standing stones were also crushed and broken up for hand-throwing, a heavy shower of well-aimed stones wounded the enemy. Then sharp-headed bulky stones came towards the hero, over the bodies of the warriors and over the stone-piles of the heroes, and over the multitude of young warriors, so that it was with broken shields the shadowy troops, and with confusion the warrior formations, raged victorious and hacked the broken bodies of the hundred troop and the pillar stones and the heroes of the men of Ireland that were gathering there, so that no sleep nor resting, nor lying down, nor eating, nor lying in bed was allowed to them for seven days and for seven nights. They were jumping and kicking and gadding about like a great drove of cattle suffering from the heat and from being constrained, such was the effect that the powerful thunder feat had on the men of Ireland, after Cú Chulainn had inflicted it on them.

Then on the eighth day a great weariness and fatigue seized Cú Chulainn, as great as the terror he had brought to the four great provinces of Ireland. Then Cú Chulainn came after this throughout the men of Ireland, and a general outburst rained on the men of Ireland, and there was not a shield nor a battle helmet of a hero, nor body armour, that was not pierced in that onslaught. Medb saw this and she blamed and rebuked, and exhorted, incited, urged and challenged the men of Ireland against Cú Chulainn. And when Mac Nia mac Finn mac Rosa saw this, he came for combat with a sharp-edged lance that was long and stiff, and resolutely he approached him and swiftly cast like a sudden gust his broad spear as straight as a sword towards Cú Chulainn, so that it hit the top of his right leg, so that the upper leg was torn and lacerated by the swift cast of the champion; the Liath Macha was full of wounds and torn skin from the swift casts. And at length he cut the flesh and extracted the spears that were in the back of the horse. Erc mac Cairbre eagerly took a throw that was swift and nimble towards him, the spear was sharp, poisonous blue and grey-pointed, it pierced the top of the left leg of the warrior, it was there that the lance supported by a broad head struck Laeg between his loin and his navel. And he cut equally deep in order to extract the lances from the great wounds. The young kings avoided wounding one another at that place, since it was not very far off from these places that the aiming was. And the rest of the men of Ireland escaped from them in every direction, and left the battlefield to him.

'I fell by that throw, O Cú Chulainn,' said Laeg, 'and it was not from the wounding I got at that battle, nor from the combat, the like of which we were in before.' 'Pity, O Laeg,' said Cú Chulainn, 'for it was not your cry of pain when wounded, but the great injury to you. For unless I was first pierced all over, no man on Earth would have shed your blood.' 'If that is so,' said Laeg, 'then let me accompany you before you fall from weakness and exhaustion. For since today we sought out by force the camp of the four great provinces of Ireland, none of the men of Ireland will be allowed through fear to draw blood from me, and as I am today without lord and chief I make my departure, and it is sad to be departing and separating from each other, O beloved foster-brother,' said he. 'Glory and blessing to you,' said Cú Chulainn, 'for no lord ever got nor will get a servant of such fame that was better than you. And I give my word and may all throughout Ireland hear that I will avenge you today. And I give my word since we bound our friendship together on that first day, neither to separate nor to quarrel together during day or night until this very moment. And take my blessings with you to yourself, and to Emer and Conchobar, and tell them of my conflict and of my campaign of vengeance against the men of Ireland.' 'Alas then, O Cú Chulainn,' said Laeg, 'it will be said before the young heroes of Emain that I am a servant without a lord and without a master today.' 'Do not say it,' said Cú Chulainn, 'for if you were to say that it would break my heart.' 'Alas then,' said Laeg, 'for that is not what I would have wished.' And Laeg and Cú Chulainn bade farewell to each other, and although Laeg made his farewells then, he was reluctant to depart from his master, and came before him tired and wounded. He was looking out to see what form of attack he would bring to the men of Ireland and what form of violence they would bring to him.

Then he came, bravely, with a strong body ready for vigorous feats, to below where the gillies were, and with a well-prepared and daunting plan killed the servants through slaughter and maiming, so that many a lad of the men of Ireland fell in vengeance for his worthy servant. And he came then in lasting fury and battle anger, and full of wrath, and menaced the horses of the men of Ireland, so that many a horse of the men of Ireland fell in vengeance for his worthy horse. And after this he came passionately, with a sudden onset and a vehement rush, to where the men of Ireland were, and neither heroes nor bones nor battle armour could take him as he smote and struck, neither one person nor a multitude from the one place facing against him, and in full stride he threw himself upon the fleeing host, and those ahead and those in their wake were seized and killed, and great was the destruction, and many a man of the men of Ireland fell by him in vengeance for his sores and wounds, and there was none there without loss of feet or hands or half a head or one eye, or without a lasting blemish on him.

When Medb saw the dead bodies on the battle field and the slaughter brought about on the men of Ireland by Cú Chulainn, she asked in a loud, distinctive voice: 'Where is Lugaid mac Con Rí?' 'I am here,' said Lugaid. 'It was promised to me that Cú Chulainn would fall by you on the poisonous spear that Bolcán made and gave to you in order that Cú Chulainn should fall by you.' 'If I promise something, then it is right that I fulfil it,' said Lugaid. And Lugaid rose, a skilled hero, lion-like to that place, as a result of the urging of Medb, and he seized the large-shafted, sharp-headed and long-headed lance, and cast a long throw at the battle warrior, so that the broad-headed, easily thrown lance landed as far away as the sleeping Dub Sainglend, whom it pierced. It then struck Cú Chulainn between his loin and his navel; the sharp point of the spear smashed then and the blue spear cut with force all the way to his navel. The Dub Sainglend fell then, and it struck the Liath

Macha, alone by the chariot, and the poisonous spear was in her throughout the battle. Cú Chulainn leapt out of the chariot then and went against the men of Ireland, and swiftly dispersed them east and west, north and south from him, and they did not dare to be near where that spear was thrown, and his entrails flowed out by his feet, and the raven Badb landed upon his feet, and the raven bent over to eat part of the small intestine under his foot, but Cú Chulainn wrenched his gut away. And laughter burst forth from Cú Chulainn and this laugh was to be his last. And mists of white death came towards him, and he came to a pool that was close by. It was from there that he washed himself, and after that the pool was called the Pool of the Washing.

When Laeg saw the deserted plain from which the host had dispersed, and Cú Chulainn nursing himself, he came towards him. And when Cú Chulainn saw Laeg, he was well-pleased. Laeg tended to him, he tied and prepared the wounds that were passing blood, that were a mass of gore, and the broad green pool of water becomes very red with blood, and he was not long thus when he saw an otter drinking his blood, and as Cú Chulainn saw the otter drinking the blood from his body, he killed it with the throw of a stone. 'Take victory, O Cúcán,' said Laeg. 'Your life is not over yet, and you will avenge the men of Ireland.' 'Alas, O Laeg,' said Cú Chulainn, 'no person can ever be killed again after that animal. And it was a hound I killed on the first hunt I made and it was prophesied that the killing of a hound would be my last exploit; and dear Laeg,' said Cú Chulainn, 'take me towards the great pillar stone that is over there yonder, it is there that I shall die. Arrange my sword, the Crúaidín Cadutchenn, and put my shield and my spear close to each other. And if the men of Ireland see me in the distance, fear will not allow them to come and behead me; and tell Conall of all this.' And it is thus that it was done. Thus they came to the pillar stone and Laeg did not dare touch nor go near him until they reached the pillar stone. And he tied his chest to the pillar stone, and he placed his hand towards his heart and adjusted him.

'Alas then,' said Cú Chulainn, 'I vow and I swear by the high gods, that it is not possible for a stone heart or for bones or for iron to have the strength that was in me today, and if it be known might it be a heart of blood or of flesh that was in me, for I did not do half the things that I could have done either in valour or in deadly deeds.' Then Cú Chulainn set his face to the men of Ireland and placed his shield beside him, and put his spear before his shoulder and took his unsheathed sword in his hand. Life parted from his body then in front of the pillar stone. It is then that the hero and his weapons fell, the honour and the valour, the defender and the power of Ireland. Laeg went from there then and saw the Dub Sainglend rising from the mists, and he came towards her and cut the spears out of her, and there were tears of dark blood flowing down her cheeks, and Laeg went on her, and they came out on the battlefield sad and wounded after their chief, and they came towards Emain Macha. And that is how Cú Chulainn died.

As for the men of Ireland, they were three days and three nights facing Cú Chulainn, and fear prevented them from going and pulling the very blue dart that was in him. Cú Chulainn was three days and three nights standing in front of the pillar, and the Liath Macha was across the plain ready and irresolute, eating and walking towards and continuously striking the host, and no hound nor wild animal dared approach him then. The men of Ireland said: 'Cú Chulainn is deceiving us, yet he has succeeded in bringing the men of Ireland yonder together.' 'Where is Badb the daughter of Cailitín?' said Medb. 'I am here,' said Badb. 'Rise,' said Medb, 'and let me know whether Cú Chulainn is alive or dead.' 'I will go there,' said Badb, 'I will find out if the news is bad.' As a shape-changer she has come, that is, in the form of a bird fluttering in the air above. 'If he is alive, I will kill him with the first throw of a sling, and neither a bird nor an animal will come between us and the air, unless to die, and if he is dead I will descend in front of him, and you will hear my outcry.' She came as a crow, as a scaldcrow upon the remote firmament above, and gradually she came closer from above until she came within range of him, and she let out three great shrieks, and landed out in front on a thorn tree, so that the thorn of the crow is the name of the thorn trees on Mag Muirthemne. When the men of Ireland saw that they said, 'It is true, Cú Chulainn is dead and we can approach him.'

It is then that they approached Cú Chulainn, and his sword was upright in his right hand and he gripped it tight as he died, and none of the men of Ireland could release the sword from him, and Lugaid mac Con Rí said: 'Cut the tendon from the hand, and the sword will fall from him.' Thus it was done by them, and the sword fell athwart, and thirty kings' sons were there, the sword cut and shattered their thirty right hands, and that is the last deed that Cú Chulainn did. 'Behead Cú Chulainn,' said Medb. The men of Ireland looked to see who was the rightful person to behead Cú Chulainn and said that it was Lugaid mac Con Rí. 'O Lugaid,' said Medb, 'behead Cú Chulainn, since it was Cú Chulainn who killed your father.' Then Lugaid rose and cut off the head of Cú Chulainn. It is then that there arose beautiful and wonderful colours from the head of Cú Chulainn: there grew one of two heads of hair on him, the first ruddy and as red as the sun, the second as white as snow on a very cold night. Then the men of Ireland held council there to find out to which province they would take the head of Cú Chulainn. The host said that it was to be placed with Medb and that she was entitled to take the head to Cruachain. 'I will not take it,' said she, 'but Erc mac Cairbre will take it when he has sovereignty of the centre of Ireland [Tara],' 'I will take it with me,' said Erc, and he brought it to Tara, and the men of Ireland left Tara and each other then for the borders of their own provinces, and they ordered strong men and champions and warriors to guard behind and in front of it, so that Conall Cernach would not carry the body off. And that is the story so far.

As for Emer, she was on the ramparts of Emain every day, watching out by the plain and listening to the stories. And the young woman was not long there when she saw a lone horseman coming across the plain of Emain towards her, and slow and spiritlessly he came. The lady was trembling and fearful as she watched, and she recognized that it was Laeg that was there. 'That is true,' said Emer, 'it is Laeg yonder and the Dub Sainglend, and they have left Cú Chulainn and the Liath Macha to die on Mag Muirthemne under a pool of blood and a mass of gore, and it is sad indeed that it is not Cú Chulainn and the Liath Macha coming towards me, for it is many the day that he came along that way, boastful and proud, towards Emain.' The womenfolk and the assembly of women, the poets and the learned men of Emain came out towards him and asked the tidings from him. He told them from start to finish, and the womenfolk let out a heavy sad cry throughout Emain, and they made one wail and outcry throughout the whole province. Emer and Laeg came to Dún Delca, and found the fort burning, and the women came to the place where Cú Chulainn was, and they pitched a beautiful many-coloured tent over the body of Cú Chulainn, and the women wailed and lamented in a mournful way over the body.

Then Lebarcham was brought to Emer. 'Rise, O Lebarcham,' said Emer. 'Find out where in the wide world Conall Cernach is and tell him that Cú Chulainn has been killed by the men of Ireland.' There and then Lebarcham bolted out and ran fast to Inver Mór on the borders of Cooley, and she saw a ship setting about in the wide harbour and she recognized it as the Engach, the boat of Conall Cernach, and Lebarcham came towards it and Conall came up from below the deck and came before Lebarcham, and bade her welcome. 'Welcome to you, O kingly warrior,' said Lebarcham, and as she spoke she was hand in hand with Írial mac Conall and under his protection. 'What news have you, O Lebarcham?' said Conall. 'The story I have,' said Lebarcham, 'is that Cú Chulainn has fallen by the men of Ireland.' 'That is painful news,' said Conall, 'and it pierces my heart in the middle of my chest.' Then he added: 'get my horse and harness my chariot, so that I may go and see what number of the men of Ireland killed my foster-child on the plain of Muirthemne.' Conall's horses were harnessed, namely, the Derg Drúchtach and the Conchann Crónfada, and the chariot was yoked on them, and Conall leapt into the chariot and very eagerly he travelled. Then the white horse became exhausted and Conall's chariot fell upside down. An immense anger came over Conall then and he hit the horses with a rod that was in his hand, and he took out his frenzy on the Conchann Crónfada, and the horse fell down dead. Conall rose regretfully after that fall and fitted the chariot onto Derg Drúchtach, then he leapt on it, for he is one of three horsemen that bridled a single horse in Ireland, namely Lug Lamfada, who killed a tribe of Fomorians at the battle of Mag Tuired, and Subaltach Sídech on the Liath Macha before the host of the Táin Bó Cuailnge and Conall himself on the red onslaught [Dergruathar], which feeds his vengeance for Cú Chulainn.

Conall came before the meadow of Emain and across Áth na Foraire, on Sliab Fúait, and reached the smooth and lovely plain of Mag Muirthemne, and as he reached the plain he saw the destruction, the hacked bodies. Red with blood were the pools on the plain from the destruction of the men of Ireland, as were the horses and the charioteers and the kings. Conall visited the dead bodies on the battlefield and examined them. 'Terrible is the death of my foster-child by the men of Ireland,' said Conall, and he counts a hundred furrows and a hundred dead before each ridge, and there was no more counting after that. And he traversed the battlefield as it was, until the Liath Macha came to him and her body was pierced with spears. There were waves of blood against her sides and against the yoke on the left side of the chariot. 'It is seldom,' said Conall, 'that the Liath Macha was yoked on the left side, and for you, O Liath Macha, to be waiting for me, though I am your worthy lord, after your own lord. I will yoke my chariot to you so that we may go to avenge Cú Chulainn on the men of Ireland and on the host.' Conall approached the territory, travelling with the Liath Macha; then the Liath Macha departed from him, and she did not turn back, and she came within the battlefield, and the experts and the learned ones told her that she would not leave the end of a meadow without a curve on that one day. And she came to Linn in Léith; there she bounded till she drowned.

Then Conall came before the body of Cú Chulainn, and he held his body in front of him, and he let out a moan and a wail. 'Cú Chulainn should be buried now,' said Emer. 'You should not do that at all,' said Conall, 'until he is avenged on the men of Ireland, and until his head is recovered. For there is not a province in Ireland that I will not search for it, for I will bring it back and by force if necessary. For it is great the crying that I hear now, and it is great the shrieking that is about Mag Muirthemne and the Meadow of Conall, and it is great the wailing and the outcries throughout the province after Cú Chulainn. For he was a good man to guard a province and to answer a cry, and to hack bodies in the presence of a mass of blood, and my senses carry a heavy cry for my hound gone from me, and Lugaid mac Con Rí is entitled to maim Cú Chulainn, since it was he who killed the Clanna Dedad in the company of Cu Ri and Fiamain, and it is sad for me without Cú Chulainn to answer this cry, to be just one horse and charioteer before them.'

It is then that Conall moved before the camp of the men of Ireland, and he came towards Áth na Muilt, towards Áth hir Diad, towards Glenn Mór and towards Glenn Bolgán, and Conall looked beyond and saw smoke at one side of the way beside him. 'It is true then,' said Conall, 'that there is a great number of men yonder, yet there are no members of the Ulaid there.' And he came hither and Connla saw the lone horseman as he rose from the side of the hill; it was this Connla who was a foster-brother of Lugaid mac Con Rí.

He came to Lugaid and told him that the lone horseman was approaching, and when Lugaid was thus informed he waited after the host, keeping watch, until Conall attacked them without warning. There was great plunder and many hostages were taken out from the province. 'I see one horseman approaching, O Lugaid,' said Connla, 'and a great furious red assembly before the horseman, and I never before saw one man greater, nor more kingly nor more beautiful nor more princely who came here with more speed than this horseman whom I see coming towards you.' And his chariot came close by. 'I recognize him,' said Lugaid. 'He is the kingly warrior of Ireland, namely Conall Cernach mac Amergin, and no welcome comes in windfalls by him, although he has not come as an enemy before, either from the sea or from the land, and although he is a friend to us, he is a poisonous friend.' Then Conall pledged Lugaid that he would reach within the company like a storm before them, and Lugaid gave his word that he would neither avoid nor shun him, and that he would be on the Plain of Argetros for contest and combat.

Furiously Conall came to the sloping streams of Brega, and as he was there he saw one hundred and fifty champions and battle-equipped warriors at the edge of the ford, well-prepared and coming towards him. And Conall sought them out. 'Who are ye, O young hero?' said Conall. 'Maine Mó-Ebirt,' said he, 'the son of much-loved Ailella and Medb, and heir to the kingdom of Connacht, and he is here.' 'Good for me to find Maine,' said Conall, 'for it was you who killed Cú Chulainn.' 'It was I who killed him,' said Maine. 'I will kill you then,' said Conall. And Conall fiercely sought the hostile tribe and thrust spears one after the other at the warriors, and Conall was holding his shield before his lance and he struck the place where the warriors were with swift blows, and made fragments of the weapons and of the swords, and he came furiously and fiercely upon the men, and he measured perfectly the strength of the tight blows through the sides of the strong warriors, so that they were hacked and lacerated and cut down in battle, and thousands of the people of Maine were killed and scattered by the furious conflict then. Conall came then before Mó-Ebirt for mutual slaughter, and struck him with a violent and mortal blow, so that he was torn to pieces, his body cut open and his bones rent, as a result of the skill of that one blow; so that one man was alive owing to the swiftness of his hands, so that none of the people of Maine escaped without slaughter or without wounding. And afterwards Conall himself beheaded Maine, and he came to a wood close by and cut a long rod of white hazel as thick as his hand, and he twisted it and made a knot on the top of it, and tied the head of Maine to the band of twisted twig. 'It is good that I have this head,' said Conall. 'I carry – upon my word it is not my choosing to be bearing a full load – the heads of the kings and chiefs and strong men of Ireland upon these withes, and the absence of the men of Ireland on them since my expedition across the sea, when there is not a fort nor a field of battle in Ireland that is not full of lamenting and grief, and my power will be used to avenge my dear foster-child on them. And it is good that I went [to] Maine after Lugaid the Munster man. And it is good that it is from the Connacht men that I drew the first blood and had my first revenge. And Sruth Maine is the name of the stream wherein Maine fell forever.'

And after that Conall came to Tara, and the young warriors of Ulster were there at that time, accompanying Fedelm Nuacrothaig, the daughter of Conchobar [his namesake] Cenn Berraide of the Ulaid. And it so happened that Erc mac Cairbre was washing in a washing tub at that time. 'Good for the Ulaid tonight,' said Erc, 'without a blood avenger or a champion from the borders, after the departure of Cú Chulainn.' A feeling of shame came over Cenn Berraide. 'That is wrong,' said he, 'for as long as Conchobar and his family live, and Conall and his family, and Fergus and his sept, and the kings of Ulster besides. The people of Ulster have a blood vengeance, and upon my word,' said Cenn Berraide, 'they are a people able to destroy and [lacuna in text] and plunder and search each province, and take hostages and captives from you and from the men of Ireland alive to the Ulaid in the absence of Cú Chulainn.' Erc took a stone the size of his hand and threw a masterly shot towards Cenn Berraide. Cenn Berraide bent his head before the stone and let it go past his side, so that it went out through the side of a wall. And Cenn Berraide arose, grabbed his armour and came out of Tara, and he saw a lone horseman coming swiftly and hastily towards Tara along a direct route, and they rejoiced greatly on seeing the face of the great kingly horseman, and they recognized that it was Conall who was coming with such speed and with such vehemence. And Conall looked ahead and saw that it was a man belonging to the Ulaid there. They rejoice and each of them goes to greet the other, and strong kisses are given to one another. 'Have you a story, O Cenn Berraide, and how is Tara?' said Conall. 'Erc mac Cairbre is here,' said Cenn Berraide, 'and I have left him in the washing tub, and you gave your word that there is no man of vengeance nor incitement alive in Ulster now after Cú Chulainn.' 'That is not true,' said Conall. 'You are alive still, and I am a man for blood vengeance and incitement.' Then Cenn Berraide told of the quarrel with Erc.

They came to Tara after that and they saw a ball game being played on the green of Tara, and it is the lords of the household of Erc that were playing, namely Mál and Midna, and the ball that they were kicking was the head of Cú Chulainn. 'What is this?' said Conall. 'Shame on you,' they said, 'have you not heard that Cú Chulainn was killed by the men of Ireland at Mag Muirthemne?' 'I have heard,' said Conall. 'If you have heard,' said they, 'well, it is his head that we are using for a ball.' 'It is unfortunate for me to be with you,' said Conall, 'and the head has come to ye as a blood fine for this game.' Conall approached them with reckless anger and thrust Cúlclais, his eager, proud, fierce spear [lacuna in text] with a sharp head, with a heavy shaft and bulky, warrior-like. It wounded them greatly, their sides were marked with wounds. All the strong warriors were severely wounded and beheaded quickly, especially a pair of fine heroes, namely Mál and Midna, he made a withe of vengeance for the game and attached Cú Chulainn's head to it, and said: 'It was not right of ye to be boasting with the head of my friend.'

'Take, O Cenn Berraide,' said Conall, 'the head of Cú Chulainn, so that it may be with Emer.' 'I will take it,' said Cenn Berraide, 'and rather than killing one hundred men of Ireland every day and every night, I would prefer to bury the head than take part in destruction.' It is then that Cenn Berraide rose [and took the head] towards Dún Delca, and took Emer's hand [and presented the cleaned] head to her, and placed it on the body [and took Emer to it], and afterwards the druids placed it in front of her breast, and there was lamenting and grieving over its head, and they sucked his lips and drank his blood, and placed a satin veil over him. ['Alas! Alas!'] said the young woman, 'his noble head looks very fine as it is today. And it is many the daughters of kings and leaders of the world would be paying tribute if they should know about this. Regardless of the wealth and pleadings of the gold-diggers of Ireland and Scotland, you are the first choice and the first love of the men of the world. And it is a pity for me to be here today after you, for there was not a woman, with or without a man, from Ireland or Scotland, or the whole world, who was not envious before your strength. For there are treasures and jewels, taxes and tributes from the ends of the Earth coming to me, telling of the power and courage of Cú Chulainn.' She vows, his hand in her hand, and, vowing, she cuts his flesh and says it aloud: 'Alas then,' said Emer, 'it is great the slaughter of kings and chiefs and strong men that met their death on the battlefield in a terrifying way from swift blows by your hands, great is the number of birds and frenzied animals that fell by you, and great is the number of treasures and riches that were bestowed on him by poets and learned men of the world.'

Emer was conversing after this and said: 'Long has it been shown to me by dreams in the night that Cú Chulainn would fall by the men of Ireland, and it was shown to me on the wall of Dún Delca that he would fall down, and that his shield would be shattered from blows to its edge, and as his sword would be broken, so would his lance, right at its exact centre, and Conchobar was shown being killed in my presence, and myself and you being beheaded. The reason I saw those dreams was that they were from the druids of Ireland, and the cry of prophecy was that I will come to the poisonous weapons of the Clan Cailitín and fall by Lugaid mac Con Rí.'

'And, O Laeg,' said Emer, 'for were we on one way, and beautiful though it be, and were we to search the whole world from sunrise to sunset, we would never find anyone like you, O Laeg, and Culann, servant of the Iubraighe and the Liath Macha and the Dub Sainglend, and me and Cú Chulainn. And it is sad for me still and Lugaid of the Red Stripes. Without a man to wage battle, to race horses or to check rivalry and warfare, after the departure of our beloved foster-father, and it is sad for me to be breaking my heart close to his breast, listening to the sincere cries of men and women lamenting the champion in piercing screams, and the young Ulster warriors wailing Cú Chulainn, and the rest of the Ulaid laid low with the *cess* and without the strength to take revenge against the men of Ireland.'

This is what the tired and mournful Laeg and Emer were saying: 'It is sad to be separated from each other now, for we were part of a gentle company of strength and all from one place.' 'That was true,' said Laeg, ' and his servants will never find another person to equal my own chief.' 'Woe is me,' said Emer, 'and Laeg,' said she, 'did Cú Chulainn not leave a message with you for me, or did he not give instructions to his chief?' 'He did not,' said Laeg, 'but he commanded that you never go with a man unless it is an Ulster man.' 'I will do that,' said Emer, 'since there will not be a man of all the men in the world after Cú Chulainn.' After that Emer said, 'I will not go anywhere until Conall comes to me.' 'Neither I nor any-one else is in agreement about these tidings,' said Laeg, and they sighed and lamented about Cú Chulainn, and for fear of Conall they did not bury him until he arrived.

As regards Conall: after [beheading] Mál and Midna he said: 'Say to Erc mac Cairbre to come out and address me, and if he comes I swear by my honour that when I reach him there is not a sufficient number to save him from me.'

This was told to Erc, and he arose at hearing it, and seized his arms and his armour, and, seeking Conall, came out of the fort, and three warrior champions in battle dress came with him. 'Well now, Erc,' said Conall, 'pleasant and easy it is since the killing of Cú Chulainn.' 'Stop playing with words,' said Erc, 'for I will not pay a blood fine nor an honour price to you, but will strike before crush-ing and wound before killing.' 'Alas then,' said Conall, 'we will nei-ther take gold nor treasures of the world from you as a blood fine, but rather your own head, and place it among all the other heads,' and he spoke a poem and stayed put.

It is then that they approached each other, Erc with his three champions and Conall on his own, that is Conall the princely war-rior of Ireland and a well-travelled man who has journeyed the world, who feels neither fear nor terror before the multitude, whether on land or sea, whether by day or night; and they threw a hard, swift shower of strong missiles all at once at Conall. And he made a wheel of venomous course from blades and sent it before the wind, so that it came furiously and mercilessly into the exact centre of the enemy. And it hammered them with strong blows, eagerly, constantly and fiercely, with the strength of a strong man, so that the sides of the warriors were badly cut. Thus it was that warriors were half-torn, and were wounded and cut up from the blows of the wild hands; horror and fear and terror seized the warriors of Erc, from the slaughter of the reckless Conall, so that they burst forth and escaped as fast as they could, without memory, without sense, without waging battle, from that place where they were, namely, the plain of strength that was Tara, so that Erc was left on his own lamenting. Conall thrust his eager, strong and unrelenting spear, the Cúlchlas with its sharp head and broad shaft the height of eight men, into the breast of Erc, so that the rivets on the head of the spear were cast through the exact middle and rapidly broke the back of Erc at its exact centre, and brought strong blows with his heavy sword across his sides causing his end, so that between his shield and his sword he made fragments of his body and his battle armour. He then cut his head off and attached it to a withe.

'It is good for me,' said Conall, 'to have that head on a twisted twig in vengeance for the head of Cú Chulainn.' And he sent the head to Tara, and after that he came to avenge their defeat, and he began killing and annihilating the people of Erc; so that a hundred heroes fell in the company of the doorkeepers of Tara. Muiredach mac Fergus, chief of the household of Erc and upholder of the people of Tara, came to avenge Erc on Conall, and Muiredach summoned Conall to combat, and left one hundred warriors at each door by the doorkeepers of Tara. A troop of champions came with him to answer the call to combat with Conall.

Conall the battle warrior approached in splendour to this combat and he seized his fighting spear of great prowess, of eager, vigorous blows, of deep dense deeds; the first warrior falls in the company of Muiredach, defeated by Conall, and in a running burst and with great speed he [Muiredach] approached the people, and as he reached the second door of the doormen of Tara, he recognized Conall coming and he challenged him to combat, and shamed him with great words of rebuke. When Conall heard the loud voice of Muiredach, he leapt impetuously, like a terrible, very sharp and reckless wave, approaching Muiredach in a wild and furious manner, and he brought an additional powerful force to his battle stroke, coupled with an excessively vigorous crushing blow, so that the first warrior falls there by Conall in the fort. Muiredach went away from him and approached the third door of Tara, and as he reached there he was at once challenged, and battle-victorious Conall approaches, and takes a deadly impetuous attack to the enemy, destroying them with a great battering, so that a troop falls by him completely rendered and hacked at that spot. And Muiredach approached with noisy haste towards the fourth door. By then a troop has fallen by each door of the doorkeepers of Tara before Conall, and Muiredach mac Fergus is beheaded in the centre of the hall at Tara after that strong attack, and after that his head is placed on a withe.

'It is good for me, O Muiredach,' said Conall, 'to place your head on this withe for the sake of inciting and challenging, and we will burn the hereditary homestead of Erc, and above it Tara, the sovereign centre of Ireland; that I will not burn.' And he said a lay and stayed put.

After that Conall came from Tara, boasting of great deeds, of the fall of battalions of champions at Tara by him, and he found out that Colla mac Faithemain had come to find Lugaid mac Con Rí, who was keeping watch on Conall, and they met each other, and they fought in a wild, furious and impetuous way, in a swift, fierce and raging manner, hacking and mangling, dragging and striking together without reserve, and Conall struck a poisonous, hateful, very strong blow at Colla in that conflict, so that it cut his head off, and he placed it on the same withe. 'Upon my word,' said Conall, 'it is good for me to have mac Faithemain reduced to dissected fragments and in layers of gore about the rushes, and for me to be carrying his head.' And he spoke a lay and remained where he was.

Then Conall came to Fiodh Rocaime, and he saw great smoke coming from the side of the neighbouring wood. 'It is true then,' said Conall, 'that there are a number of the men of Ireland there, and there are some Ulster cattle and hostages there as well.' Conall came towards the fire and the clan Calitín was there. And as he saw the horrible witches, he recognized that it was his hereditary foes who were there, namely the clan Calitín, and he said: 'I give thanks to the gods whom I worship, that I may make judgement against you,' said Conall, 'and never in my travels by sea or by land has such a windfall of wealth been placed before me or them. Even though the men of Ireland fall by me, to take the clan Calitín alone is my greatest wish in my journey through Ireland in vengeance for Cú Chulainn, and how welcome it is to come here and to take away these hateful heads towards Emain, and great is the welcome that the womenfolk as well as the women of the assembly will have, as well as the good people and the great nobles of Ulster, when they see these guests.'

It is then that Conall swiftly and furiously approached the fire, and grabbed and exhorted his spear, and relentlessly started to strike about; then the one-legged sorceresses and aerial phantoms rose and began thrashing about, together with one-handed phantoms, and they began a deadly wounding and smiting with warrior blows on the hero Conall, but when he found his confidence from their spells and devil-craft his warrior vigour returned with great power, and he started wounding, and furiously delivered his warrior blows, yet he did not release the wretchedly brave and wounded witches, so that they fell from fierce blows of lasting strength there, and he cut their six heads from them and put them on a withe.

Conall came then in good spirits after the glorious triumph, and boasting of his victory over the clan Calitín, and he came to the plain of Argetros, and Glais Chruinn, and said that he would be at Glais Chró on the same day, and as he was there he saw the battle preparations and the helmet buckles of the night watch in front of him. And there was Connla, the foster-brother of Lugaid mac Con Rí, and the household of Lugaid close by. Then the warriors and the triumphant warlike champions approached in great numbers, they fought each other with reckless slaughter, triumphantly cutting bones and hacking the bodies of each other. And they fought continuously, shooting and embedding their swift arrows and, with great skill, their sharp-edged spears towards Conall, and there was no fear nor weakness from the wounds, nor from the blows, nor from the fierce throws of the foot soldiers, but killing and performing great deeds holds sway among the fighting cries and the continual fighting of the troops, until one man comes out to them, and they do not know whether he has come to defeat them or to bring ignominy to them.

A thousand fell on the banks of the ford here and there, and Conall and Connla fought off and on. They fought by striking and wounding each other, by shield and by head and by helmet. Connla fell in the ordinary way from hard blows by Conall, and after that Conall cut his head off and after that he put it on a twisted twig, and he looked at the field of dead bodies and the dripping bare necks from the battle, and the opened bodies emitting blood, and the stream-pools of red blood flowing swiftly into the glen, so that there were clots of gore and very red blood flowing into the cold, clean sandy stream. 'The victorious stream of violent death, [Budh Glais Chró] will be the name of this glen for ever after these deeds,' said Conall.

Conall came then to the Plain of Argetros. It was there that Lugaid was making arrangements. With neither flight nor avoidance

Conall approached them at once, ready for battle; as white-bodied, hard Cliodna of the waves hurls fish throughout the land, so Conall swiftly killed and quickly shattered the Clan Dedad around him. They fell by him, arm against arm, elbow against elbow and host against host, so that he left pools of blood after him.

Then Conall and Lugaid came together for combat. 'Well, Conall,' said Lugaid, 'we are not equal, you have two hands and I have one. Tie your right hand in front of you.' Conall tied his right hand. Then they seized their broad-grooved, hard and sharp swords together, and Lugaid struck Conall, and cut and sliced open the tie and the fetters, so that both hands were immediately free. 'O beautiful, triumphant, battle-victorious Conall,' said Lugaid, 'tie your hand as promised, so that it is completely bound.' 'You cannot make me do it this time,' said Conall, 'for when I was bound by fetters, I regretted it, and the hand that is untied is good for swift strikes, so I will not tie it now.'

They waged battle and fought fiercely together, remembering each grudge and hatred, until Lugaid fell by a hard blow from Conall, 'the battle-triumphant' Cernach. Then Conall beheaded him. Then fondness for his foster-child arose in Conall and he said: 'If you had not beheaded Cú Chulainn I would be very reluctant to defeat and behead you,' said he, since he was the son of the third of the following fathers, namely Conall, Cú Chulainn and Cu Ri mac Daire.

After that Gabhál Glinde fought, and Gabhál fell from a swift struggle with Conall, and he was quickly beheaded. Glas mac Dedad fell by Conall then, and fifty of the colourful, dexterous Clan Dedad fell by him on that expedition and journey, and all the heads were put about a twisted twig. Anyhow the withe was full of the heads of kings and lords and people of the men of Ireland. He put a knot under them and left on the same path before they were found, so that he reached Dún Delca 'right to the sun', where the body of Cú Chulainn was. He left the heads on the ground and put them then on the sharp stakes of Bodb around the blossoming green. And he let out a great cry on seeing the warrior's heads on the long stakes. Emer arose then. 'May the body of the battle warrior be buried now,' said Emer, 'and tell me to which nobles of Ireland were these heads that I see on the sharp stakes of Bodb.' And she composed a poem then, Emer's lament for Cú Chulainn, and after that Conall answered her. After they both recited their lays Emer requested that Conall make a broad and extensive grave for Cú Chulainn, so that there would be room for herself, as is fitting for a lawful spouse. He raised a stone over the grave and wrote Cú Chulainn's name in ogam; then they played funeral games.

That is the death of Cú Chulainn as far as this.

Emer's lament for Cú Chulainn

At the same time as his [Cú Chulainn's] body was coming homewards from Muirthemne, his head was being received from Tara. Emer attached his head on his body and pressed her breasts against him. She seized his hand in her hand and pressed her mouth against his and said the lay.

> O hand, O disfigured hand
> whilst we were healthy
> often was it placed under my head
> O sweet to my neck this hand.
>
> O head, O disfigured head
> since you crossed the water
> many the times I have soothed
> many the beatings this head has taken.
>
> O eye, O blemished eye
> always spirited and loving
> identical will be our grave
> dug equal for both of us.
>
> O weapons, O weapons
> great the destruction you wrought
> never were you in any battle
> where you yielded to Badb.
>
> O grey (head), O grey (head)
> your master ever quick,
> long the arm that brought forth destruction
> alas now the head brings forth but spectres.
>
> O dark headed one
> I would not abandon your firm head,

CÚ CHULAINN

alas for the broken heart and shattered ribs,
the chieftain left to die on the plain.

I know where my heart is
O Cú Chulainn of the middle plain,
no longer will your face be blood-stained,
once I have washed your head.

Behold there a beloved mouth
ice-cold to the kiss, as is said of dead warriors,
alas for the smile that spread across your cheeks;
let not the void diminish your deeds.

O noble king
let none confute your valiant contest
over thirty days and nights
in front of my bosom and body.

O man, O blemished man
for a time, leader of the host of kings.
O beloved with the cold gold hair
and with the shining cheeks
the shield of Cú Chulainn together with his two spears
and his keen sword
give to Conall of the battles.
Never was a gift given such as this.
Beloved each blemish, beloved each,
on him who will not hear the sound of
the cuckoo, till Doomsday.
Until death comes to us all.

Oh for the summer days, or a tree
By a stream
Today I will not lift my head.
There will be no rejoicing, only sorrow,
Och, O hand.

That is the death of Cú Chulainn as far as this.

Glossary of Placenames

Ailbine river: known now as the Delvin River, which today forms the northern boundary of Co. Dublin, and flows into the sea by Gormanstown castle north of Balbriggan. It marks a boundary of Fine Gall, now Fingal.

Airbe Rofir: in Conaille Muirthemne, Co. Louth.

Alba: Scotland.

Amrún Fer nDeá: possibly older name for Grellach Dollaid.

Argetros: 'silverwood', an area of land in the parish of Rathbeagh, barony of Galmoy, Co. Kilkenny.

Áth Alad:; 'the ford of the piebald' on Muirthemne, Co. Meath.

Áth Fhir Diad: 'the ford of Fer Diad', now Ardee. The ford on the river Dee at Ardee, Co. Meath. The site of the single combat between Fer Diad and Cú Chulainn.

Áth Muilt: 'the ford of inciting?', also known as Áth Fhir Diad, Ardee, Co. Meath.

Áth na Foraire: on or at Sliab Fúait, presumably on a height with a good view south!

Áth n-Imfóit: on the Boyne. Possible meaning is the 'ford crossed by sods'.

Baile in Bile: 'townland of the sacred tree', but where and which tree? Was it the great yew (an tIuir) at Newry, a locality and tree familiar to Cú Chulainn.

Belach mBairdine: the Pass of Bairdine, possibly in the vicinity of Emain Macha.

Ben Gulban Gurt meic Ungarb: in Ulster.

Benn Súan: the hill of Sleep?

Berna Éle: in the territory of Ely O' Carroll, i.e. the baronies of

Clonlisk and Ballybrit in Laois, and the baronies of Ikerrin and Eliogarty in Co. Tipperary.

Bile Búada: 'tree of power'. Although there were many such trees, the great ash at Uisneach being the most notable example, the Bile referred to here was on the Plain of Lúada south of Emain Macha. The Bile Búadas were sacred trees, and often represented the centre of a tribal territory and/or an inauguration site of kings.

Black Country: between Castleblaney and the Fews Mountains.

Blackwater river: on the borders of Leitrim and Sligo.

Braine: 'projecting or prominent landscape'. On the way from Brega to Ardee.

Brí Errgi: probably in Co. Down (Hogan onom.)

Bruiden Dá Derga: 'the hostel of the two Reds'. Morris (JRSAI 65 1935) suggests that it is close to Lough Bray west of Glencree. The Dublin area known as Bohernabreena was, according to Morris, the 'road to the bruiden of Dá Derga'.

Brú of Mac Ind Oc or *Brú na Bóinne*: in the Boyne Valley, Co. Meath.

Carnmag: Moycarne, near Lough Erne, Co. Fermanagh (?).

Cathair Osrin: between Dún Dá Bend to the north and Lí Thúga to the south (Hogan onom.)

Cerma: Is this Cerna a notable burial place in Pagan and Christian times 'which lay in a straight line between Slane in Meath and Lusk in Dublin'? (Hogan.) A hill in Meath in the barony of Skreen.

Cerna: a hill in Meath which according to the Dinnsenchus was a 'place of noble sepulture in pagan and Christian times'. It lay on a straight line between Slane in Meath and Lusk in Dublin. The name is probably preserved in the townlands of Carnes East and West in the parish of Duleek, Co. Meath. Hogan (onom.) cites Cerna with Kelcarne castle and Kilcarne in the barony of Skreen. This Cerna is a townland and parish three miles south-south-west of Navan and five miles north of Tara. Here there are Templecarne and Kilcarne bridges over the Boyne.

Claithar Cell: across the Brosna and Little Brosna rivers of the Slieve Bloom and close to the Devil's Bit Mountain, Co. Offaly.

Cleitech: south of the Boyne near the Bridge of Slane.

Clíu Máil meic Ugaire: 'the territory of Mael mac Ugaire', between Knockainey and Slieve Reagh in Limerick.

Cnogba: Knowth on north of the Boyne river, three miles northeast from Slane, Co. Meath.

Conaille Muirthemne: a territory south and southwest of Dundalk.

Cooley: Cuailnge, the Cooley mountains near Carlingford, Co. Louth.

Crích na Dési Bice: 'the region of the Deasys (Bec)', this territory is south of the Shannon and in east Limerick including Tara Luachra, Knockainey and part of the Galtee mountains.

Crích Ross: embraced part of the barony of Farney, Co. Monaghan and some of Meath and Louth (O' Donovan). Here possibly in Brega south of Telltown. Ráth Cathbad and the river Conchobar were in it.

Crích Saithi: 'territory of the Saithi' extending from the Boyne to Dundalk, from Lough Neagh to the foot of the Mournes.

Crích Uatne: territory of Uaithne Uí Iffernan, on the east side of the river Shannon in the barony of Owney (?) Hogan.

Crogha: knoll on the north side of the Boyne.

Cruachain: see Mag Aí.

Cruachán Aigli: Croagh Patrick Mountain in Mayo.

Crúfóit: from fót cró, 'sod of gore'. According to Hogan, probably Croboy in the barony of Upper Moyfenrath, Co. Meath. Between the river Delvin and the river Boyne.

Cruinnloch: Cronnloch, north east of Glen Mór (which see below).

Cú Chulainn's pillar stone: situated at Knockbridge, two miles west of Dundalk. This stone still stands and is locally known as 'Cloch an Fhir Mhóir', the stone of the big man. It is here that tradition has it Cú Chulainn died. The stone is 2.9 metres in height.

Droichet na nDaltaí: 'The Bridge of the Pupils' on the Isle of Skye, Scotland. See Watson.

Drommanna Breg: in the south-east of Ulster, a boundary of the diocese of Armagh.

Drowes River: which flows from Lough Melvin into Donegal Bay.

Druim Collchaill = Áine Clíach: Knockainey, Co. Limerick.

Druim na Mármuice: 'the ridge of the great pig' is said to be Drom Beg, the hilly country in south county Louth.

Dubid: Dowth on the Boyne, Co. Meath.

Dún Dá Bend: 'the fort of the two hills'. Mount Sandel Coleraine, Co. Derry.

Dún Dá Lethglas: north of DownPatrick, Co. Down, stands a Motte and Bailey, just east of the Quoile river. To the north of this is a rath, which may explain the use of Dá in the name. Whether one or either of these settlements was the home of Celtchair mac Uthidir is open to question.

Dún Delca: 'the fort of the pin', Dundalk. The present 'Dun Dealgan' is the Castletown Motte and Bailey. It has a grand view of the surrounding countryside including the Cooley Mountains, Slieve Gullion and the Fews. A souterrain is set into the south side of the mound.

Dún Imrith: 'the fort of the run round or course' in Mag Conaille, Co. Louth. One of Cú Chulainn's two forts the other being at Dún Delca.

Dún Inbir: unknown.

Dún mac Nechtain Scéne: in Mag Breg.

Dún Rígain: unknown but between the mouth of the Bann and six-mile water river, which flows into Antrim town and finally into Lough Neagh.

Dún Scáthach: on the Isle of Skye in the south end of the Island.

Elg: a name for Ireland.

Emain Macha: ancient capital of Ulster under the kingship of Conchobar mac Nessa, where Cú Chulainn trained to be a warrior. It is two miles west of Armagh city, now known as Navan Fort.

Fedan Chuailnge: the streams of Cooley, Co. Louth.

Findcharn: or Finncharn, the white cairn on top of the Mournes, also known as Finncharn na.

Foraire: or 'the white cairn of the watcher'. From here one could see as far as the plain of Meath.

Finncora: Corofin or between Corofin and Slieve Callan, Co. Clare.

Fiodh Rocáime: 'Rocam's wood'? Possibly a wood in Leinster. If so it may be Fiodh Frosmuine.

Gáireach: 'Gary a townland in Castletown? Parish in the barony of Moycashel, about 5 miles east of Clare'. C.O'Rahilly. TBC Stowe Version

Glais Chró: 'stream of gore' close to Lough Neagh, or is now covered by Lough Neagh. Hogan.

Glais Chruinn: 'circular stream' between Conaille and Cuailnge that flows between southwest and northeast of Dundalk town.

Glen Eóin: east of Athlone, Co Westmeath.

Glen Mór: north east of Glen Eóin, east of Athlone.

Glenn Mór: also known as Glenn mbolgáin, both near Ardee, Co. Meath.

Glenn na Márdaim: 'the glen of the Ox' it is synonymous with Glen Brega and Mag Breg or the plain of Brega. It is said that there was an effigy to this ox on the plain of Brega and that it was taken charge of by the women of Brega.

Glenn na mbodur: 'the valley of the deaf', near Emain Macha, Co Armagh.

Glond Áth: Glondath, 'the ford of the dead', on the Delvin river.

Gort na Mórrígáin: the field of the Mórrígan, near Dunleer, Co. Louth.

Grellach Dollaid: Girley, near Kells Co. Meath as suggested by Hogan (onom.) The Fews also mentioned by him as well as Lower Iveagh, Co. Down.

Ibor Cind Trachta: 'The yew wood at the head of the strand', Newry, Co. Down.

Invermór: on the Cooley side of Dundalk Bay, Co. Louth.

AnIrluachair: range of mountains stretching from Killarney in Co. Kerry to Millstreet in Co. Cork.

'Land of Curoi Mac Daire': associated particularly with Caherconree, Slieve Mish, Co. Kerry, between Dingle Bay and Tralee Bay.

Lind Lumnig: 'the pool of Limerick', the Lower Shannon from Limerick to the sea.

Lí Thúga: 'perhaps the abode of the Fir Lí, west of the Bann'. (Hogan onom.) Li is the Irish for the river Bann. The Bann flows out of the Atlantic Ocean from west of Portstewart into Lough Neagh, and the mouth of the Bann was known as Túaginber.

Lochán in Tonaigh: 'the pool of the wasting', according to local tradition there was a pool in this field at Knockbridge where Cú Chulainn's standing stone is. Knockbridge is two miles west of Dundalk, Co. Louth.

Loch Cuan: Strangford Lough, Co. Down.

Loch Gur: Co. Limerick.

Loch Ectra: between the Mournes and the Fews.

Loch Linnhe: which flows between Lismore Isle and Morvern in Western Scotland.

Loch Luatha = Cruinnloch: 'a day's march from Telltown'. Hogan.

Luglochta Logo: the gardens of Lug. Possibly present day

Drumanagh near Rush and south of Loughshinny. It is a promontory fortress with an entrance of three ramparts. It would be an ideal 'playing field'.

Machaire Conaill: the meadow of Conall, between Slieve Breg and Dundalk, i.e. between Monasterboice and Dún Delca.

Machaire Mór na mMuman: 'the great plain of Munster' extending from the river Owenogoffy, near Nenagh, to the Galtee Mountains. (Hogan onom.)

Mag Aí: 'plain of the sheep', a large plain about Tulsk Co. Roscommon known also as Cruachain Aí and Cruachain Connacht (the ancient royal centre of Connacht).

Mag Alchuing: in Ulster. (Hogan onom.)

Mag Brega: the Plain which includes the east of Co. Meath and the north of Co. Dublin. 'The Plain between the Liffey and the Boyne.' (C. O'Rahilly.)

Mag Eogan Inbir: unknown.

Mag Fidga: a plain inhabited by the Aes Sidhe.

Mag Finn: 'Keogh's country or the Bredagh, parish of Taghmaconnell, barony of Athlone, Co. Roscommon.' Hogan.

Mag in Scáil: 'plain of the scattering'. Medb was from here.

Mag Lúada: between the Bile Búada and Emain Macha.

Mag Macha: 'the plain of Macha', known as the Moy, near Armagh city, the parish of Moy lies on both sides of the Blackwater river and includes the town of Moy in Co. Tyrone. See Keating, *History of Ireland*, vol iv.

Mag Muirthemne: Cú Chulainn's territory extending form Dún Delca, Co. Louth to the Fews, Co. Armagh.

Mag Tetrai: the Plain of Tethra, the king of the Fomorians. In Brega.

Mag Tuiread: 'plain of weeping'. Two primordial battles of Irish mythology were fought here. Places associated with these battles include Cong, Co. Mayo, and Moytura east and west, Co. Sligo. Moytura is also a village on the shores of Lough Arrow, Co. Sligo.

Maigue river: flowing through Co. Limerick to the Lower Shannon.

Máirimdill: the ancient midden heap at the back of Telltown, Co. Meath.

Mannchile, later Muincille: the storehouse of Mannach, the hospitaller. Possibly North-east Co. Dublin or East Brega in Meath.

Muir Miss: the sea at Tralee Bay (?) Co. Kerry, north of Slieve Mish.

Nenagh river: river of the grandson of Cathbad, Co. Tipperary.

Ochaine: Trumpet Hill in Conaille Muirthemne. East from Dundalk and facing the sea from the north.

Óenach Senchlocair: 'the assembly at the old stony place' between Lough Gur and Tara Luachra. Probably Monasteranenagh, near Croom, Co. Limerick, 'one of the chief burial grounds in Ireland before Christianity' (Hogan onom.)

Oircel: (a trough!) between the Fews and Slieve Gullion.

Ollarba: the Larne water flowing into Larne Lough.

Port Nóth of Cú Chulainn: the landing place of the boats of Cú Chulainn, at Dundalk Harbour.

Ráth Celtchair= Dún Dá Lethglas.

Ráth Imil: bBy Dundrum Bay, Co. Down, or perhaps in the Mournes close to the source of the Bann river. This (perhaps) is where Lóegaire Búadach's fort was.

Rathmooney: near Lusk, Co. Dublin, the fort of Fergal Manach, father of Emer (who was Cú Chulainn wife).

Ráth Soilech: 'The earthen fort of the willows', an old name for Armagh city.

Ros na Ríg: modern parish is called Rosnaree. It is situated on the Boyne, two miles south east of Slane, Co. Meath.

Scenmenn Monach: Scenmenn Manach (Stowe) – between the river Delvin and the river Boyne.

Seanmag Léna: 'the old Plain of Léna'. 'Léna was killed and buried there' (Hogan onom.) On the Plain of Mag Léna, Co. Offaly, with Moylena village on it. It is close to Durrow, Co. Offaly.

Senáth: close to Athlone, Co. Westmeath, possibly Mag Derg which is east of Athlone.

Síd Truim: 'Síd Truim was the ancient name for Cashel. 'There is a townland of Sheetrim in Co. Armagh, and the name also refers to a hill east of Slane, Co. Meath.' (Myles Dillon, notes to Serglige Con Culainn.)

Slemna Maige Ítha: 'the smooth plain of Íth', near Raphoe, Co Donegal, where Íth, uncle of Míl and ancestor of the Milesians, died.

Sliab Cáin: now Slieve Reagh on the borders of Counties Limerick and Cork.

Sliab Edlicon, also known as Sliab Bladma (Hogan): which is Slieve Bloom in Offaly.

Sliab Fúait: a mountainous range known as the Fews, close to

Newtown, Hamilton, Co. Armagh. Sliab Fúait is also named as the highest mountain in the Fews. Cú Chulainn would have travelled this road many times between Dún Delca and Emain Macha.

Slige Midlúachra: the great road from Tara to Emain passing through Drogheda, Dundalk and from Dundalk along the R177 which becomes the A29 in Armagh. Once one crosses the border it is less than four miles to the Dorsey (the gate into Ulster) at Drummill Bridge, from here one crosses the Dorsey River, towards Newtown-Hamilton and over the Fews towards Armagh City. Emain is two miles west of Armagh City.

Slieve Felim Mountains: East of Limerick City, Co. Limerick.

Smarmore: south of Ardee, Co. Meath, where warriors were treated during battles; 'the marrow fields of the women of the Prophetess Fedelm'.

Tara: 'any high place' originally called Temain Breg. Tara is in Co. Meath, five miles south of Navan. It was the chief inauguration site of the kings of Meath and of Ireland.

Tara Luachra: 'Fort of the Rushes or Marshes' and residence of the Curoi mac Daire of the Clann Dedad, burial place for the kings of Kerry. Close to Castle-Island, which was formerly Oilean Ciarrai, exact location is doubtful. The plain surrounded by mountains with the Shanowen River running through its centre beside Castle Island may be its location. Again a small stream near Dysart, close to Castle Island, is said to be the site of a ford (Beal Átha na Teamhrach) leading to it. An ancient road is said to have gone from here to Taur Hill over the Cork border. Finally, the topographical name would fit in with this area.

Tech Mid-chúrta: the so-called Banqueting Hall at Tara, though this is disputed now and the area consisting of the above is more likely to have been a circus for horses or a stretch for annual sporting activities during the Feis at Tara.

Téite Brecc: 'the speckled house', this is the house at Emain Macha in which weapons were stored.

Telltown: the Tailten games and fair were held here in August. Telltown is in Co. Meath beside the river Blackwater and near Donaghpatrick, four miles northwest of Navan.

Temair na hArda: Tara of the Ards Peninsula, Co. Down, i.e. Tara Fort, a hilltop fortress overlooking Millin Bay, royal residence of the Uí Echach or HorseKeepers, known as the Uí Echach Arda, while Tara Fort was known as Ard Ulaid. It is situated east of Strangford Lough.

Termag Trogaigi: a haunt for the Aes Sídhe.

Tethbe: Teffia in Co. Westmeath. This territory known as the foxs' country includes the town of Granard. It extended as far south as Durrow in Offaly and also comprised part of Longford.

Trácht Éise: 'the strand of the track'. Is this the same as Baile Strand near Seatown east of Dundalk? It would seem to be from talking to local historians not to mention Lady Gregory's version of the Death of Aífe's One Son, where she refers to it as 'Baile's Strand'.

Tráig Baile: 'Baile Strand', situated on Dundalk Bay near Seatown. See Trácht Éise.

Tráig Tola: 'indented coastline' possibly east of Tara Fort on the Ards Peninsula to the south of Millin Hill, Co. Down. But mention is also made of associations of Conchobar mac Nessa with Mag Inis or Lecale, if so Tráig Tola may be close to Benderg Bay and Killard point, which would fit in with 'indented coastline'. Killard Point is at the south east of The Narrows, which form the entrance to Strangford Lough.

Tyrrhenian Sea: sea enclosed by Corsica, Italy, Sicily and Sardinia.

Uanúb (white foam river): The river, which joins the Dee, a couple of miles north of Dunleer, Co. Louth.

Uisnech Mide: west of Mullingar, Co. Westmeath, known as the Hill of Uisneach, this was the ancient centre of Ireland and a place for druidic assembly. It was also known as Cnoc Úachtair Erca, 'the hill of the high heavens' and Cnoc Úachtair Fhorcha, 'the hill of the foremost fires'.

Glossary of Persons, Peoples, Gods and Goddesses

Aed, Aed and Fingin: the three horn blowers of the craeb ruad.

Aed Abrat: 'fire of the crow', a fairy prince or chief from the Isle of Man.

Aífe: a warrior princess from the Western Isles of Scotland, against whom Cú Chulainn fought. However, eventually they became close and had a son whose name was Conlaí.

Aílill mac Máta: king of Connacht, and generally referred to as simply Ailella. As king he takes a subordinate role to his wife, queen Medb. His name: Ailill has been compared to the Welsh ellyll, 'an elf or demon', and his surname may mean a monster or a pig.

Amergin: the seer of the sons of Míl who came from Galicia in Spain. He fought the legendary Tuatha Dé Danann at Telltown, Co. Meath. He is said to have built the causeway at Avoca, Co. Wicklow. His name has been defined as meaning 'wonderful birth' or 'wonderful child'.

Atharne, Drec and Drobél: three druids of the craeb ruad.

Bass mac Omnaig: a suitor who sought Emer's hand.

Bel: may well be similar to Balor or Balar mac Doit, a mythical god of the Fomorians who was slain by Lug mac Ethlean. He was a sun god and is alluded to by his single or later 'evil eye'.

Be Néid: the wife of Néid or Néit, the god of battle.

Blaí Briugu: the hospitaller. He was the hospitaller to the king whom he had to entertain for a certain time each year. He was also entrusted with providing food and medicines during contests and wars. His full name is Blaí or Blad Briuga mac Fiachna.

Boand: from bó finn meaning white cow, Boand is often referred to as the white cow goddess. Bovinda is the name Ptolemy gave her, and her original name may have been Bou-vinda. She was the wife of both Nechtan mac Labraid and the god Nuadu, she also lived with the Irish Zeus, namely the Dagda. The river Boyne is called after her, as she followed it back to its source and was submerged in it, thus becoming the divinised river. Bruig na Bóinne, the Boyne Valley region which includes Newgrange, Knowth and Dowth, is called after her.

Bodb: the son of the Dagda, commonly referred to as Bodb Derg. He is lord of Bruig na Bóinne, the Boyne Valley mounds. He is associated with Síd ar Femen, the modern Slievenamon in Co. Tipperary. He is also the reputed owner of supernatural pigs, which reappear as soon as they are eaten.

Bolcán: a smith who made arms for the Clan Cailitín.

Brea mac Belgain: a chief from southeast Ulster.

Breoga: father of Ith from Galicia who came to Ireland. Breoga or Breogan is still a noted ancestor god in Galicia, in north west Spain, today. He was the ancestor of the sons of Míl, the progenitor of the Gaels.

Bresal Bric: 'Bresal the Speckled' was son of Fiachra Fobic of Leinster. A king who was in the (14th generation) from Cathaer Mór king of Leinster. He is an ancestor of the Osraige and of the Leinstermen.

Bricriu: the satirist of the Craeb Ruad, whose fort was at Dundrum Co. Down. He was similar to Conan Maol the satirist of the Fenian sagas. A noteworthy phrase of his is: 'clearer to me a whisper than to anybody else a shout'. He was trampled to death whilst acting as umpire between the Donn bull of Cooley and the white-horned bull of Cruachain Connacht.

Brigit: one of a triad of goddesses all called Brigit. Goddess of the arts, and a mother goddess, associated with the triskele and 'Brigit's Cross'. St. Brigit, as abbess and foundress of the monastery of Kildare, carried on many of the customs associated with the pre-Christian Brigit.

Cacht, Maine, Crimtan, Bres, Nár and Lóthar: members of the craeb ruad.

Cailitín: chief of the Clan Calitín. He together with twenty-seven sons were felled by Cú Chulainn. His three sons and three daughters, with Medb's help, vowed to avenge their father's death.

Cairbre Nia Fer: king of Leinster and credited with being of Gaelic stock.

Cairbre Niad fer mac Rois: king of Tara and of Leinster. He permitted the Picts (the Cruithin) to settle around Tara in Brega. He eventually expelled them from here so they moved west to Connacht and to the Aran Islands. O' Rahilly states that they were not the Picts but rather the Fir Bolg. He is said to be an ancestor of St. Brigit of Kildare.

Cathbad: famous druid at the court of Conchobar mac Nessa. According to early accounts he was the real father of Conchobar mac Nessa. He foretold a child's future by placing his palms on its mother's womb. He had a druidic school at Emain Macha, and his own son Genann was also a druid.

Celtchar mac Uithechair: a member of the Craeb Ruad or Red Branch Knights of Ulster. Dún Celtchair, a large fort near Downpatrick, Co. Down, is named after him. He was famed for his spear, the Iuin Chelchair.

Cermait Milbél: (Cermait: 'honey mouth') a son of the Dagda and a noble youth of the Tuatha Dé Danann.

Cethirn mac Fáebarderg Fintain: Cethirn of the 'Red Sword Edge'. A member of the 'craeb ruad'.

Ciri, Biri and Blaicne: the three sons of Éis Énchind, three warriors of Aífe who fought the sons of Scáthach in Scotland.

Clanna Dedad: a race of people synonymous with the Érainn. A people of pre-Gaelic descent.

Cleitech: the keeper of a notable síd near the bridge of Slane, north of the Boyne. Here Cormac mac Airt was laid to rest after a salmon bone stuck in his throat. Although Cleitech is mentioned as a battle hero, his association is more with the 'house of Cleitech': an Otherworld resting place.

Cliodna: sea goddess associated with Glandore, west Cork.

Colla mac Faithemain: champion of Tara, beheaded by Conall Cernach in vengeance for the death of Cú Chulainn.

Conaing and Glaisne: members of the craeb ruad.

Conaire Mór: High king of Ireland, was killed at Bruiden Dá Derga. There was a seven- year interregnum after his death.

Conall Anglonnach mac Iriel Glúnmáir: an Ulster chief.

Conall Cernach: foster father of Cú Chulainn and leading member of the Craeb Ruad or Red Branch Knights. A collector of taxes from the Scottish kingdoms of the Western Isles of Scotland.

Conchobar mac Nessa: king of Ulster (Emain Macha), at Navan Fort two miles west of Armagh city. Possibly the natural father of Cú Chulainn. Died from the calcified brain ball of Mes Gegra which was thrown by Cet, a cattle raider. The name Conchobar is still current as Conor and in the surname O' Connor.

Condere mac Echach: an eloquent spokesman at the court of Conchobar mac Nessa. He attempted to reason with Conlaí, Cú Chulainn's son who had arrived by boat at Baile Strand, Dundalk Bay, Co. Louth.

Conlaí: son of Cú Chulainn and Aífe of Scotland. Was eventually killed by his father in combat at Baile Strand, Dundalk, Co. Louth.

Connla: foster brother of Lugaid mac Con Rí who was one of a party that had killed Cú Chulainn. He was beheaded by Conall Cernach.

Cormac Conn Loinges: a son of Conchobar mac Nessa. He saved his father's life when Fergus mac Roich went to kill him due to the king's treachery. On the night he was born the druid Cathbad laid the following taboos upon him: to be borne by horses yoked with an ashen yoke; to swim at one time with the birds of Loch Lo; to pass dryfoot over the Shannon. His name means 'head of the exiles', and he is said to have been an incestuous son of Conchobar mac Nessa. He was exiled when he sided with the aforementioned Fergus mac Roich.

Crimthann Nia Náir: a king of the Érainn for sixteen years. Associated in pre-history with Tara Lúachra, CastleIsland, Co. Kerry. A fortress of his Dún Crimthainn was said to have been situated at Howth, Co. Dublin.

Crom Deroil and Crom Darail: two pupils (not very bright!) of the great druid Cathbad.

Cruind mac Agnoman: Husband of Macha and the one who urged her to race against horses, which led to her death. Prior to dying she gave birth to twins (Emain Macha) and cursed Ulster.

Cú Roí mac Dáire: Cú Roí means 'hound king'. His fortress has been associated with Caher Conree, Co. Kerry. He was a king of Munster. He was beheaded by Cú Chulainn, who then eloped with his wife, Bláthnat.

Cúan and Cett: two sons of Scáthach, the warrior instructor from the Isle of Skye.

Cú Cuillesc: a satirist who was speared by Cú Chulainn after posing a number of questions to him.

Cúcán: pet or familiar name for Cú Chulainn.

Culann mac an Gabhann: the smith to Conchobar mac Nessa. He is generally simply referred to as Culann. Tradition states that he had his house on the slopes of Sliab Cúilenn (Slieve Gullion, Co. Armagh). Cú Chulainn (formerly Sétanta) received his name from Culann at this house. He was the armourer to the Red Branch Knights or the Craeb Ruad.

Conchobar mac Fachtna Fatháig: king of Ulster, more usually known as Conchobar mac Nessa. Fachtna Fatháig was his father and Ness was his mother.

Cumscraid of the great hosts: a member of the court of Conchobar mac Nessa.

Cúan, Ceth and Cruife: the three sons of Ilsúanaig and three warriors of Aífe of Scotland.

Cuscrad and Cormac: members of the retinue of Emain Macha at the time of Cú Chulainn and Emer.

Cúsraid Mend Macha mac Conchobar: son of Conchobar mac Nessa. Apparently he was so handsome that his appearance was enough to make women stammer.

The Dagda: lord of the Tuatha Dé Danann and chief god in the pantheon of Irish gods. Like Ajax, in death the Dagda recedes from power and fame. He is not a vengeful god.

Dam Dreman and Dam Dilenn: warriors from the Western Isles of Scotland killed in combat by Fer Diad.

Deichtine: daughter of Conchobar and mother of Cú Chulainn. A standing stone to her at Castletown just north-east of Dun Delca is known as Lia Lingadon.

Delbáeth mac Eithlend: a noble youth of the Tuatha Dé Danann.

Derbforgall Uí Rúad: daughter of Rúad, a king of Western Scotland. She fell in love with Cú Chulainn and followed him back to Ireland in bird shape. Cú Chulainn suggested that she take the hand of Lugaid Réo Derg as a companion. This she did.

Dési Beg: the present day Deasys. They occupied a part of Limerick at this time (c. first century A.D).

Domnall Míldemail: also Domnall Míldemon, Domnall the Warlike. Cú Chulainn went to him in Scotland to complete his military education.

Dornoll Olldornae: 'Dornoll of the large fists'. She was the daughter of Domnall Míldemail. She fell in love with Cú Chulainn.

Her love was not reciprocated and she vowed to avenge herself on him.

Dubthach Dóel Ulad: a noted warrior of the 'craeb ruad' or Red Branch Knights from Emain Macha, Co. Armagh.

Dubthach mac Lugtach: also known as Dubthach Doel Ulad or Dubthach the Dreaded from Ulster. After he died, his lands were flooded by Loch Neagh. He was a warrior of Emain Macha.

Éis Énchind: a warrior from the Western Isles of Scotland whom Cú Chulainn killed in combat. Known as Éis Birdhead.

Emer: the daughter of Fergal Manach from Lusk, Co. Dublin and the wife of Cú Chulainn. She is referred to as 'Emer, the beautiful one of the yellow hair'. In the Book of Leinster (LL123a,20) is the oldest version of Emer's lament for Cú Chulainn.

Enna Aignech Cerna: Enna the plunderer; Cerna = 'swollen' from a wound he received. He fought at the battle of Carmann (now Wexford) where he killed Aengus Ollmugaid, Aengus the Great Destroyer. He is associated with Rath Gríad (the fort of the champion) at Cerna in the parish of Duleek, Co. Meath.

Eochaid Íuil: a chief, real or imagined, from the Isle of Man.

Eochu Bairche: a warrior whom Cú Chulainn met on the Isle of Skye, he instructed him as how to act whilst in the house of Scáthach.

Éogan Inbir: a chief from pre-history, associated with the Isle of Man.

Erc mac Cairbre: foremost warrior and king of Leinster. His territory included Rathmooney and Drumanagh. He cut through the left leg of Cú Chulainn with a single spear cast.

Errgi Echbél: from Brí Errgi, Co. Down.

Ethne Aitencháitrech: 'an adult acquaintance', wife of Conchobar mac Nessa. In the Heldensage (Thurneysen) referred to as 'mit den Giuster-Schamhaaren'.

Ethne Inguba: wife of Cú Chulainn or simply an 'adult acquaintance'.

Fáenglinni mac Dedad: a warrior of the Clanna Dedad from West Munster.

Fáilbe Find: a companion of Labraid Lúathlám and king or chieftain from the Isle of Man.

Fedelm: also known as Fedelm Nói-cruthach, 'nine-shaped'. She was a prophetess to queen Medb of Connacht. In Irish she is known as a banfaith or seer and it is in this capacity that she answers Medb when Medb asks her to predict the outcome of the Táin. She replies: 'I see red, red, red'.

Fand: wife of Manannán mac Lir and daughter of Aed Abrat from the Isle of Man. She fell in love with Cú Chulainn and he with her.

Fandle mac Nechtan Scéne: the last of the three sons of Nechta who challenged Cú Chulainn when he set down in a fort in their territory.

The Féni: from singular Féne, a freeman.

Fer Bárth and Láirin and Drust mac Serb: Ulster warriors who were part of a tax- gathering band of Ulster warriors along the Western Isles of Scotland. These tax collectors were led by Conall Cernach and Lóegaire Búadach.

Fer Caille: a member of the Ulaid.

Fer Diad mac Damáin: a great Ulster warrior, who trained with Cú Chulainn on the Isle of Skye, where Cú Chulainn was his gillie. However his name suggests that he was one of the Domnainn of Connacht or of east Leinster. He is also known as Fer Diad Conganchnes or Fer Diad of the Horn Skin, the latter being part of his armour.

Ferceirtne: name of a poet or poets. Mentioned as poet in the company of Cú Chulainn, also as composer of a poem quoted in 'Orgain Denda Rig'.

Fergna mac Findchonna: hospitaller to the kingly court of the Ulaid.

Fergus mac Roich: king of Ulster in the first century B.C. and king of all the mac Rorys or great horse men. Left the kingship after bringing the sons of Uisliu back from Scotland. He went to Connacht as he was betrayed by Conchobar. He, as legend has it, recited the Táin Bó Cuailnge to Senchán Torpéist, the poet. This happened after Senchán called up his spectre from the grave. Fergus was killed by Lugaid, when Ailella saw them swimming together in Findloch (white lake, as Carrowmore lake in the barony of Erris, Co. Mayo).

Fésse: mentioned in the 'wooing of Emer' as a great housewife and spouse. Possibly connected to the area around the Boyne valley.

Fiachaig and Findchad: members of the craeb ruad.

Fíachna and Follomain: members of the craeb ruad.

Fiachra mac Fir Aba: a member of the Craeb Ruad or Red Branch Knights and one who related part of Cú Chulainn's boyhood deeds.

Fíal: daughter of Fergal Manach. She describes the horses leading the chariot of Cú Chulainn and Laeg and its occupants.

Fíamain mac Forai: an Ulster warrior who trained with Cú Chulainn in Scotland under Scáthach.

Find, Eochaid and Illand: the three pipers of the craeb ruad.

Find, Erúath and Fatemain: the three cupbearers of the craeb ruad.

Find mac Rossa: a king of Leinster.

Findabair (Finnabair): 'fair eyebrow' daughter of queen Medb and king Ailella, she was offered in marriage to Fer Diad as a reward for fighting Cú Chulainn. Froech was the common law husband of Findabair; at least this is inferred by an ogam inscription found at Cruachain.

Findchad fer Bend Úma mac Fraeglethain: an Ulster chief.

Findchóem: foster mother of Cú Chulainn, it was she who nursed him as a child. She was a daughter of Conchobar and a sister of Deichtine.

Fintan mac Néill Níamhglonnaig: a chief from Mount Sandle, Coleraine, Co. Derry.

Flesc, Lesc and Lúam: the three cupbearers of Nechtan mac Labrad, husband of Boand of the Boyne.

Fóill mac Nechtan Scéne: one of the three sons of Nechta Scéne, who had his fort between the rivers Liffey and Boyne.

Folloman mac Conchobar: a son of Conchobar mac Nessa, king of Emain Macha.

The Fomorians: a race of people coming from the sea. Literally 'under the sea' or also interpreted as 'sea-men'. Christian writers thought that they were descended from Ham the son of Noah. With their god Balor, they can be traced back to the Middle East and can be ascribed to the Phoenicians. Balor has strong associations there, where the Fomorians are regarded as pirates.

Furbaide: one of the sons of Emain Macha at the time of Cú Chulainn and Emer.

Furbaide: nephew of Queen Medb and son of Clothru.

Gabalglinni mac Dedad: known as the ancient of Clanna Dedad. He was blind for thirty years and was being looked after at the fort of the Dedad.

Gabhal Glinde: beheaded at Tara by Conall Cernach in revenge for the death of Cú Chulainn.

Garb: Fomorian associated with Malahide Bay, Co. Dublin.

Genann Gruadsolus: Genann of the 'brow of light', son of Cathbad the druid and one who consoled Cú Chulainn towards the end of his life.

Germán Garbglas: a chief whom Cú Chulainn and Fer Diad fought against in the Western Isles of Scotland whilst under the tutelage of Scáthach.

Glas mac Dedad: the last man to be beheaded by Conall Cernach at Tara in revenge for the killing by the 'men of Ireland' of Cú Chulainn.

Grice: a chief from Croagh Patrick, Co. Mayo.

Gulban Glass mac Gráci: from Ben Bulben, Co. Sligo.

Ibar mac Riangabra: charioteer to Cú Chulainn. When Cú Chulainn was a child Ibar pointed out the various places of note within the kingdom of Ulster. He was with Cú Chulainn when the latter went on his first military expedition.

Ibor Boichlid: slew the sons of Garb, who were Fomorians from Malahide Bay, Co. Dublin.

Ibur, Scibur and Catt: three brothers who defended Emer from Cú Chulainn during their courtship.

Labraid Lúathlám ar Claideb: 'of the fast sword-hand'. Some say he was a fairy king, others a possible king or chief from the Isle of Man.

Laeg mac Ríangabra: Cú Chulainn's charioteer. A large cairn just north of Laytown is where he is said to have been entombed. Some say that Laytown is Baile Leag in Irish. He was killed from a spear thrown by Erc mac Cairbre, which struck him between the loin and navel.

Lath and Luath Gaible mac Tethrach: two of the many suitors who sought Emer's hand.

Lebarcham: a messenger, handmaiden and satirist at the court of Conchobar mac Nessa. Her parents are recorded as being Aí and Adairce.

Lí Ban: 'beauty of woman' and wife of Labraid Lúathlám ar Claideb.

Lóch Mór mac Egomas: an Ulster warrior whom Cú Chulainn slew with the 'gae bolga'. He also wore the 'conganchnes' or horn-skinned armour associated with Fer Diad.

Loegaire Buadach: member of the Craeb Ruad, or Red Branch Knights, close friend and companion of Cú Chulainn, who shared many adventures with Cú Chulainn in Scotland. Died in defence of a poet called Aed mac Ainninn.

Lug: god of the harvest, a sun god and spiritual father of Cú Chulainn. He is associated with Luglochta Loga or Lug's gardens at Drumanagh, a place in the territory of Fergal Manach, Emer's father. His feast day is the first of August. His full name is Lug mac Ethne.

Lug mac Ethnenn: one of the principal gods of the Tuatha Dé Danann. He is the divine father of Cú Chulainn. Like many Irish gods he reputedly died at Loch Lughborta by Caendruim close to the hill of Uisneach, Co. Westmeath.

Lug Scimaig: held a great feast for Lug mac Ethlenn after the battle of Mag Tuired, during which Lug mac Ethlenn was crowned king of the Tuatha Dé Danann.

Lugaid and Lúan: sons of Lóch Mór who were on the ship with Cú Chulainn, sailing towards Ireland after their training in Scotland.

Lugaid Lámderg mac Léti: Lugaid of the 'Red Hand'. A king of the Dal nAraidne or Picts at the time of Cú Chulainn.

Lugaid mac Con Rí: son of Cú Roí mac Dáire, who was armed by Medb to avenge the death of his father by Cú Chulainn. He speared Cú Chulainn between the loin and the navel.

Lugaid mac Nois mac Alamaic: a legendary king 'from the west' with twelve charioteers from Munster. Emer Manach was betrothed to him. However, on hearing of Cú Chulainn's intentions vis-à-vis Emer he turned back from Fergal's home and left.

Lugaid Réo Derg: High King of Ireland. Lugaid of the 'Red Stripes'. He acceded to the kingship of Tara as a result of an old ritual known as the tarb fes. He was a foster son of Cú Chulainn and the tales have it that he received the precepts or moral instructions from Cú Chulainn prior to his inauguration. A fort of his is said to have been on an old site of the Bailey Lighthouse, Howth, Co. Dublin.

Mac Nia mac Finn mac Rosa: his spear lacerated Cú Chulainn's leg and wounded him.

Macha: together with Badb and the Mórrígan, she makes up the Mórrígna, a trio of war-fertility goddesses. Emain Macha (Navan Fort) Co. Armagh is called after her. Thus her name is synonymous with the ancient capital of Ulster.

The Mairtine: a tribe from Munster, that slew Conall Cernach, in revenge for the death of Cú Roí mac Dáire.

Mannach: the hospitaller from Muincille in north Leinster.

Medb: queen of Connacht, the most powerful of the pre-historic personages. In mid English her name is Mead. In Sanskrit, mádhu, 'honey, sweet drink'. With Boadicea of Britain she remains the most striking and persistently memorable of queens in these islands. She is at the heart of the early history and mythology of Ireland, but particularly of Connacht. She was killed by her nephew Furbaide, as revenge for the death of her sister Clothru on Inis Clothrand in Loch Ree.

Míl: from Galicia, in North West Spain, his sons are said to have been the original Gaels who entered South Western Ireland.

Morann mac Móin: a celebrated judge associated with the Bretha Nemed or collection of laws. He was called upon to give instructions to the king at particular times. His mother was a Pict. The 'Testament of Morann', known in Gaelic as Audacht Morann, is attributable to Morann. It is part of a literary genre known as precepts or moral instructions to a king or prince. If he existed at all he existed in the first century A.D.

Mórrígan: one of the three daughters of Iron Death, and one of the war fertility goddesses to the Tuatha Dé Danann, collectively as a triple goddess known as the Mórrígna. She sits on the shoulder of Cú Chulainn after his death.

Muiredach mac Fergus: chief of the household of Erc mac Cairbre at Tara. He was beheaded 'in the centre of the hall' at Tara by Conall Cernach.

Naoise mac Uisliu: one of the famous children of Uisliu, who was beloved of Deirdre, betrayed and met his death due to the scheming of Conchobar mac Nessa. He trained with Cú Chulainn on the Isle of Skye.

Níam: daughter of Celtchar mac Uithechair and mistress to Cú Chulainn.

Nuadu: a king of the Tuatha Dé Danann. His arm was hewn off in battle. In St. Patrick's Cathedral in Armagh (Church of Ireland) a statue pertaining to Nuadu is to be seen. His full name is Nuadu Argatlám (Nuadu of the Silver Arm). He is more popularly known as Nuada. The vowel ending 'U' denotes a god, i.e. Éire, Ériu.

Óa and Adarc: the parents of Leborcham, handmaiden and satirist at the court of Conchobar mac Nessa.

Óengus: Mac ind Óc or Óengus Mac ind Óc, more popularly Aengus

Mac ind Óc or just simply Aengus. His father was the Dagda and his mother was Boand. He is the harper to the gods and is buried in the Boyne Valley. From whence he once inspired poets!

Redg Rotbél: a chief from Raphoe, Co. Donegal.

Riches: a female satirist who tried to have Cú Chulainn killed but died in the attempt.

Rind mac Níuil: a Scottish warrior killed by Cú Chulainn in Scotland.

Róimid Rigóinmit: jester to the court of Conchobar mac Nessa.

Roncu: the fisherman to Conchobar mac Nessa.

Rúad: one of the kings of the Western Isles of Scotland, whose daughter was held to ransom by some Fomorian pirates.

Ruad mac Forníuil: a warrior from the Western Isles of Scotland, killed by Fer Diad.

Rúad mac Rígdúnd: legendary king of Munster whose story led to the Delvin river (on the borders of Dublin and Meath) receiving its name.

Sainrith mac Imbath: 'son of the ocean', was according to legend father of Macha of Emain Macha.

Scandlach: a leading woman within the Ulaid at Emain Macha.

Scáthach: 'the shadowy one', a female warrior queen from the Isle of Skye, Scotland. She trained Cú Chulainn in warrior craft, particularly in the use of the *gae bolga*. Comparisons have been made between her presenting the *gae bolga* to Cú Chulainn and the presentation of King Arthur's sword by the Lady of the Lake.

Scél mac Bairini: the doorkeeper at Emain Macha, noted as a great storyteller. His name in Irish means teller of tales.

Scennmenn Manach: a shape-changer and sister of Fergal Manach.

Scibur and Ibur and Cat: three brothers of Emer, three men that were spared by agreement between Cú Chulainn and Emer, when Cú Chulainn came to take Emer away from the present territory of Fingal in Leinster.

Senach Síaborthe: a chief from the Isle of Man.

Sencha mac Ailella: one of the three 'valour holding heroes of Erin'. Known for his beauty both in form and in speech. He was an orator and a diplomat to the Craeb Ruad. A foster son of Conchobar mac Nessa, in whose court he was both an instructor and wise man.

Sétanta: Cú Chulainn's tribal name, his tribe being the Sétantii from north-west Britain. Sétanta has been translated as 'one who knows the way'.

Sétanta mac Sualtam: Cú Chulainn's name prior to becoming Cú Chulainn.

Sualtam mac Roich: foster father of Cú Chulainn. He tested Cú Chulainn's vigour at Dún Rudruige (Dun Rory, on former site of Dundrum Castle, Co. Down) in a possible rite of passage known as the 'Champion's Covenant'. He was king of Cooley thus had the right to all the cattle there. He was decapitated by the edge of his own shield as the horse he was riding, the Liath Macha, reared up. According to legend the severed head cried out: 'Men are wounded, women are captives, cows are driven away'. This was the call to arms for the Ulaid at the Cattle Raid of Cooley.

Tethra: king of the Fomorians to whom Fergal Manach is said to have been related.

The Three O' Chletigs: the three orators of the craeb ruad.

Tigernach Tétbannach mac Luctai: king of East Munster.

Tinnell mac Boclachtnai: a chief from Ulster.

Triath: a king and chief of the Boyne valley.

Trisgatail Trénfhar: a member of the 'craeb ruad' and a bodyguard to king Conchobar mac Nessa. Reputedly capable of killing people merely by looking at them.

Tuachall mac Nechtan Scéne: one of the three sons of Nechta, who challenged Cú Chulainn when he stopped in their territory.

Tuatha Dé Danann: a people regarded by scholars as completely mythical. Their goddess is Danu or Anu. The gods and goddesses of Ireland are almost all connected to them. Some say they came from Greece, some from Syria or Scythia and others that they came from Denmark. They are the architects of our mythology; they live in the sídhe from whence they leave each samain or hallowe'en. From the sídhe they ladle out their magic, spells and measured inspiration.

Úathach: daughter of Scáthach; she fell in love with Cú Chulainn. Eventually Cú Chulainn acceded to her wishes and lived with her.

Ulbecán or Wulfkin the Saxon: who according to legend was a foster-father of Cú Chulainn. As a foster-father Ulbecán taught Cú Chulainn melodic speech.

Úma mac Remanfisig: a chief from Cooley, Co. Louth.

Notes on Irish Words Used in Text

Ces: a debility or sense of inertia. Often referred to as ces noínden Ulad or the nine-day debility or trance of the Ulaid. Often associated with the spell Macha cast on the Ulaid, which attacked them when a crisis arose. Sometimes associated with the ancient custom known as the couvade. In the latter meaning the ces is associated with the pangs of labour in childbirth.

Cumal: A female slave, more generally a unit of value for all forms of exchange.

Eneclann: originally 'face-clearing', later to mean compensation for any illegal act carried out upon one.

Fidchell: lit. 'wood intelligence'. A board game often associated with chess but can also mean draughts or backgammon. The origins and rules of fidchell would appear to be unknown.

Gae Bulga: Cú Chulainn's most famous spear. The spear of Bulg, the god of lightning.

Geis, pl. geasa: an injunction or taboo. Breaking a taboo often resulted in death.

Imbas forosnai: an ancient rite of divination, whereby the future could be prophesied.

Liss: the anglicised version of the old Irish word les or modern Irish lios. It means the space about a dwelling enclosed by a bank. More popularly, a ringfort or sometimes locally a fairy fort.

Ollamh: an expert in art and science, a professor. The highest grade of 'fili'.

Samain: lit. 'summer's end', a time of feasting, of holding conventions. At this time the spirits of the dead arose, the great meeting at Tara was held at this time every three years. Food was stored, marriages took place and during the long winter evenings the storyteller perfected his craft.

Serrda: a sickle-like blade attached to a chariot. Whether its origin is in the word Serrdai (the Syrians) or not is a moot point.

Síd: a fairy hill or mound, an abode of supernatural beings, known as the 'shee' in English, as in banshee, the 'woman of the mounds'. Also a tumulus or cairn.

Sídhe: (see síd).

Sliotar: a hurling ball.

Tech Mid-Chúarta: the Banqueting Hall at Tara, literally the House for the Circulation of Mead. Now regarded as a 'circus' for sport assemblies.

Bibliography

Royal Irish Academy, *Dictionary of the Irish Language* (Dublin, 1983).

Van Hamel, A.G. (ed.), *Compert Con Culain and other stories* (Dublin, 1978).

Guyonarc'h, Christian, J., *Textes mythologiques irlandais* (Brittany).

Dillon, Myles, *Serglige Con Culainn* (Dublin, 1975).

Carmichael Watson, J., *Mesca Ulad* (Dublin, 1983).

O'Rahilly, Thomas F., *Early Irish History and Mythology* (Dublin, 1946).

Hull, Eleanor, *The Cuchullin Saga* (London, 1898).

Kinsella,Thomas, *The Táin* (Dublin, 1969).

Stokes, Whitley, 'The training of CúChulainn', *Revue Celtique,xxix,*109–152.

Thurneysen, R., *Die irische Helden und Königage* (Halle).

Best, R., and Bergin, O. (eds) *Lebor na hUidre* (Dublin, 1929).

Best, R., and O'Brien, M.A. (eds) *The Book of Leinster vol.2* (Dublin, 1956).

Mallory, J.P. (ed.) *Aspects of the Táin* (Belfast, 1992).

Lynn. C.J., 'The Iron Age mound in Navan Fort: a physical realization of Celtic religious beliefs?', *Emania*, 10. pp. 33–57.

McCone, K., *Pagan Past and Christian Present* (Maynooth, 1990).

Ridgeway, W., 'The date of the first shaping of the Cuchulainn saga', *Proc. Brit. Acad*, 1905.

Strachan, John, *Old Irish Paradigms and Selections from the Old-Irish Glosses* (Dublin,1949).

Thurneysen, R., *A Grammar of Old Irish* (Dublin, 1993).

BIBLIOGRAPHY

Gregory, Augusta, *Cuchulain of Muirthemne* (London, 1902).
Aitchison, N.B., 'The Ulster Cycle: heroic image and historical reality', *Journal of Medieval History*, 1987.
Gantz, Jeffrey, *Early Irish Myths and Sagas* (London, 1981).
Marshall J.D.C. *Forgotten Places of the North Coast* (Armoy, Co. Antrim, 1987).